The Maoris at Trench Practice, Ghain-Tuffhia Camp, Malta. (1915).

THE MAORIS IN THE GREAT WAR

A History of
The New Zealand Native Contingent
and Pioneer Battalion

GALLIPOLI, 1915
FRANCE AND FLANDERS, 1916-1918.

BY JAMES COWAN.

Published by the Maori Regimental Committee.

WHITCOMBE & TOMBS LIMITED
AUCKLAND, CHRISTCHURCH, DUNEDIN, WELLINGTON, N.Z.,
MELBOURNE AND LONDON.
1926

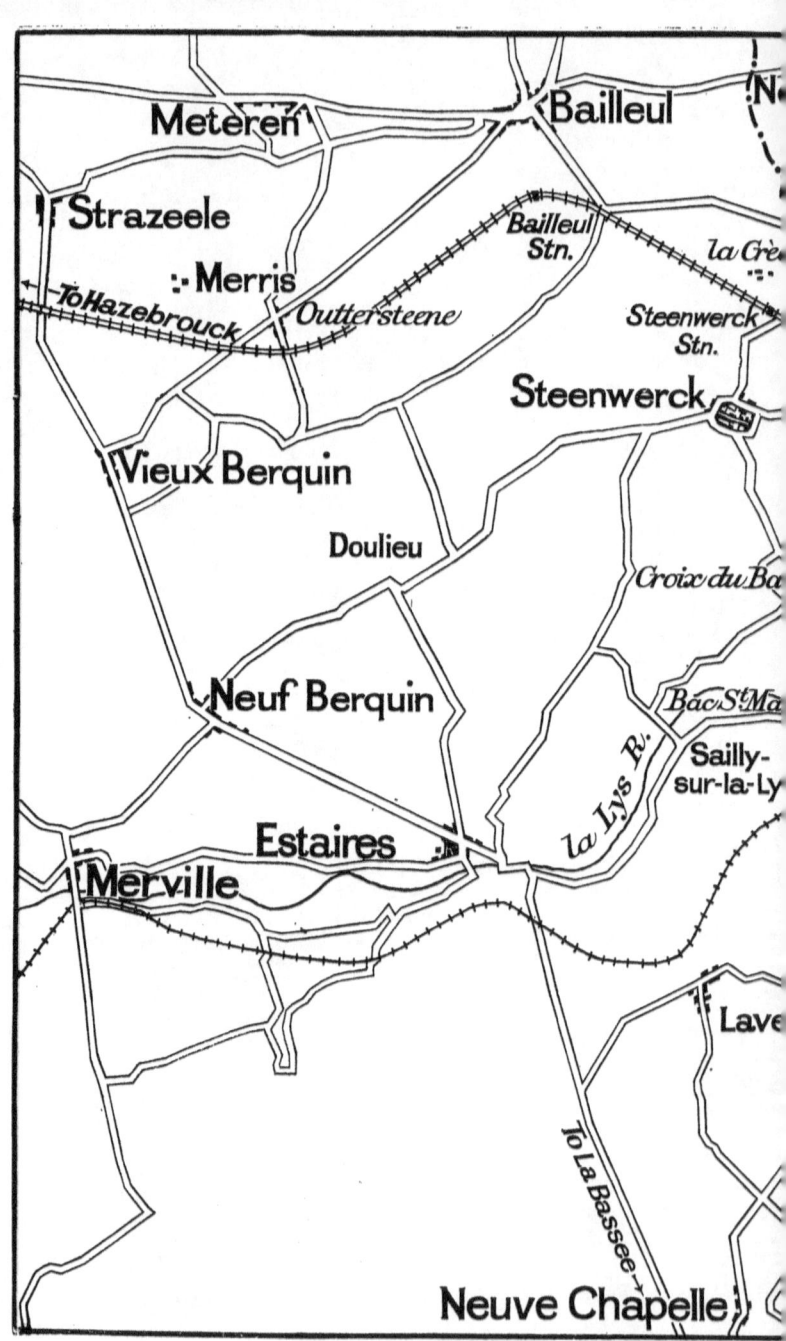

VICINITY

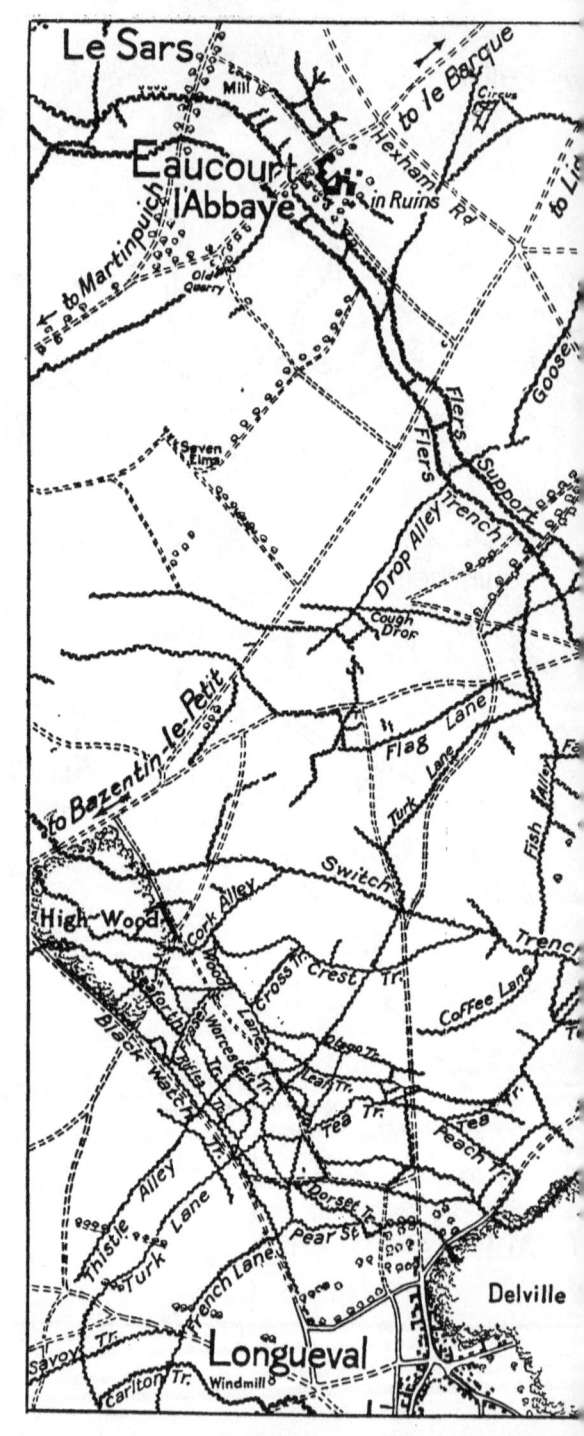

MAP OF ENTRENCHMENTS, BEZANTIN

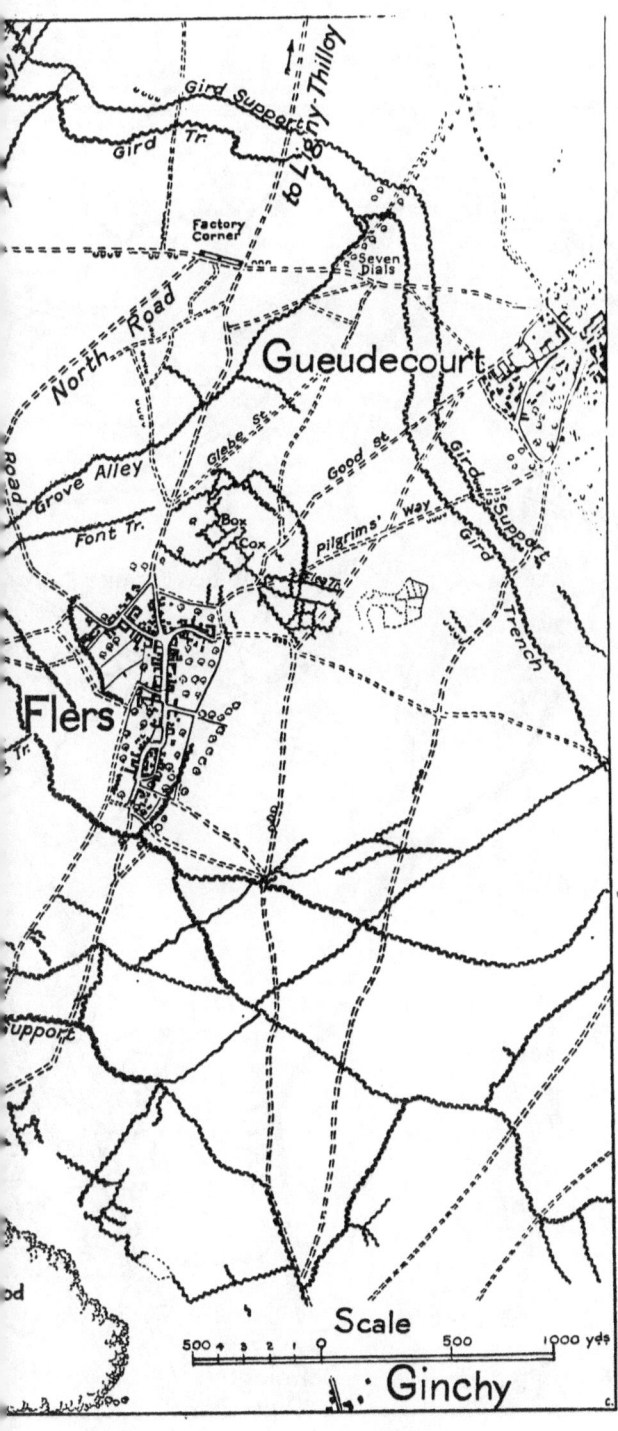

—Flers—Gueudecourt, September, 1916

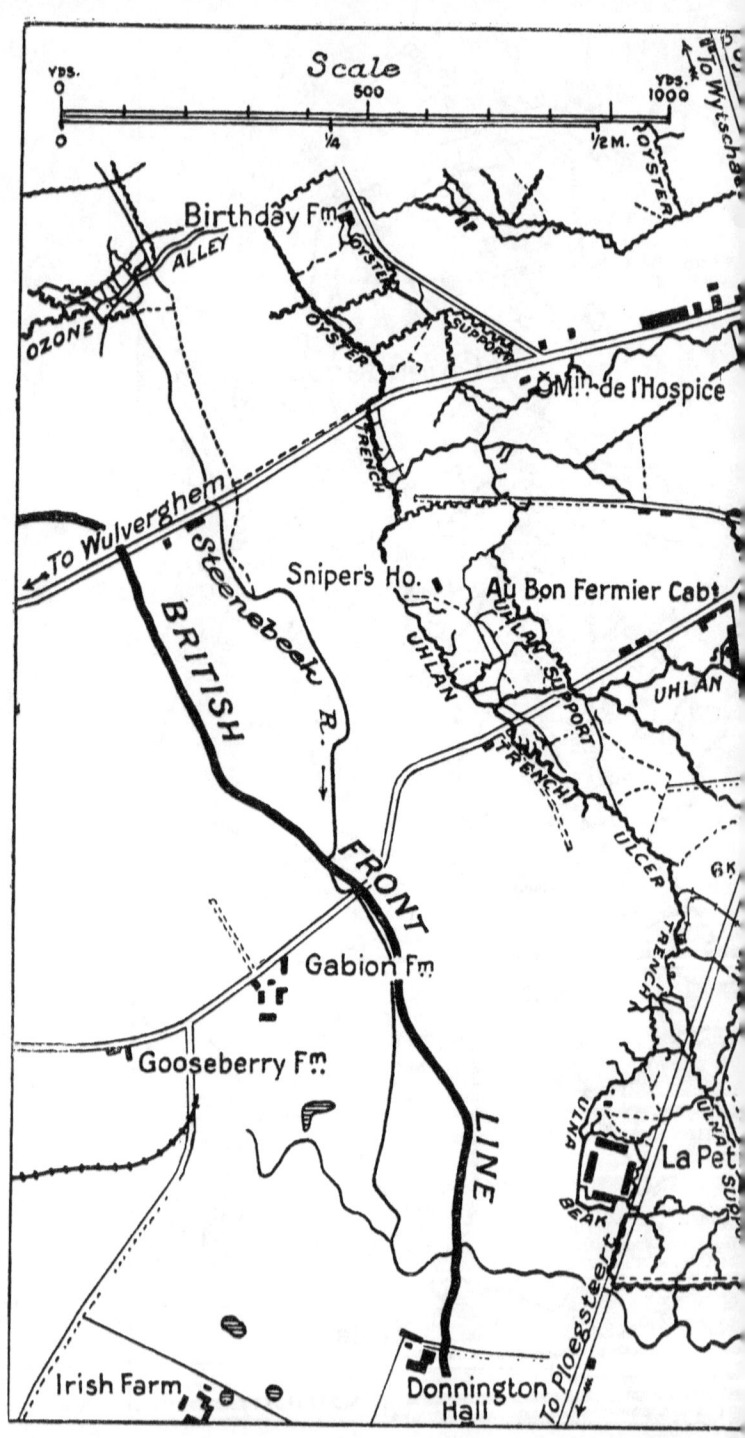

MESSINES

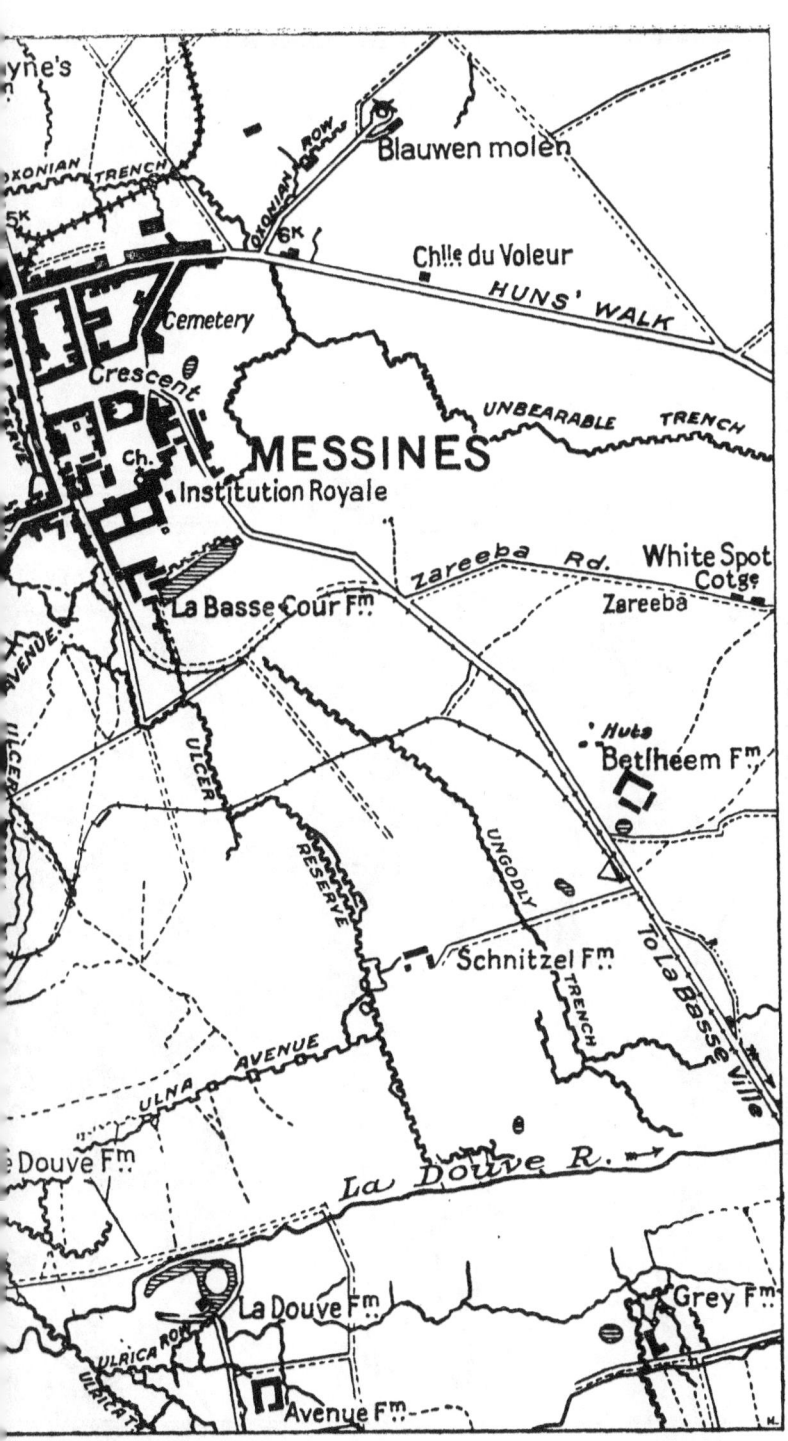

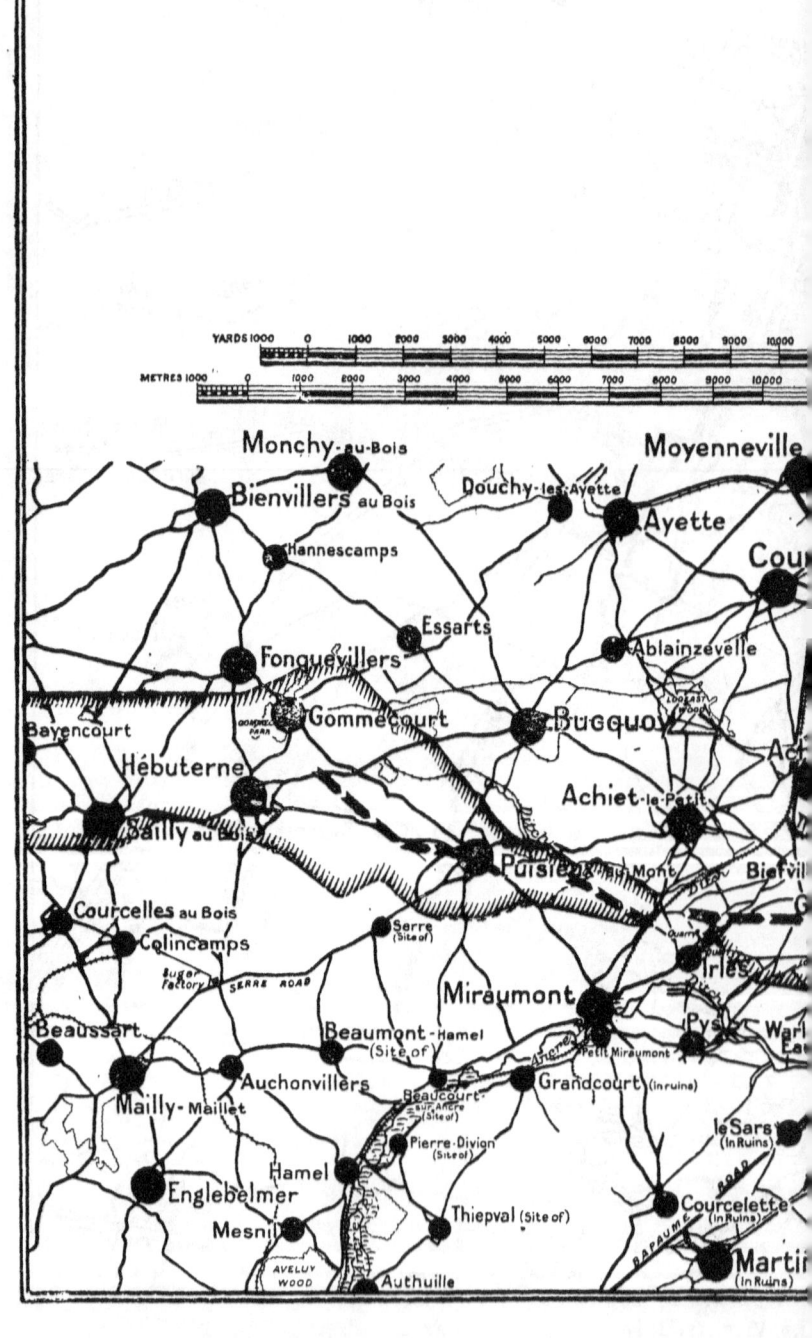

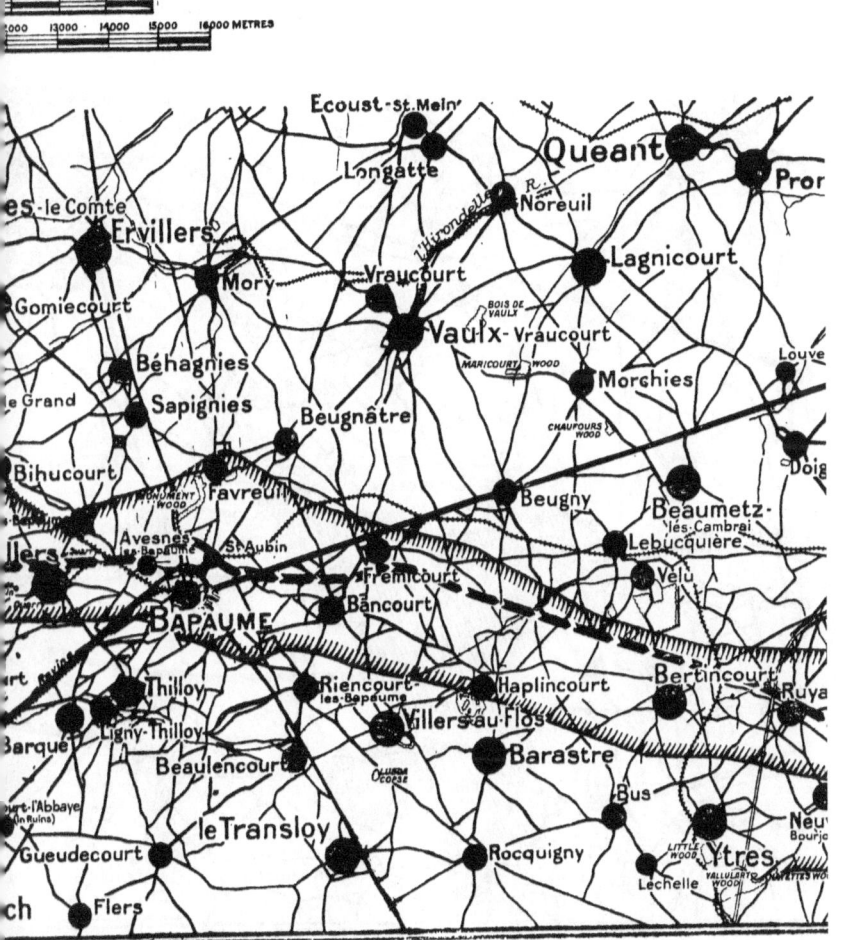

MAP SHOWING THE COUNTRY OVER
IN THE ADV

HEBUTERNE TO LE QUESN

Captures: 9,000 prisone

The shaded sections represent cap

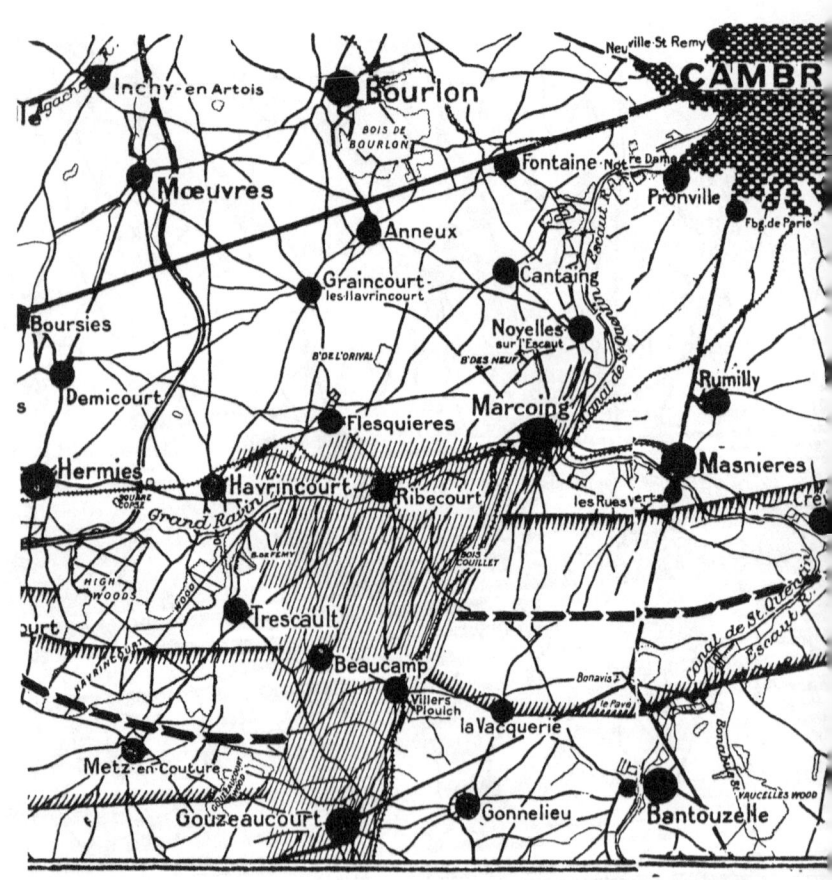

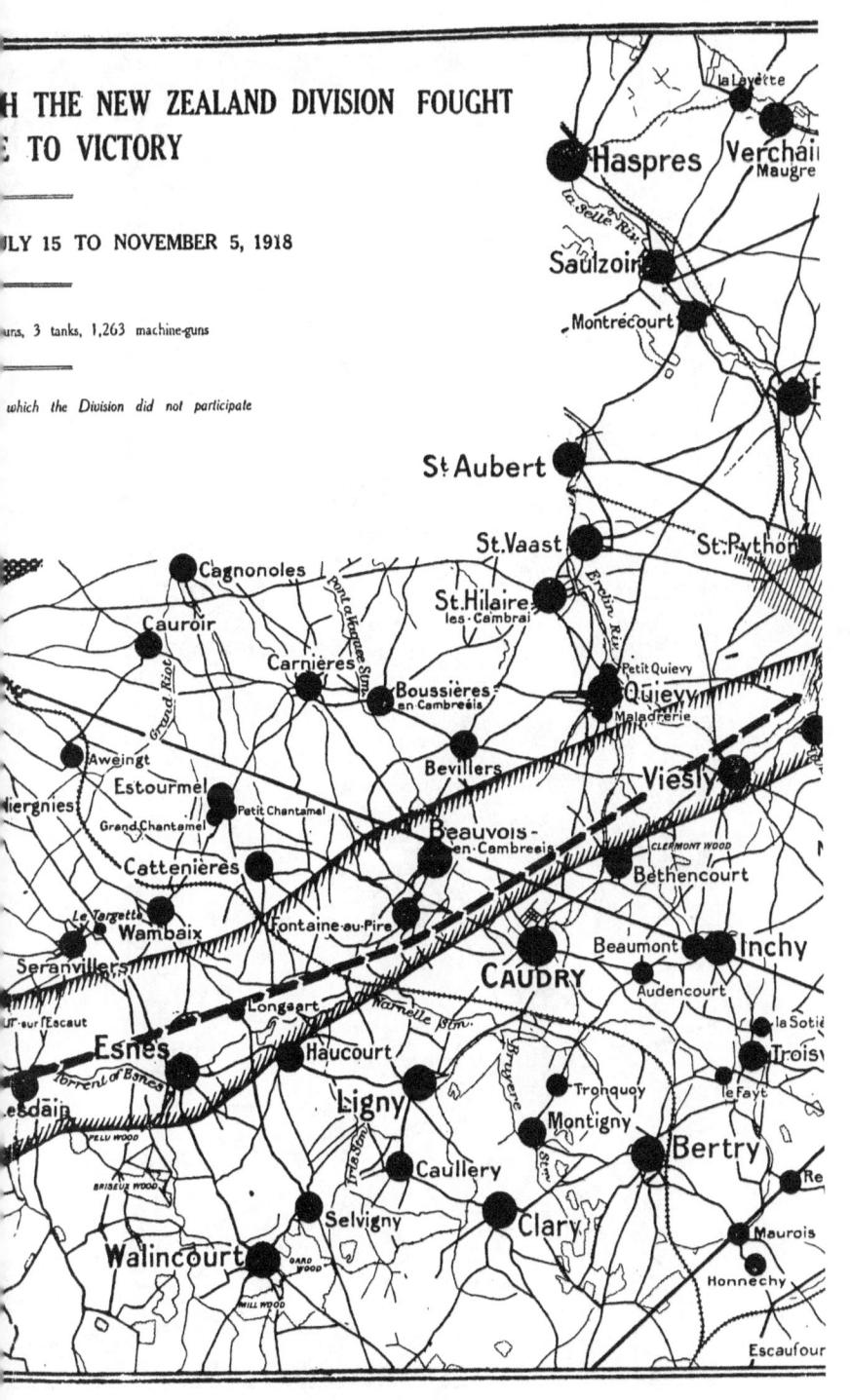

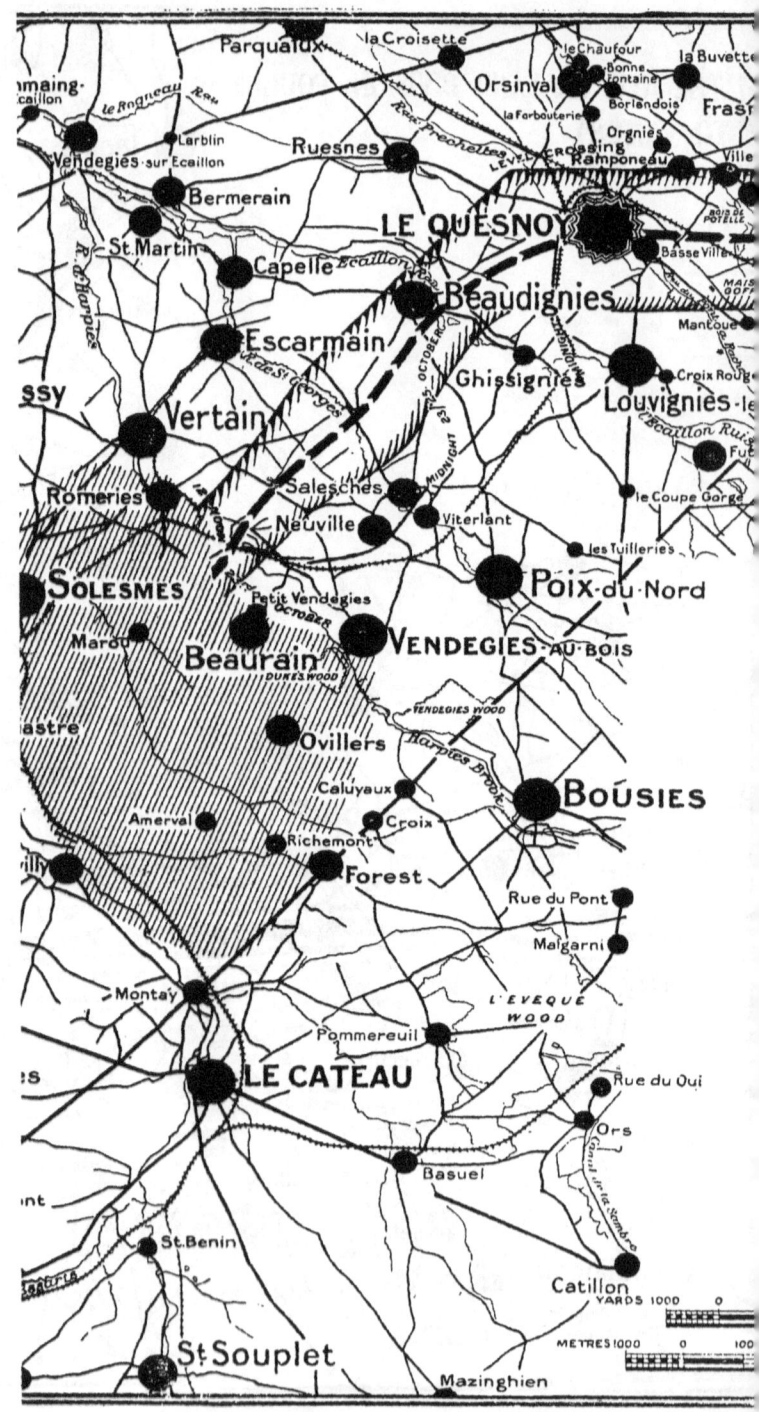

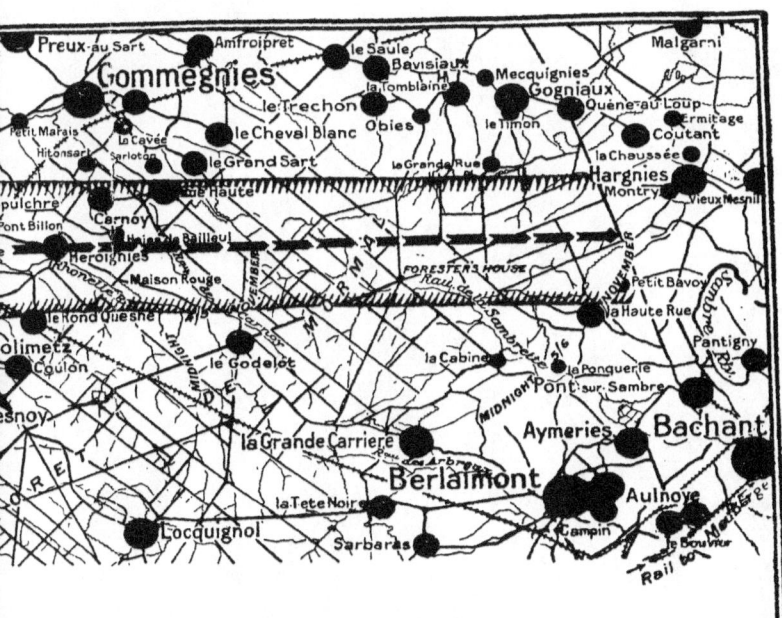

SUCCESSIVE STAGES:

Time	Date	Location
4 p.m.,	July 15	First Advance, East of Hebuterne.
Midnight,	August 17-18	Western outskirts of Puisieux-au-Mont.
,,	,, 21-22	Beyond Puisieux-au-Mont.
7 p.m.,	,, 23	Western outskirts of Irles—Bihucourt. (Not N.Z.)
Midnight,	,, 24-25	Biefvillers.
,,	,, 25-26	Western outskirts of Bapaume—Favreuil.
2 p.m.	,, 29	East of Bapaume
Midnight,	September 1-2	East of Bancourt and Fremicourt.
,,	,, 2-3	Villers-au-Flos—Beugny.
,,	,, 3-4	East of Bertincourt.
,,	,, 5-6	Neuville.
,,	,, 6-7	Metz-en-Couture.
,,	,, 7-8	Eastern edge of Havrincourt Wood.
,,	,, 12-13	West of Beaucamp.
,,	,, 28-29	Gouzeaucourt—Villers-Plouich. (Not N.Z.)
,,	,, 29-30	La Vacquerie—Masnieres.
,,	Sept. 30-Oct. 1	Escaut Canal.
,,	October 1-2	Crevecoeur.
,,	,, 8-9	Esnes.
,,	,, 9-10	Western outskirts of Fontaine-au-Pire.
8 a.m.	,, 11	Western outskirts of Briastre.
Midnight,	,, 12-13	East of Briastre.
Noon	,, 23	Vendegies—Romeries. (Not N.Z.)
Midnight,	,, 23-24	Beaudignies.
,,	,, 24-25	Close to Le Quesnoy.
,,	November 4-5	In the Mormal Forest.
,,	,, 5-6	Eastern edge of Mormal Forest.

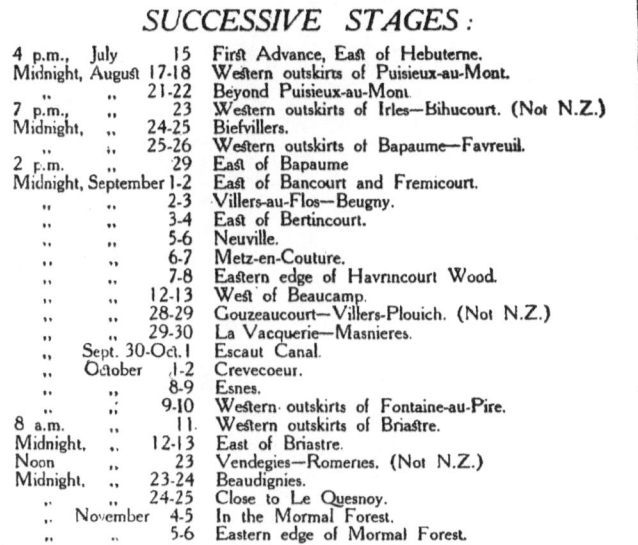

AUTHOR'S PREFACE

This narrative of the services performed in the Great War by the Maori soldiers of New Zealand has been written under instructions from the Maori Regimental Committee, approved by the Defence authorities. Official histories of the Dominion's war effort and a series of histories of the various Pakeha units have been published, and the present book supplies the completing volume of our regimental records. References to the Maori Contingent at Gallipoli and, after its organisation as a Pioneer Battalion, in France and Flanders may be found here and there in the official and regimental histories, in the eloquent despatches of Sir Ian Hamilton and the reports of other commanders, but a connected and detailed story of the gallant Maoris and their South Sea Islands cousins was required. This volume has been compiled mainly from the official War Diaries of the Battalion commanders, and has been augmented from various sources, chief of which are the excellent diaries kept by Major Peter H. Buck (Te Rangihiroa), D.S.O., M.D., who served continuously from 1915 to the end of the war. Lieut.-Col. W. O. Ennis, D.S.O., who was four years on active service, assisted with notes and kindly read the proofs and made useful suggestions. His death by accident in Auckland was an untimely end to a fine career, a tragedy deeply regretted by old comrades. Departmental files of the Hon. Sir Maui Pomare, Native member of the Executive Council and Chairman of the Maori Recruiting Committee and Regimental Committee, have also been drawn upon for information regarding the raising and organisation of the corps. My thanks are due to Sir Maui and his Committee and the New Zealand Regimental Canteen Funds Trust Board for the facilities given, and to Major L. C. Forgie, Secretary of War Records and Trust

Funds, Defence Headquarters, and Captain Jervis, in charge of the Records at Mt. Cook Barracks, for their kind help. From numerous Maori sources, too, came assistance in the compilation of this narrative of our Native countrymen's deeds on the hills of Gallipoli and in the great labour of pioneer duty with the armies in France.

The principal maps used are those which appeared in The History of the New Zealand Division in France, The New Zealanders at Gallipoli and The History of the New Zealand Rifle Brigade.

JAMES COWAN.

Wellington, N.Z.
March, 1926.

OFFICERS OF THE N.Z. PIONEER BATTALION, 1919.

This photograph of the officers of the Pioneer Battalion was taken in England shortly before return to New Zealand early in 1919. In the front rank (left to right): Chaplain Pene te U. Hakiwai, Lieut. Karauti, Captain P. Ferris, Captain P. Tahiwi, Lieut.-Col. W. O. Ennis (O.C.), Captain Broughton, Captain Mulholland (surgeon), Lieut. Paku, Lieut. H. Wilson, Lieut. Hetet.

CONTENTS

	PAGE
Chapter 1—Introductory: The Maoris offer for Service Abroad ..	1
Chapter 2—Recruiting and Organisation of the Maori Contingent	9
Chapter 3—The Maoris at Anzac, Gallipoli, 1915	24
Chapter 4—The Battle of Sari Bair, Gallipoli	34
Chapter 5—The last weeks at Gallipoli	59
Chapter 6—Formation of the Pioneer Battalion	70
Chapter 7—Arrival of the Pioneers in France (1916)	76
Chapter 8—Maori Raiding Parties (1916)	81
Chapter 9—The Pioneers' Work on the Western Front (1916) ..	88
Chapter 10—The Pioneers' Work on the Western Front (1917) ..	103
Chapter 11—Cook Islanders in the Field	106
Chapter 12—The Pioneers in the Battle of Messines (June, 1917).	108
Chapter 13—The Pioneers' Work in Flanders (July-September, 1917)	116
Chapter 14—The Third Battle of Ypres (October, 1917)	124
Chapter 15—Work on the Western Front (January-May, 1918) ..	132
Chapter 16—The Summer of 1918—Western Front	139
Chapter 17—Final Stages of the War, 1918	143
Chapter 18—The Capture of Le Quesnoy—The Armistice	151

APPENDICES

The Maori Roll of Honour	162
List of Decorations	172
The Maori Contingent after Sari Bair	175
"Te Ope Tuatahi"—A Maori Recruiting Song	179
Index	182

List of Illustrations

	FACING PAGE
The Maoris at Trench Practice, Malta—*Frontispiece*	
Officers of the Maori Battalion	IV
Lieut.-Col. G. A. King, D.S.O.	XII
Lieut.-Col. C. G. Saxby, D.S.O.	1
Lieut.-Col. W. O. Ennis, D.S.O.	4
Major H. Peacock	5
Hon. Sir Maui Pomare, M.P.	12
Hon. Sir James Carroll, M.L.C.	13
Hon. A. T. Ngata, M.P.	16
Mr. Tau Henare, M.P.	17
Mr. H. W. Uru, M.P.	20
Party of Ngati-Tuwharetoa Soldiers	21
The Last of the German Cruiser "Emden"	24
In the Mediterranean	24
The First Maori Contingent, 1915	25
The Maoris' Camp in Malta	28
Officers "Doing their Bit," Malta	28
After Skirmishing Practice, Malta	29
The First Mail from New Zealand, Malta	29
Officers Comparing Notes, Malta	32
General Chaytor, at Malta	32
In the Training Camp, Malta. Practicing the Charge	33
Foot Inspection, Malta Camp	33
At Old No. 3 Post, Anzac, Gallipoli	36
The Sari Bair Battlefield, Gallipoli	36
One of the wounded, Gallipoli	37
No. 1 Outpost Dressing Station, Anzac	37
Major P. H. Buck (Te Rangihiroa), D.S.O.	44
Chaplain H. W. Te Wainohu	45
Scene in the Battle of Messines Ridge	112
An example of the Germans' Work	112
Opening a Communication Trench	113
The Market-Woman	113

	FACING PAGE
Around the Christmas "Hangi"	120
Meat for the Fighting Men	120
Chaplain Wainohu and some of the Boys	121
Mr. Massey and Sir J. G. Ward inspecting the Pioneers	128
Mr. Massey addressing the Pioneers	129
A Haka for the Chiefs, Bois de Warnimont	129
Inspecting the Pioneers, Bois de Warnimont	140
Sir Joseph Ward addressing the Pioneers	140
Cheers for Mr. Massey	141
Mr. Massey at Etaples, 1918	141
Chaplain P. te U. Hakiwai	144
German Shell Bursting, Puisieux	148
German anti-Tank Rifle	148
Pioneers at Trench Improvement	149
Meal-time, Grevillers	149
Timi enjoys one of Sir Joseph Ward's cigars	156
New Zealand Ministers addressing Soldiers	156
A Presentation Gun, Rarotonga	157
Sir James Allen addressing Rarotonga Soldiers	157
Maori War Memorial Church, Kahukura, Waiapu	160

PLANS.

Barb-wire Defences near Ypres, 1918	132
Frezenberg Post Entrenchments	133

MAPS.

Anzac, Gallipoli, 1915
St. Omer and Hazebrouck
Armentieres and vicinity
N.W. France
Entrenchments, Bezantin Ridge, etc.
Messines and vicinity, 1917
Scene of the New Zealanders' work, end of 1917
Area of action, summer of 1918
The Final Advance, Hebuterne to Le Quesnoy

PREFACE

(By the Hon. Sir Maui Pomare, K.B.E., C.M.G., M.D., M.P.)

On this Anzac Day eight years ago nearly a thousand Maori Pioneers were toiling and fighting in the trench-seamed barb-wired Western Front in the most fearful struggle of man against man that this war-soaked globe had ever seen. From beginning to end a total of over 2,200 Maoris and several hundred South Sea Islanders of allied Polynesian blood wore khaki and obeyed the bugle call of the Empire which until that world-wide "Fall in" sounded had been but a vague name to most, and to many indeed quite unknown. The eleven years which have elapsed since the Hokowhitu a Tu sailed from these shores for Egypt and Gallipoli have given us the length and breadth of vision needful to estimate at its full value not only the service which our Maori people gave to their country and their allies but also the reflex of that service on the position of the Maori as a social and political entity in the life of New Zealand.

Our people's voluntary service in the Great War gave a new and glorious tradition to the story of the Maori race. It gave the crowning touch to the sense of citizenship in the British commonwealth; it satisfied in the one fitting fashion the intense desire of the Maori to prove to the world that he was the equal of the *pakeha* in the fullest sense—physically, mentally and spiritually. The rush of the Maori to offer his life in the nation's service not only gave proof that his hereditary fighting temper was as strong as ever at the call of danger; it enabled him to exhibit the supreme qualities of citizenship, a larger patriotism than mere clanship; endurance, valour and self-sacrifice in the highest degree.

Our people were quick to realise their sacred obligation to join in the great cause. Within a few hours of the sounding of the war *tētere*, the Government received eager offers from men of the Maori race. At that time it was not considered wise for us to participate in the actual fighting, and so the Hokowhitu a Tu left these shores for garrison duty, but the galvanic current of battle stirred the warrior blood of ancestral chieftains in their veins, and they asked that they might be allowed to go to the firing line. They were given the opportunity at Malta to continue on garrison duty if they so chose. The order was given, "Those who wish to remain on garrison duty slope arms." Not a rifle moved, not an eye blinked. That was the spirit of Anzac unity. And so over the Aegean Sea they went and fought and endured in the Homeric fields of old, and the spirit of Helen watching from the crumbled walls of Troy saw the deeds of her warriors outdone by a handful of men from thousands upon thousands of miles away, from an undreamed-of land under the Southern Cross.

Two days of the War years stand out above all in one's memory. One was the day in February, 1915, when those splendid lads of the First Maori Contingent marched through Wellington streets on the farewell ceremonial parade. The other was the day in August of that year when the news came of their share in the battle of Sari Bair. The casualty list of the most glorious August in our history brought grief to many Maori homes; but that grief was submerged in the higher thought that the Maori had proved himself; that the Gallipoli test had found him ready and had for ever joined his name and *mana* with those of his *pakeha* brother. Henceforth he was the racial peer of any man on earth.

This history tells the story of Gallipoli and France in detail in so far as concerns the Maori Contingent, or the Pioneer Battalion as it became after Gallipoli. Others besides our historian Mr. Cowan have told how gallantly the Maoris took their share of those terrific days on the Peninsula, where they had to encounter not merely human foes but killing heat, insect plagues, disease-saturated dust, thirst and sickness. They could well have said after that ordeal: "We are few men, but well hardened." Mr. John Masefield joined our lads with the fighters of the Empire in his "Gallipoli"; he wrote of the Sari Bair storming parties:

"Men of all races were banded together there. There were Australians, English, Indians, Maoris and New Zealanders made one by devotion to a cause, all willing to die so that their comrades might see the dawn make a steel streak of the Hellespont from the peaked hill now black against the stars."

Those deeds of our men on Gallipoli Peninsula, their long purgatory in the trenches, their heroic labours as Pioneers in France under the test of sustained shell fire, established them as compeers of the trained British soldier. It satisfied also their people at home that the olden fame of the warrior race was safe in their hands. There was in their indifference to terrific odds, their steadiness under devastating fire, the spirit of Rewi Maniapoto's reply to his kinsmen who counselled a night retreat from beleaguered Orakau: "We sought this combat; wherefore then should we retreat? If we are to die, let it be in battle; if we are to live, let us survive on the field of battle."

And of those whose destiny it was to fall on the field of honour it can be said, as a famous Greek said of his countrymen long before Orakau or Gallipoli: "So they gave their bodies to the commonwealth and received, each for his own memory, praise that will never die, and with it the grandest of all sepulchres, not that in which their mortal bones are laid, but a home in the minds of men."

The story is told of one of our olden warrior *kaumatuas*, Tamakehu a Toroiti, that when dying he called his sons together and commanded them, "Be brave that ye may live." To-day our noble dead live in our hearts because they were brave. Of Britain's soldiers who fell, a poet has written:

"They shall not grow old as we that are left grow old,
Age shall not weary them, nor the years condemn "

That sentiment was one with the belief of some of our own sages; in the calm Reinga land there is eternal youth.

To the kinsfolk of our immortal dead I echo these thoughts.

And have not those men of ours a message to New Zealanders to-day? They have, and let me express it in one of the idioms of our tongue: "*Nga whakanēnene kainga parea ake; nga whetewhetengu whakawāteangia.*" "The bickerings of the home must be put aside, the misunderstandings set right." Giving it a broad application, the heroic dead yet speak to us: "Make this beloved country of ours, the country for which we gave our lives, a better and a happier land for the children, for all who are to come after us." That is their message. Let us not disregard it.

Maui Pomare

Native Member of the Executive Council,
Minister for the Cook and other Islands, and
Chairman of the Maori Regimental Committee.

Anzac Day, 1926.

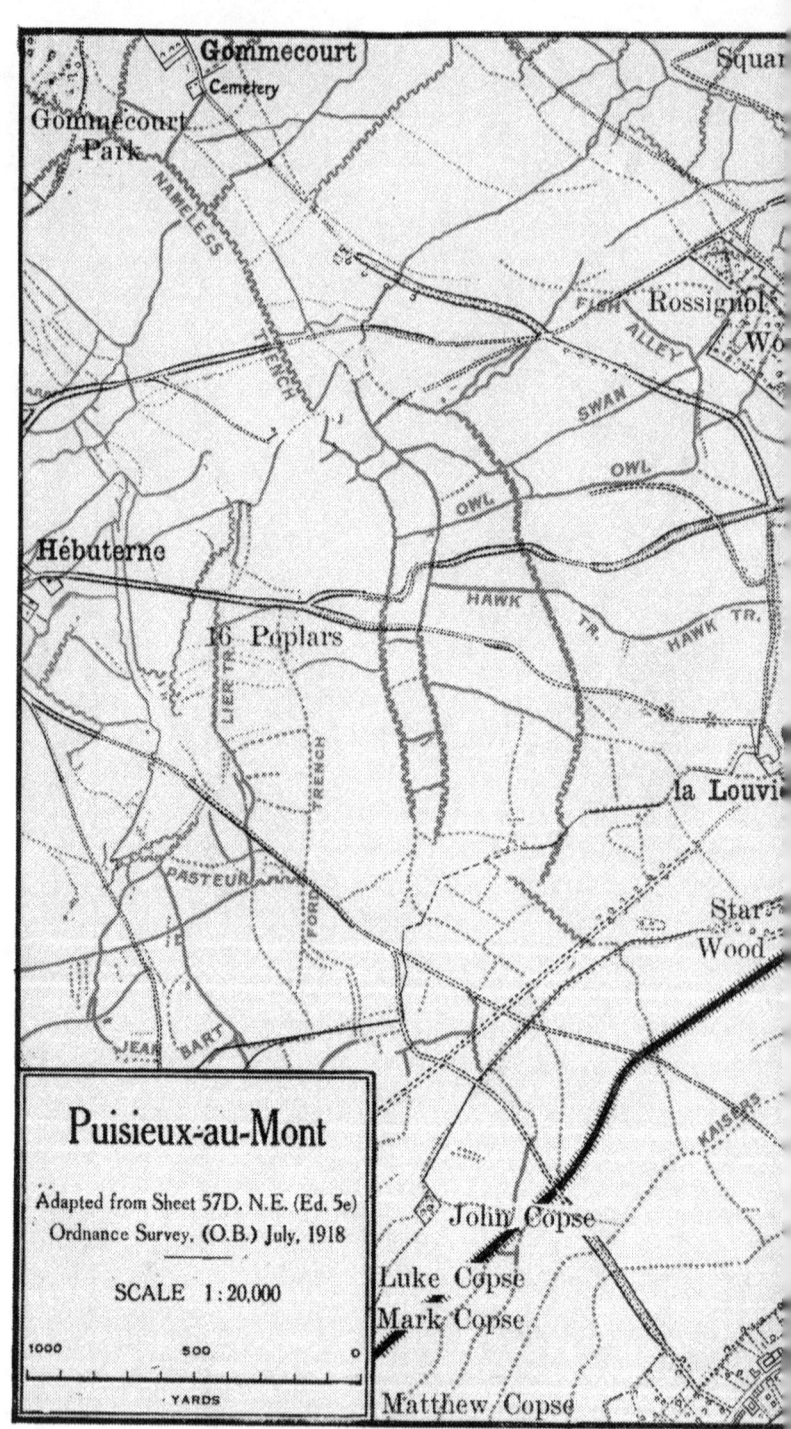

Area of Action, Summer of 1918.

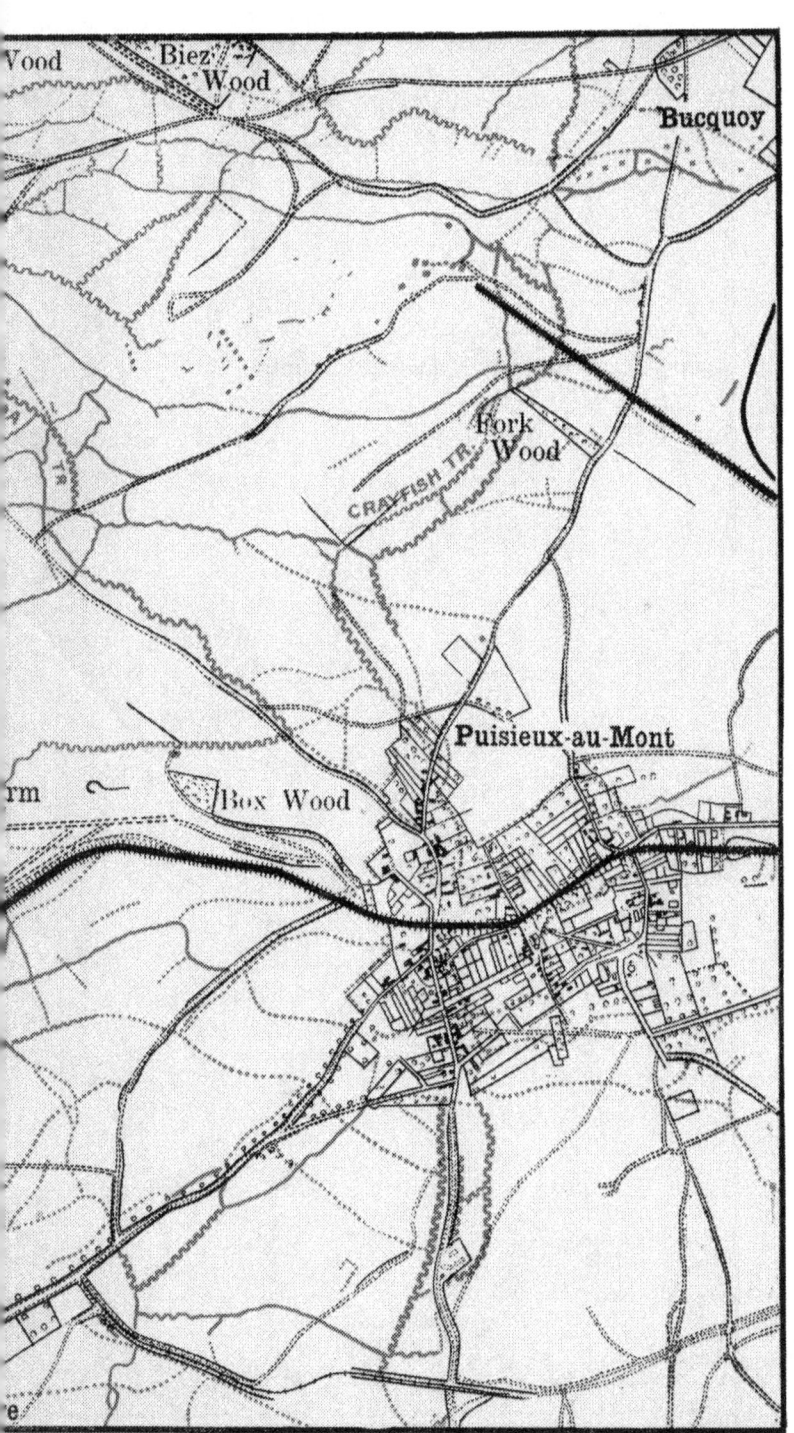

[*Copyright*

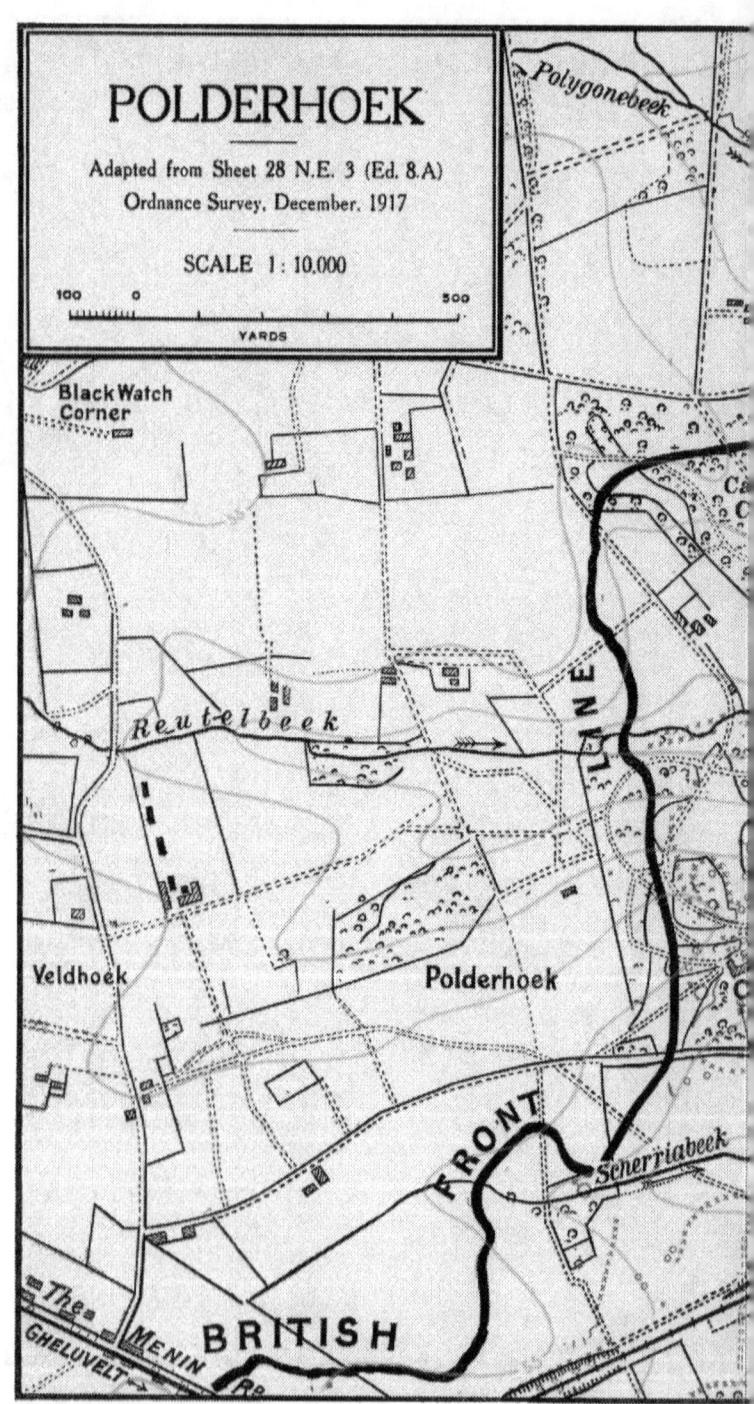

SCENE OF THE NEW ZEALANDERS' WORK AT THE END OF 1917.

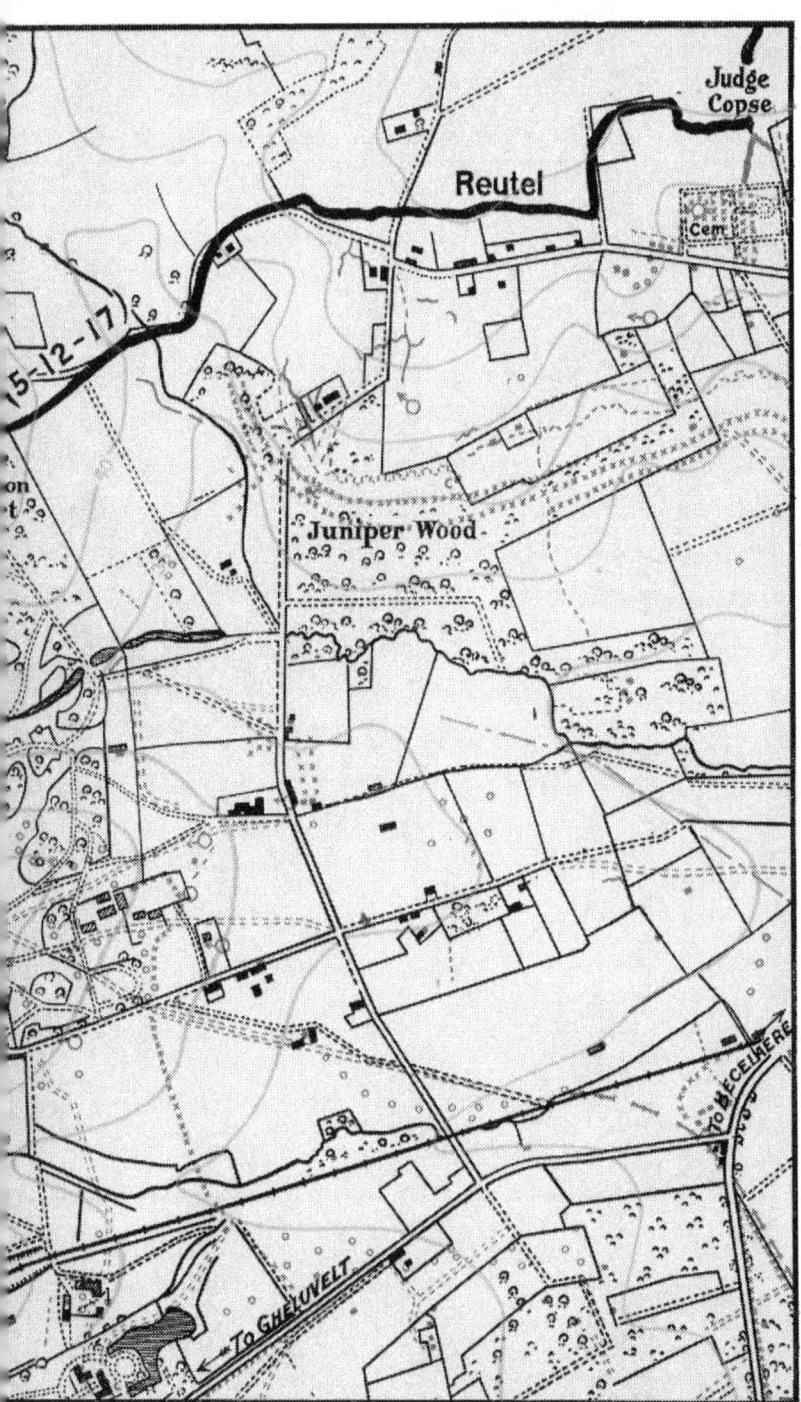

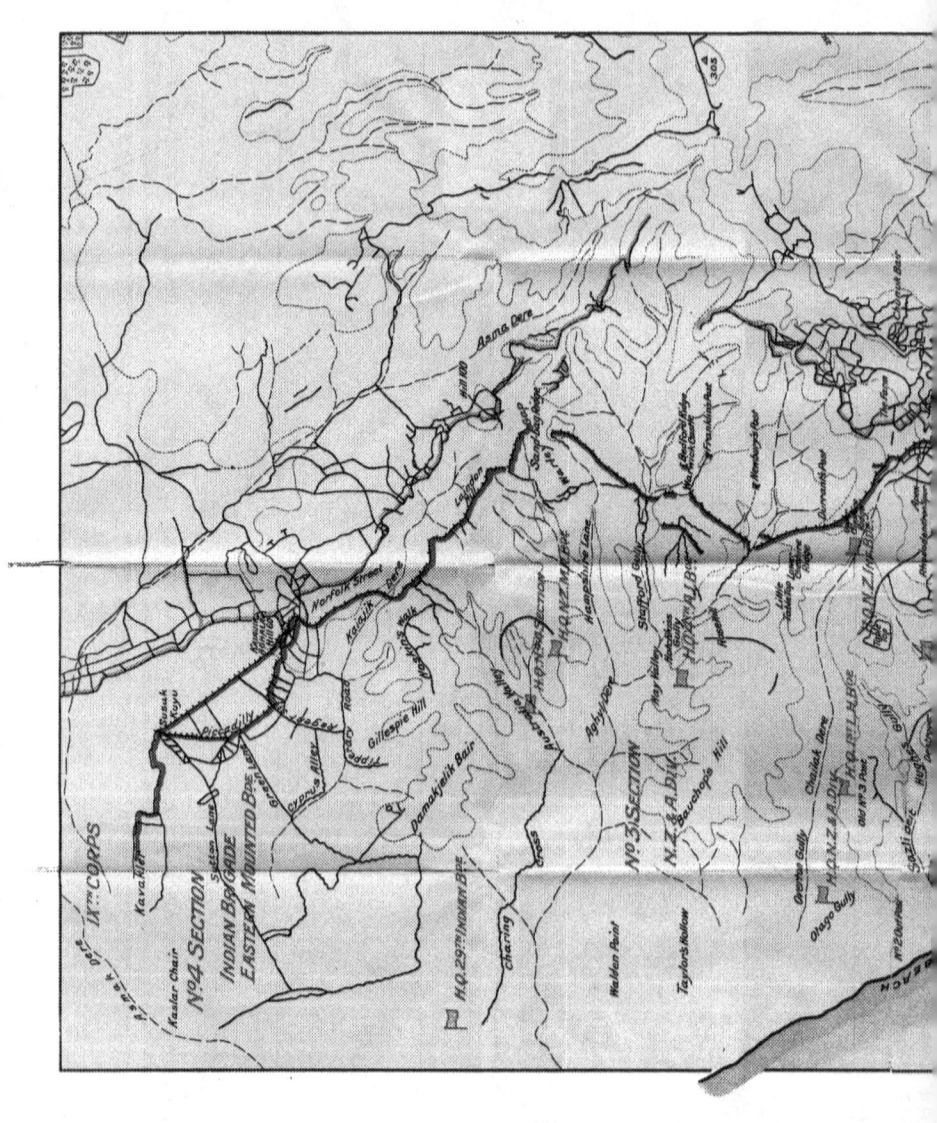

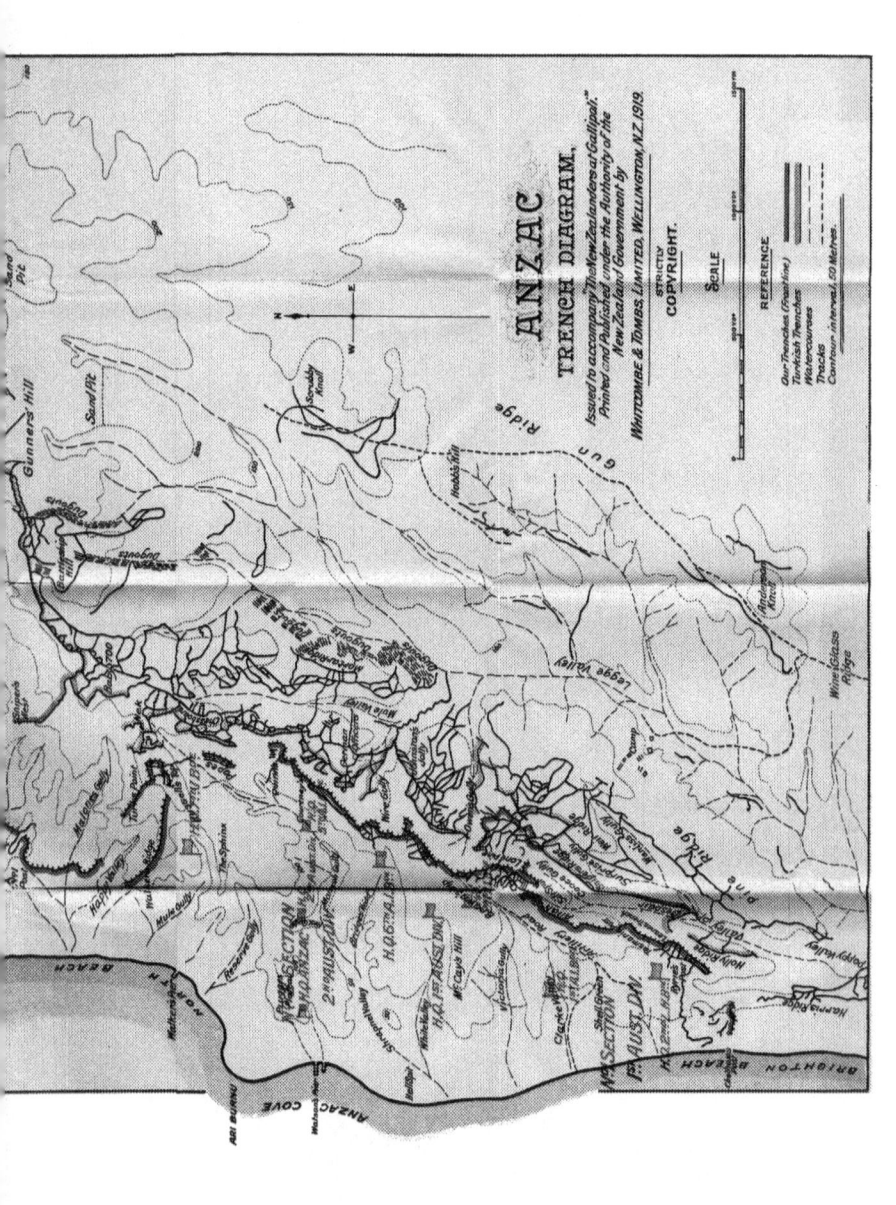

LIEUT.-COLONEL G. A. KING, D.S.O. AND BAR, AND CROIX DE GUERRE.

The D.S.O. was awarded for distinguished services on Gallipoli. Lieut.-Col. King, when Captain, was appointed to the command of the Pioneer Battalion in France in 1916; was several times mentioned in despatches, and after the Battle of Messines was decorated by General Anthone with the Croix de Guerre. Killed in Action, October 11th, 1917.

LIEUT.-COLONEL CONRAD G. SAXBY, D.S.O.

Served on Gallipoli and in France, 1915-1918 Appointed to the Command of the Pioneer Battalion in August, 1917. Died of influenza just after the signing of the Armistice.

CHAPTER 1.

INTRODUCTORY.

THE MAORIS' OFFER FOR SERVICE ABROAD.

With centuries of military traditions behind him, it was natural that the Maori should have been eager to shoulder rifle alongside his Pakeha compatriots in the Great War. He knew what it was to give up all for a cause, an idea. In the olden Maori polity the tribe came first; the tribe had first claim on the strong arm of the clansman, and the tribe stood behind every one of its members. No freeman of the *hapu* or *iwi* could suffer injury from a member of another clan and appeal in vain to his kinsmen for help in exacting justice. The whole strength of the collection of families which formed the tribe was at the disposal of the paramount chief and the war-captains once a certain line of policy had been decided upon. Here was Empire in miniature. It was easy for the modern Maori to appreciate the importance of united action in defence of the congeries of great families called the British Empire. He was quick to perceive the truth of the motto that unity is strength, and to realise that his duty as a citizen of the Empire was to come into alignment with his white brothers and cousins against the common danger. But a still more powerful impelling force was the thought that flashed from tribe to tribe that here at last was the great opportunity of showing what the present-day Maori could do in the field of battle.

For many years after the end of the last New Zealand wars the Maori had regarded his race as a dying one, doomed to extinction, as he phrased it, like the huge *moa* bird of his ancestors' days—**Ka ngaro i te ngaro o te moa.** Government statistics for a time went to support this melancholy belief. But the tide turned; the census showed an unexpected increase in native population. This increase became more marked each year under the new health regime established by the State health officers, notably Dr. Pomare and Dr. Te Rangihiroa, and the Maori took up heart again. In 1914 the Maori people numbered approximately 50,000, and the latest estimate of population is over 54,000. The Maori is adapting himself to the requirements of the Pakeha civilisation, and being socially and politically the full equal of the Pakeha his confidence in himself and his future is reinforced by a determination to acquit himself like a man in company with his British fellow-citizens.

There were those who, in their ignorance of the race, professed to doubt whether the modern young Maori was as good a man as his fighting father and grandfather. The Maori we used to see, the tall, straight-backed old athlete, tattooed to the height of the *moko* art, alert and active even in his old age, the old scout and bush warrior skilled in all the work of entrenchment, ambuscade, fort-storming and forest tactics, was for all purposes a perfect fighting man. A very few of these survive, in the villages of the King Country, the Urewera, the Bay of Plenty Coast. But the modern Maori, reared in a semi-Pakeha environment, college-bred, interested more in the new ways, new tasks and new amusements, thinking too little of his ancestral traditions—would he acquit himself as well as his grandfather on the field of battle? Some said no. But we who had known the Maori from earliest years, who had had Maori playmates at school and had lived and worked and travelled with native friends, knew better, knew that the hereditary love of war and the national traits of pride and courage had not been extinguished by a few years of non-necessity for exertion in ways military.

That the young Maori was no degenerate, softened by the peaceful life, was quickly made manifest when the First Contingent went into action at Gallipoli in 1915. Not merely were the native New Zealanders superior to all the coloured troops—a distinguished General said that the famous Ghurkas were but children as compared with the Maoris—but they proved superior to many of the white troops in directions which suited the genius of the race. They were as grim and thorough as any Highland regiment in attack work with the bayonet, and they proved themselves equal to the tremendous nerve-test of sustained shellfire, the greatest test of all. They were the only native troops who hung out the whole of the bitter trench work in France in 1916-18. They were fully the equal of their forefathers in fortitude and endurance as in dash and energy. They were most willing workers. A New Zealand officer who watched them in France said, "They did everything with a rush and immense determination; everything seemed a pleasure to them."

Coming of a race of fort-builders, the Maori soldier was a natural military engineer, and he entered into his work of entrenchment-making in France with the utmost interest. Not only did he work more quickly at the toil of digging-in than any other soldier of the King—this was the observation made by British officers—but he took a scientific pride in the construction of his field works. This was to have been expected of a people famous for their skill in *pa*-building in the olden wars. The grandfathers of some of these men had constructed the great stockades in the Bay of Islands country which had withstood British artillery—such as it was in the Forties—, the kinsmen of some had laid out the elaborate system of trenches which had baffled General Cameron at Paterangi, in the Upper Waikato, in 1864; those works, by the way, were pronounced by a British officer to be stronger than the Redan in the Crimea. There is a field-work at Puraku, near Rotorua, built in 1867 by a Ngati-Raukawa war-party, which bears a most remarkable resemblance in the details of trenches to the fighting-saps and communication trenches cut by our men in France and Flanders in 1916-1918. Field-engineering, in fact, came easy to the Maori; he could and did in many cases improve on the work of the British Army men.

With the exception of the Waikato, Taranaki and Urewera districts, the Maori tribes were denuded of their young men during the war. As in the Highland glens, the English shires and on the New Zealand farms, the native villages were deserted by the able-bodied: it was a matter of shame to be found lagging behind. Alike on the cocksfoot-grass slopes of Akaroa and the maize paddocks of Auckland, the women and girls at harvest took the place of the men. In Rotorua there were scarcely any but the older people, the women and the children; every Arawa who could pass the doctor and look fit to carry rifle and swag went into camp to train for the great adventure. The age limit was liberally construed. There is a young Maori at Matata who enlisted with the Arawa in the First Maori Contingent, fought at Gallipoli in 1915, was invalided home, married an Arawa girl, and volunteered for further service abroad, when his wife stopped his wandering by informing the authorities that he was only seventeen. But it was the custom of the Maori to enter the firing line in the early teens. Many a man of the old generation went on his first war trail at the age of twelve. Rihara Kou, a venerable Ngapuhi warrior at Kaikohe, who farewelled his youthful kinsmen—29 young men went from Kaikohe to the Front—was only thirteen when he helped to defend Ohaeawai and Ruapekapeka stockades against the British troops seventy-one years before. In some cases father and son joined the Contingent. One of the grandsons of the early-days Danish trader Philip Tapsell and the chieftainess Hine-i-turama of Maketu, Bay of Plenty, took his two sons with him when he enlisted and the three fought in the bayonet charges on the blood-reddened slopes of Sari Bair. That celebrated pair of Maketu, by the way, founded quite a tribe; their descendants number about a hundred, and of this little halfcaste clan, called Te Whanau-a-Tapihana ('The Offspring of Tapsell') 28 men served in the Great War. Another small clan of the Arawa, the Ngati-Manawa, living at the Rangitaiki river, on the western border of the Urewera country, lost five young men in the war. The Ngati-Manawa had ever been noted for their pluck and enterprise in war. In the Sixties of last century, when they fought gallantly on the Government side under the Mair brothers and their own chiefs against the Hauhaus, they could muster only about forty fighting men, and some of these were young lads, but they were all reliable and fearless fellows. The young and able-bodied of Ngati-Porou, too, joined practically to a man.

Many times there had been suggestions to send Maoris overseas for military service on distant shores. The military genius of the race was recognised a full century ago, and this recognition was first manifested in a very curious way in the days when the Maori was, in war-time, a ferocious and dreaded

LIEUT.-COLONEL WM. O. ENNIS, D.S.O.

Served as Captain with the First Maori Contingent, Gallipoli, 1915; Major Pioneer Battalion, Western Front, 1916-1918. Commanded the Battalion, November 1918 till the return to New Zealand. Staff Superintendent, New Zealand Railway Department. Accidentally killed at Auckland, February, 1926, aged 55 years.

MAJOR H. PEACOCK, N.Z. PERMANENT STAFF.

Major Peacock was in command of the Training Camp near Narrow Neck, Devonport, Auckland, from 1915 to the end of the War. Died at Paeroa, 1924.

raider who not only killed but ate his enemy; his principal item of commissariat was his foe's body. In the year 1829, according to Mr James Bonwick in his book, "The Last of the Tasmanians," a project was brought forward by Mr Horace Rowcroft and seconded by Major Gray, at Hobart, to introduce a number of New Zealanders into Van Diemen's Land, as Tasmania was then called. It was contended that as the Maoris would sell slaves for a musket each they would be quite willing to catch blackfellows at the same rate. "Their great intelligence, their crafty policy, and their warlike bearing, with the use of weapons better adapted than 'Brown Bess' to forest contests, made the plan acceptable to many." Mr Rowcroft added a plea of "benevolence," as Mr Bonwick called it. It was truly Pecksniffian benevolence. The Maoris were then regarded as about the greatest savages and cannibals that the world could furnish; so, without reflecting upon the consequences of contact to the Tasmanians, he declared that "much good would result to the New Zealanders by their intercourse with us, and would probably sow the germ of civilisation among an energetic and enterprising people." But the humane Colonel Arthur feared the massacre of his black subjects and rejected the proposals. The colonists and officials of Tasmania, in the end, succeeded in exterminating the poor aboriginals without the help of Maori musketeers.

Nearly thirty years later there was another Maori Contingent suggestion. Governor Gore Browne, in 1858, gave approval to a proposal made by Captain Charles Brown, of New Plymouth, that a Royal Maori Corps of from 300 to 600 men should be raised to serve at the Cape of Good Hope against the Kaffirs. The Governor sent the proposal to the British Government, but it was discouraged by the War Office and nothing more was heard of it. It is not likely that many Maoris were eager for such an enterprise; indeed, I believe Captain Brown's pretty scheme was really put forward and supported by a number of colonists because if accepted it would comfortably dispose of some hundreds of fight-loving brown neighbours who would otherwise be a possible source of trouble in New Zealand.

In a despatch to the Secretary of State for the Colonies

in 1849, Governor Grey said that the Maori, in the opinion of experienced officers, was infinitely superior to the North American Indian in weapons, in knowledge of the art of war, and in skill in planning and perseverance in carrying out the operations of a long campaign. The Natives were, in fact, even better equipped than the British corps for the warfare of the country. That was written after experience of three small campaigns—the war with Ngapuhi at the Bay of Islands, the fighting at the Lower Hutt and at Pauatahanui and Horokiwi, Wellington, and the Whanganui war of 1847. More formidable campaigns were to come, the wars that began in 1860 and lasted for more than ten years, and the experience of these wars, in which the Imperial and Colonial troops far outnumbered their opponents, thoroughly justified Sir George Grey's early respect for the Maori as a soldier and a tactician and strategist.

On several occasions Britain's wars, during the last forty years, inspired the Maori with a desire for overseas service. One of these offers had a touch of comedy. The news that an Australian contingent of troops was being despatched to Suakim, on the Red Sea, to aid the British forces in the Soudan War, in 1884, prompted a Ngati-Haua warrior, Hoté Tamehana, to volunteer the services of himself and a party of his tribe to fight the *iwi mangumangu* in North Africa. Hoté was the son of a celebrated patriot, Wiremu Tamehana Tarapipipi, the Maori "Kingmaker," and brother of Tupu Taingakawa, the present head of Ngati-Haua and leading man in the old Kingite cause. Hoté had fought against the Queen's troops in the Waikato and Taranaki wars. Fired by new-born loyalty, he rode in from his *raupo*-thatched village at Korakonui and entering the telegraph office at Kihikihi township, on the King Country frontier, wrote a telegram to the Government offering himself and twenty of his young men of Ngati-Koroki and Ngati-Haua for the Soudan campaign. "Twenty men!" said a settler to whom he showed the message before handing it in; "Why not make it two hundred?" "*Ka pai, ka pai!*" Hoté exclaimed, "That's good, very good. I'll make it two hundred men," and two hundred the telegram made it. The Government did not accept the offer, but Hoté got into trouble with the members of his tribe for committing them to foreign service without consulting them.

In the year 1896 the Arawa tribesmen, who had fought gallantly for the white Queen against the Hauhaus in the campaigns of the Sixties and the 1870-72 expeditions, discussed the matter of volunteering for service in South Africa. It was in the days of the Anglo-German crisis following on the invasion of the Transvaal by the Chartered Company's force under Dr. Jameson and its defeat and capture by the Boers. A meeting was held in the tribal meeting-house "Tama-te-Kapua" at Ohinemutu to consider the question of "the difficulty which has arisen between the Queen of England and other tribes," and many speeches were made for England and against all England's foes. Several speakers exhorted the Arawa to enlist for South Africa, but as there did not appear to be any call for their services the tribe contended itself with expressions of loyalty to the Crown. "My country right or wrong " was the sentiment of the meeting.

During the South African war there were many offers from Maori volunteers, but although numerous men of part Maori and part English blood served in New Zealand Contingents it was not thought necessary to enlist a Maori Contingent. Conspicuous among those who were eager to serve was the Ngati-Porou chief Tuta Nihoniho, a man of true soldierly instincts and training, who had fought against the Hauhaus on the East Coast from 1865 to 1871. To relieve his disappointment he sent a present of a greenstone *mere* to Lord Roberts. In the mid-eighties, when there were alarms of possible war with Russia, Tuta raised and commanded a Maori volunteer corps, the Ngati-Porou Rifles, which was in existence for four years.

In the Great War.

The Maori Contingent, reorganised as a Pioneer Battalion after its Gallipoli service, consisted of the following:—

First Maori Contingent—February 14th, 1915	518
Second Draft—September 19th, 1915	312
Third Draft—February 6th, 1916	110
Reinforcements to October 18th, 1918	1287
Total of all ranks	2227

The South Sea Islands troops enlisted for service with the New Zealanders were:—

Niué (Savage Island) natives—February 6th, 1916	148
Rarotonga and other Cook Islands natives— first draft February 6th, 1916	50
Rarotongans—second draft, November 16th, 1916	115
Rarotongans—third draft, June 3, 1918	145
Total	458

The Maori Roll of Honour.

The following is the official list of deaths in the Maori Contingent and the Pioneer Battalion, on active service, 1915-1918:

	Officers.	Other Ranks.
Killed in Action	8	122
Died of Wounds	4	62
Died of Sickness	2	130
Other causes	1	7
Totals	15	321

Grand total, all ranks—336 dead.

In addition to these casualties, 734 members of the Maori force were wounded, making the total casualties 1070, or nearly 50 per cent. of the total number of men sent overseas.*

---

*See Appendices for a complete list of the fatal casualties in the Maori force during the war.

CHAPTER II.

RECRUITING AND ORGANISATION OF THE MAORI CONTINGENT.

The first proposal to send a Maori force to the War was made in the beginning of August, 1914. The news of the proclamation of war between Britain and her Allies and Germany aroused the *kaingas* from the far North to the Wai-Pounamu, and telegrams to the Government offering Maori assistance to the Empire came pouring in from all parts of the country. The Arawa of Rotorua and the Ngati-Kahungunu of Te Wairoa and other parts of Hawke's Bay were the first to volunteer, followed quickly by Ngati-Porou, by the tribes around Gisborne and by Whanganui and Ngati-Apa. The first reply of the authorities was to the purport that the rule of the Imperial Government had been that no native race should be used in hostilities between European races. It was soon announced in the cablegrams, however, that Indian troops were being sent to France and also that native soldiers from Africa were to assist the French. On learning of this the Maori tribes, through their members of Parliament, renewed their request to be permitted to serve the King in the field of battle. The Prime Minister replied, expressing his great pleasure and gratitude at the offers of the loyal Maoris and stating that he would place the proposal before the Imperial Government. On September 16th he announced that His Majesty's Government had accepted the Maoris' aid and had agreed that a Native Contingent of 200 men should be sent to Egypt. A little later this suggestion was altered. The War Office proposed that there should be two Maori forces, each of 250, one to go to Egypt and the other to Samoa.

The principle of Maori participation in the War having thus been established, to the great satisfaction and pride of the people, the next step was the selection of the war-parties. On the suggestion of the Hon. the Minister for Defence, the Maori members of Parliament set about the work of raising the necessary men. On September 18th a meeting of members was held in the room of the Hon. Sir Maui Pomare (then Dr.

Pomare; his knighthood was conferred upon him in recognition of his patriotic services in the organisation of the Maori forces, and his work for the welfare of the race). A recruiting Committee was formed, consisting of the Hon. Sir James Carroll, Sir Maui Pomare (Western Maori), the Hon. A. T. Ngata (Eastern Maori), Dr. Peter H. Buck, whose Maori name is Te Rangihiroa (Northern Maori), and Mr Taare Parata (Southern Maori). This committee at once began its task of allotting the proportions of the Contingent of 500 thus: Tai Tokerau (Northern District) 100 men; Tai Hauauru (Western Maori) 180; Tai-Rawhiti (East Coast) 180, and the Wai-Pounamu ("Waters of Greenstone"—the South Island) 40. Thenceforth the Maori Committee kept steadily at work throughout the Great War. Two of the original members were replaced by others soon after the war began. Dr. Buck went on active service, and his place as member for the Northern Maori District was taken by Mr Tau Henare; and Mr. Parata died, to the great regret of his colleagues, and was succeeded by Mr. Uru.

The Committee issued through the "Kahiti"—the Maori Gazette—a notice to all the tribes, calling for volunteers between the ages of 21 and 40 years willing to serve the King for the duration of the war. "E te iwi, whitiki! Whiti, whiti e!" the appeal of the "Komiti Whakahaere" concluded. It was the old war-cry of the chiefs when danger threatened: "O tribe, gird up your loins! Rise up, rise up!" And the Maori people rose eagerly at the challenge and appeal. Volunteers came from the remote gumlands of North Auckland, from the farms and forests of the Kaipara, from the shores of the Bay of Islands and the Hauraki, the King Country and Bay of Plenty coast, the lakeside villages of the Arawa, the sheep farms and rich agricultural country of mis-named Poverty Bay and Hawke's Bay; from the shores of the great central Lake Taupo, the terraced banks of the rushing Whanganui and the plains of Manawatu and Wairarapa; then across Cook Strait the call was answered from the little townships and farms of the Ngai-Tahu. From Parengarenga, the most northerly harbour in the Dominion, down to the old whaling and sealing stations on the shore of Foveaux Strait, came athletic brown lads, intensely elated at the prospect of fighting shoulder to shoulder with their white fellow-New Zealanders against the common enemy

Those *Pakeha* New Zealanders who knew the Maori well were delighted to think that he was being given an opportunity to display his fighting qualities after many years of peace. One, an old missionary in Auckland, said: "If they are true sons of their fathers, they will be brave and gallant fighters, they will show courage and resource in battle, and they will treat wounded enemies and women and children with kindness and courtesy. I would not be afraid to trust the Maori in war. He will be truly British." A veteran of the wars of half a century previously, said: "I could not wish for better fighters and comrades than the Maoris with whom I fought. When they trusted the white man they could be relied on absolutely. As scouts, of course, there was nothing to touch them. The present generation of Maoris will probably make splendid soldiers." Another old New Zealand colonist, referring to the military traditions of the Maoris, said: "These traditions, stories of great and glorious deeds of warfare, are the best guarantee we have that the Maori, even under the strange and disturbing conditions of modern warfare, will be a soldier of whom the Empire may be proud. All Maoris are intensely loyal to their race and intensely jealous of its reputation, and now that the Maori race is merged in the British Empire, that loyalty and that jealousy are transferred to Britain. The proposal is to send the natives to Egypt to do duty there, and I know that these men will do their duty thoroughly; but if they are sent to the fighting line there will not be a man of them who will shrink from laying down his life for the Empire of which he is a part. I know that these men will welcome any chance to bring new glory to the Maori race, even at the sacrifice of their own lives."

The Defence Department and the Maori Committee jointly made arrangements for the medical examination of volunteers and their enrolment for service, and the first camp was established in the middle of October, 1914, on the grounds of the racecourse at Avondale, the olden Whau, a few miles west of Auckland city. The first Maori detachments to enter camp were small parties from Mangonui, North Auckland, and from the Auckland district. On October 19th a party of 50 young men arrived from the South Island and 36 from the Hauraki and Ngati-Maniapoto tribe. On the following day 92 recruits came in from the West Coast, representing the tribes of Whanganui, Ngati-Apa, Ngati-Raukawa and Ngati-Toa. These young soldiers were quickly followed by ninety composed of Te Arawa, of the Lakes District, Maketu and Matata, Ngai-Awa from Whakatane, Whakatohea from Opotiki, and the Whanau-a-Apanui and kindred tribes as far as Tikirau (East Cape). The famous fighting Ngati-Porou followed; these young men were from the Tai-Rawhiti villages from the East Cape southward toward Gisborne. The Ngati-Kahungunu from Hawke's Bay and some more Ngapuhi from Kaikohe and other Northern districts completed the 500 men in training under canvas at Avondale.

These young Maoris, the pick of the race, gathered from all corners of the Dominion, entered with the utmost eagerness and zest into their soldierly duties under *pakeha* instructors. All who visited the camp were pleased with the cheerful temper of the men, their great alacrity at all tasks ("fatigue it was their pride," to quote Kipling's sergeant in "The Men Who Fought at Minden"), and the quickness and intelligence they brought to bear on the work in hand. Their physique was the theme of praise by inspecting military officers. On parade they attracted great admiration for their stature, their muscular development and their alertness and soldierly bearing. On October 24th, Sir James Allen, Minister for Defence, inspected the Opé Maori, and addressing the recruits expressed his great pleasure at the Maori being the first Native race to offer for service abroad, with the exception, of course of the men of India, who were soldiers already. He praised their quickness and pride in soldierly training and said he was sure they would acquit themselves as creditably as their *pakeha* fellow-soldiers. The Minister made mention, too, of the number of college-bred young Maoris in the Opé, boys from Te Aute, Waerenga-a-Hika Mission School, St. Stephen's (Parnell, Auckland), Hikurangi (Wairarapa), Otaki, and the Three Kings Wesleyan College, Auckland.

HON. SIR MAUI POMARE, C.M.G., M.P., M.D.
Member of the Executive Council, Minister for the Cook and other Islands; Chairman of the Maori Recruiting Board and Maori Regimental Committee.

Hon. Sir James Carroll, M.L.C.
(Maori War Medal)
Member of the Maori Recruiting Board and Maori Regimental Committee.
(Died at Auckland, October 18th, 1926.)

RECRUITING AND ORGANISATION.

The proposal to send the Maoris away in two companies, one to Samoa and one to Egypt, was debated among the tribes, and was strongly opposed by the principal men. The feeling gathered weight that it would not be judicious to divide the contingent, and the unanimous opinion was soon expressed that the Maori should be sent to Egypt as being near the seat of war. The men naturally were anxious to reach the actual battlefield and were not enthusiastic about garrison duty. Sir Maui Pomare and his committee conveyed to the Prime Minister a general request that the whole of the force should be sent to Egypt, and this request was sent on by the Government to the British Secretary of State for the Colonies. On November 7th a cablegram from London to the Governor stated that the wishes of the Maoris and the New Zealand Government had been acceded to, and that all the Maoris would be despatched to Egypt.

The Contingent was now divided into two companies, A and B, composed as follows:—

A Company (Northern Maori, West Coast—South Island):

Platoon (Ropu) 1—Men from the North Auckland district, extending from Tamaki (Auckland isthmus) to the Rerenga-Wairua (Spirits' Leap, in the extreme North).

Platoon 2—Tamaki to Pari-ninihi (the White Cliffs, North Taranaki), including Ngati-Maniapoto, also the Hauraki and Tauranga tribes and Ngati-Tuwharetoa of Taupo. (These were the tribes of Tainui stock).

Platoon 3—West Coast: Waitotara, Whanganui and inland tribes from Taihape to Manawatu.

Platoon 4—Horowhenua to Wellington, also the South Island.

B Company (Rotorua and East Coast):

Platoon 5—Te Arawa.

Platoon 6—Te Awa-a-te-Atua (Matata) to the East Coast and Waiapu.

Platoon 7—Uawa (Tolago Bay) and Gisborne.

Platoon 8—Ngati-Kahungunu, from Te Mahia to Napier and Wairarapa.

The organisation of the Contingent having been completed, training was carried on steadily in infantry work under Captain Peacock and Permanent Force instructors. Squad, platoon and company drill, route marching, musketry, bayonet practice, assault practice, trench digging, night attacks and all other details of instruction kept the Contingent busy until its departure for the Front.

Several veteran officers with Maori War services were anxious to lead the Contingent, and it was at first proposed that Colonel T. W. Porter, C.B., who had a distinguished record in the New Zealand and South African campaigns, should go in command. No better choice could have been made. Colonel Porter had served continuously in the Maori Wars from 1865 to 1871 as an officer of native forces; he knew the Maori temperament as few *pakehas* did, and the men would have placed complete confidence in such an experienced and sympathetic leader. However, it was considered that he was too old for further active service. Another veteran extremely anxious to serve was Captain Gilbert Mair, N.Z.C., perhaps the most dashing and enterprising of all our New Zealand-born and bred soldiers. He had won his New Zealand Cross by a most gallant feat of arms, his defeat of Te Kooti near Rotorua in 1870. Mair was the hero of the Arawa; from 1866 to 1872 he had led them on active service. Even in his old age he was the most active of men; at seventy-eight years of age he made a long horseback journey through the rough Urewera country over the old fighting trails, with the present writer. Yet another volunteer was Major J. T. Large, who had served with the Wairoa friendlies and the Ngati-Porou in the East Coast and Urewera campaigns. Rejected in New Zealand in 1914, he went to Australia and tried unsuccessfully to join the forces there; and by way of demonstrating his fitness for active service, in spite of his age, he undertook a long walking tour through the North of Auckland. But it was the day of the young man; the old warriors were reminded that their place lay in the homeland; and they loyally accepted the position and exerted themselves in recruiting and in lending a helping hand to the fortunate ones chosen for the battlefield of Tu. Colonel Porter, in the latter part of the war, was engaged by the Government to carry out special work, as an Inspector of Recruiting Services, and he also gave useful gratuitous service as Commandant of the New Zealand National Reserve.

Early on February 10th, 1915, the Contingent packed up and bade farewell to the camp and set out on the long trail to the Old World. The Hokowhitu a Tu, "The Seventy Twice-told Warriors of the War God," the Maori chiefs christened the force, in allusion to the favourite number of a war-party, 140, for a desperate attack in the days of old. Marching through Auckland city, the men went aboard the troop-steamer "Warrimoo," which sailed for Wellington. On Saturday, February 13th, the Maoris landed at Wellington and with a *pakeha* contingent paraded in Newtown Park for final review and farewell. An official account of that memorable good-bye parade, published in Maori in the Government "Kahiti," described the march and the park ceremonials thus: "The *Pakeha* people who beheld the march of that 500 will never forget the sight, the spectacle of that splendid war-party, those tall strong men, their fine marching—it was equal to the drill and appearance of the best soldiers in the world. There were some who said that the Maori soldiers were the finest body ever seen on parade in Newtown Park. There they bade farewell to their assembled relatives; they displayed their skill in the accomplishments of their ancestors—the *haka*, the *tutu-ngarahu* (war-dance), canoe-paddling songs and other chants; excellent their leaping in the war-dance, their drill of hands in unison, their *waiata*-chanting."

There were speeches of exhortation and affection from the Maori chiefs, counsel to uphold the warrior fame of the Maori and touching songs of farewell from the native assemblage. The Maori was about to take that long, long, sea-road to the faraway land of his birth in the mists of time; he was to see, perhaps, the veritable shores of Hawaiki-nui, of Hawaiki-roa, of Hawaiki-pa-mamao, the shadowy land of legend whence his fathers came, sailing ever eastward to "the gateways of the day." Somewhere there on the south coast of Asia, the Arabian littoral, his long-ago ancestors had sojourned, from a score of countries perhaps had drawn some of their racial traits; maybe it was from the sea-going Arabs of the Red Sea coasts that they derived their skill and enterprise as sailors. Now the Opé Hokowhitu a Tu was retracing the way to the first of many Hawaikis; it was a crusading army, upholding the name and fame of the Maori to the whole world. It might well be that those splendid young men would return no more. They paraded proudly before their fellow-countrymen, Maori and *Pakeha*. There was the spirit of the ancient Roman in their last march-past: "Ave Caesar, morituri te salutant!" They marched away to the sound of high and pathetic farewells: "Haere, haere! Haere, e hoki! Haere ki te ahi e ka mai ra i Oropi! E tama ma, kia kaha, kia maia, kia manawa-nui! Haere ra!"

Early on the morning of February 14th, the Maori troopship, which was commanded by Captain Edwin, quietly moved out from her Wellington berth and steamed away for Suez via her only Australian port of call, Albany. As the Indian Ocean was reported free of danger since the destruction of the German cruiser "Emden," by H.M.A.S. "Sydney" at Cocos Island (November, 1914), there was no warship escort for the "Warrimoo" and her consorts the *pakeha* troopships "Maunganui," "Tahiti" and "Aparima." (The last named ship was afterwards sunk in the English Channel.) Captain Edwin took his ship close in to Cocos and gave the Maoris a good view of the battered enemy raider lying on the reef. There was one death on board during the voyage across the Indian Ocean, Corporal Mikaera Te Moananui

When passing through the Red Sea the Maoris heard the distant noise of a bombardment. It was a British cruiser shelling a Turkish position on the coast. On the voyage the musical talent in the Contingent was assembled and a band was formed under the direction of Captain Pirimi Tahiwi and Lieut. Stainton.

The Maoris disembarked at Suez and entrained for Cairo, where they were loudly welcomed by the *pakeha* New Zealanders, and marched out to Zeitoun Camp. A week there, and then came orders for Malta, whither the transport *Runic* carried the Maoris, to begin garrison duty at Ghain Tuffiah Camp (about 16 miles from Valetta).

Hon. A. T. Ngata, M.A., LL.B.
Member of Parliament for Eastern Maori District, and Member of Maori Regimental Committee.

Mr. Tau Henare, M.P. for Northern Maori District.
Member of the Maori Recruiting Board and Regimental Committee.

Major Peacock, who had trained the Contingent in the Avondale camp, had been given command of the force for the voyage and overseas service, but, to his own great grief and to the deep regret of his men, he was taken seriously ill on the passage and had to be landed in West Australia, and invalided home. The Maoris were very sorrowful over this misfortune, for Major Peacock was not only an excellent instructor and capable leader but he had a real liking for the Maori people, and his sympathetic attitude heartened them greatly. His place was taken by Major Herbert, who was given the command of the Contingent on arrival in Egypt and retained it at Gallipoli until after the battle of Sari Bair (August, 1915), when he was appointed to the command of a British battalion. Major Peacock, on resuming duty in New Zealand, was placed in command of the training camp established at Narrow Neck, overlooking Rangitoto Channel, Auckland. Here the work of training Maori and South Sea Islands recruits was carried on after the evacuation of the Avondale camp. His death when in charge of the Paeroa Defence District in 1924 was a matter of grief to all his old comrades and indeed to all who had known him, whether in his military or his private capacity.

Recruiting the Reinforcements.

As time went on, the heavy wastage of the battlefields and the sickness, due to the conditions under which the War was waged, necessitated considerable reinforcements to keep the Contingent, or, as it became, the Pioneer Battalion, up to field strength. When the Battalion was in France in 1917, two returned soldiers, Lieuts. Te Awarau and Puke Cross, were engaged as recruiting officers in the North Island, going from tribe to tribe and addressing the people. A notable unofficial recruiting agent was Ruatapu-nui, the Urewera long-haired prophet aforetime, who, after getting the worst of a tussle with the police at Maunga-pohatu—a fatal affray in which one of his sons was shot dead—and serving a term of imprisonment, became a staunch supporter of the King's authority, and brought in towards the end of the war some fifty volunteers, his young men from Ruatoki and other settlements. The

Arawa were particularly enthusiastic and self-sacrificing supporters of the British cause; even the elderly men were anxious to enlist. On August 9th, 1915, Hone Te Awe-Kotuku wrote to Sir Maui Pomare from Te Ngae, Rotorua: "We, the parents of those who went to Egypt, are sorry that we were left behind. We now hear that those up to 55 years are being listed. That age of life includes most of us, and the whole of the Arawa are agreed." To this the reply was that only men between the ages of 20 and 40 years were being enlisted.

There was one important exception to the general eagerness of the tribes for active service abroad. This was Waikato, embracing most of the people under the *mana* of Rata Mahuta, the great-grandson of the famous Potatau te Wherowhero, the first Maori King. The Maori Kingdom, dating back to the Fifties of last century, was now but a shadow of its olden greatness, but the memory of the Waikato war, when ten thousand British and Colonial troops were required to subjugate the Kingites, was ever before Waikato, for in that war they lost the greater part of their lands, confiscated by the Crown. "Give us back Waikato," had been their cry for fifty years. They neither forgot nor forgave that act of wholesale confiscation; and their perpetual grievance against the Government was made their excuse for declining to volunteer for the great war abroad. The Waikato, with their numerous clans, Ngati-Mahuta, Ngati-Naho, Ngati-te-ata, Ngati-Tipa, Ngati-Tahinga and others, and the Ngati-Haua—the tribe of that fine patriot of former days, Wiremu Tamehana Tarapipipi, the Maori King-maker—could have furnished a company of first-rate fighting men, athletic and enterprising. But the influence of their elders, the old diehards, who still regarded the Potatau family as their royal line, was sufficiently strong to prevent most of the young men from volunteering for the Opé Maori. They put up a passive resistance, declaring that, while they were willing to defend New Zealand from attack, they did not wish to serve outside the country.

The Maori Recruiting Committee, jointly with the Defence Department, made strenuous efforts to bring Waikato and allied tribes into line with the rest of the nation. Sir James Allen, Minister for Defence, Sir Maui Pomare, and several high chiefs of the tribe visited Waikato, argued with Rata, his "Premier" and chief adviser Tupu Taingakawa (the great Wiremu Tamehana's son), and appealed to the people to make common cause with their fellow-countrymen against the nation's foes. One of the most eloquent advocates of recruiting was Te Heuheu Tukino, M.L.C., the paramount chief of Ngati-Tuwharetoa, of the Taupo country. Te Heuheu was loyal to his race and at the same time a thorough-going advocate of Maori participation in the great struggle overseas for the liberty of the world. The principal burden of persuading Waikato to enlist lay on the Hon. Sir Maui Pomare. In one of his speeches at a meeting with Waikato under Rata, at Waahi village, Sir Maui addressed his countrymen and constituents as follows:—

"Waikato, I return your greetings, according to the customs of our race. I have listened with an attentive ear to your words—the reasons why you are resisting the law. It is bad. You are not only grasping shadows, but you are kicking against the pricks. I will show you presently that you are untrue to the traditions and unfaithful to the sacred words of your great and illustrious dead.

"You say conscription is against the Treaty of Waitangi. I ask you to consider Clause Three of that Treaty. What does it say?—'In consideration thereof (that is, in the Maori version, agreeing to the Government of the Queen) Her Majesty the Queen of England extends to the Natives of New Zealand her Royal protection, and imparts to them all the rights and privileges of British subjects.' Now, our ancestors signed that treaty. They agreed to the Government of the Queen. I ask you this question,—What is a Government for? Is it not for the purpose of making laws? And what are laws for? Is it not for the protection of the members of the State? And are not the laws made for us to obey? Then, in order to keep the Treaty inviolate, we will have to keep the laws made by the Government that our ancestors accepted.

"The British monarch extended us the Royal protection. Has not that bargain been kept? Have we not been protected from that time to this? 'And imparts to them all the rights and privileges of British subjects.' Is it not our privilege and our right to fight for King and country? I want to point out to you that no right and no privilege can exist without the corresponding responsibility. Now do you see how the Treaty favours conscription, and how you have erred in regard to its provisions?

"Now in regard to Potatau. Do you recollect his coronation oath? When my predecessors made him King of the Maori tribes, do you remember what they said, 'Potatau, we make you King. Henceforth you and Queen Victoria shall be united—the law shall be the carpet [*whariki*] for your feet and the religion of Christ your joint religion for ever.' And what did Potatau say? 'Yes, for ever. There is but one eye to the needle, through which the white, the black, and the red threads must pass.' You tell me to-day that Potatau's needle must have more than one eye; for you contend that there should be a different law for the Maoris, that conscription should not apply to them. 'Beware of Kura's urn, lest the dust from the feet of your ancestors arise and smother you.'

"It is true that Tawhiao (the second Maori King) spoke the words, which you have quoted, regarding the banishing of war from New Zealand, but were not these words uttered by him at a peace conference with the *pakeha?* Has not war been banished from these shores? Is there fighting between *Pakeha* and Maori to-day? 'I have sheathed the sword.' Mark, he did not turn the sword into a ploughshare, neither did he destroy it, but he sheathed the sword. Why? In order to protect the sword from rust and from being blunted, so that whenever the time should arise, when it should again be wanted, it would be found still keen and bright.

"Tawhiao returned all fighting across the sea. Where is the fighting now? Is it not across the sea? Therefore, in order to keep his words sacred, in order to keep the fighting across the seas, you must enlist, you must see that your sons fight across the waters, and not allow the foe to fight here. 'Beware and do not shift the landmarks of your ancestors, lest the gods curse you.'

"Now I come to your fourth reason—the shedding of blood is against your religion. I ask, are you Christians? Did not Christ say, I come not to bring peace but a sword? Did he

Mr. Henare Whakatau Uru, M.P. for Southern Maori District.
Member of the Maori Regimental Committee.

Group of Ngati-Tuwharetoa Soldiers taken at Opaea, Taihape, under the command of Lieut. K. H. Hakopa.

not say to Peter to catch a fish, and when the fish was gutted was not a coin with Caesar's superscription found on it? And did not the Founder of the Faith say, 'Render unto Caesar the things which are Caesar's, and unto God the things which are God's.' Now, Caesar is demanding from you the things which are his. Are you Christians?

"Which of you, having a child who is being tortured to death by another, will hand him a Bible and say, brother, love your neighbour as yourself. It is our Christian duty to root out all evil, and the greatest evil of the age is the German evil.

"You say the *Pakeha* must right the wrongs which he inflicted by the confiscation of our lands during the Maori war. I will not go into the merits or otherwise of your claim, because I know some of the confiscated lands were paid for by the 'Takoha' monies. That question involves a legal wrangle, which I hold you still have the option of bringing before a legal tribunal. That is a family quarrel. Put aside the petty quarrels of the family, and take hold of the battles of the Nation."

Conscription Applied.

However, Waikato were obdurate, and as the other tribes, especially Te Arawa, Ngati-Porou and Ngapuhi, and also the Defence Department, considered that some degree of compulsion should be applied, the conscription principle embodied in the Military Service Act, 1916, was extended to the Maori race, by "Gazette" notice on June 26th, 1917. This Act provided for the compulsory calling up of suitable recruits for the Expeditionary Force. Waikato as a tribe held out to the end, on principle—though the refusal of the old people to sanction volunteering greatly chafed many of the young men—and it was deemed necessary to assert the law, in fairness to the other tribes, by compulsorily taking several young men to camp at Narrow Neck. One of these was young Te Rau-angaanga Mahuta, brother of Rata. Once in camp Te Rau entered cheerfully upon his training work, and so enamoured was he of soldiering duty under the wise and sympathetic command of Captain Peacock, that he wrote to his people announcing his conversion to the principle of service and appealing to them to fall in with the Government's wishes. He got his stripe as Lance-Corporal, and very likely would have obtained a commission, but by this time (August, 1918) the war was nearing its end, and Waikato's services, willing or otherwise, were not required.

After the application of the Military Service Act to the Maoris, three ballots were held. The first took place in May, 1918. The number of recruits actually produced by these ballots was small; most of those who served were volunteers. The Maoris called up in the three ballots, up to August 17th, numbered 479; of these 136 were passed fit. There were 51 men awaiting medical examination in November, 1918, 117 men had not been traced, and 146 had been classed C2. Nearly 80 names were struck off the lists after inquiry. The compilation of the Maori roll was a task of great difficulty. The Government statistician found it impossible to get the Maoris to complete their registration schedules, and other means had to be adopted of preparing a list of First Division natives of military age. For this purpose every Maori drawn in a ballot received, with the notification that he had been so drawn, a military order to parade on a specified date for medical examination.

The Polynesian Volunteers.

The men who came from the Pacific Islands to serve with the New Zealand forces were all volunteers. In response to the offers of assistance made by the Administration of the islands adjacent to New Zealand, voluntary recruits were accepted for service with the Maori section of the New Zealand Expeditionary Force. In some cases the Administration paid the cost of transport and equipment, and, further, paid the men themselves. Rarotongans, Niue men, Gilbert Islanders, Ellice Islanders, and others were brought over to New Zealand in such numbers as the Administrations decided on and received their training in this country before embarkation for active service abroad. Military and medical officers in the service of the Administrations of the island groups were appointed as attesting and medical officers respectively, so that, in the majority of cases the recruits were attested after having passed medically fit in the islands. Thus only fit men were sent to New Zealand and the procedure saved both Governments considerable expense. Of those sent to New Zealand 631 had embarked for active service or were in a camp of training in New Zealand on Armistice Day.

Throughout the period of the war, the welfare of the lads in the trenches was the constant thought and care of a hard-working committee of native ladies, under the presidency of Lady Pomare. In every *kainga* which had sent men to the war, the women and girls made or gathered together comforts for their loved ones on the battlefields, and these were sent to the central committee in Wellington, which toiled, too, at sewing and knitting for the soldiers. Large quantities of such articles as shirts and socks, packages of cigarettes and sweets, and cases of mutton-birds from Stewart Island and *toheroa* shellfish from the west coast of North Auckland, were despatched to the Battalion, and the periodical arrival of these proofs of the loving thought of the people in far-away New Zealand was a matter for great rejoicing in the billets and dug-outs of war-swept France and Flanders.

CHAPTER III.

THE MAORIS AT ANZAC, GALLIPOLI.

The Maori Contingent under Lieut.-Col. Herbert spent several weeks in camp on Malta before receiving the anxiously awaited orders to join the New Zealand Expeditionary Force at Anzac Cove, on the war-rent peninsula of Gallipoli. The men were steadily employed in training, and a more willing and better disciplined corps it would have been hard to find. At Malta, a valuable officer of the Contingent, Captain F. Burton Mabin (later Lieut.-Colonel), Paymaster, was seconded for duty in charge of a large convalescent camp, at the request of the Governor of the island, Field-Marshal Lord Methuen, who desired a colonial officer to take charge, as there were so many New Zealand and Australian troops constantly arriving. The New Zealand G.O.C., General Godley, approved of this appointment, and for three years Lieut.-Colonel Mabin carried out his duties as camp commandant—he was in charge of six camps at various times—and he was cordially thanked for his services by the Governor and by the Colonial soldiers under his care. Malta at this time was an immensely important and busy place. There were at one time two hundred different units of the Empire and Allies in the camp under Lieut.-Colonel Mabin's command. These men and their places of origin were of a wonderful variety. There were New Zealanders and Newfoundlanders, Nova Scotians and Bermudians, Canadians, Australians, French, Italians, Greeks, Serbs, East Africans, Somalis, Indians and Chinese; these in addition to very large numbers of troops from England. The arrival of survivors of submarined transports enhanced this variety and the excitement of the camps. In one lot there were 150 officers and 2000 men of the torpedoed troopship "Cameronia."

At last, in June, 1915, after many weeks of expectation and hope deferred, orders for departure for the scene of battle were received and promulgated, to the intense delight of the men. The constant coming and going of troops, the arrival of many wounded from Gallipoli and the news of the hard

THE LAST OF THE "EMDEN."

The Maori Troopship went in close to the wreck of the German cruiser "Emden," destroyed by H.M.A.S. "Sydney" at Cocos Island, and Captain Pirimi Tahiwi took this kodak snapshot, an evening view.

IN THE MEDITERRANEAN.

Some of the officers of the Maori Contingent, on board the transport from Alexandria to Malta, to take over garrison duty, 1915.

THE FIRST MAORI CONTINGENT, ON WELLINGTON WHARF, FEBRUARY 13TH, 1915.

fighting, had created a restless feeling among the Maoris; they did not relish being kept in safe garrison while their countrymen were in the thick of it, grappling with the Turks. Now, however, they were to take their turn in the fiery test of war, and satisfaction and elation filled every heart.

The Maoris' home letters were often phrased in poetic and touching language. Private Huirua Rewha, of Ngapuhi, wrote from Malta to his father and mother at Rawhiti, Bay of Islands:—

"Come to me, go from me, my letter of love to my parents, Rewha and Mae. Vaguely the thought steals through my mind that this is my last letter. That is why I greet you thus. So, again, goodbye to all at home, to all my relations who live there, and whom I did not see before leaving. Only if luck guides my steps shall I return. For the order has come that we are to move to the forefront of battle, to enter the scorching flame of the firing line. For many days have we been quite ready. We Maoris are now off to strike—to finish what we came here for. The head officers of our party are here after greeting us, and are now instructing us in methods of warfare. Your letter of love has come to me. I am well; my only grief is I hear nothing but the English voice. It is so; therefore, I must not grieve. I now feel my spirit, my soul, my whole body are not mine now. Never mind."

The transport conveying the Maoris from Malta (via Alexandria) also had on board the New Zealand Mounted Field Ambulance Detachment, the Australian Light Horse Field Ambulance, and 84 Royal Garrison Artillery from Malta. The strength of the Maori Contingent was 16 officers and 461 other ranks. On the morning of July 1st, the troopship entered Mudros Harbour, the port of Lemnos Island, and the Maoris gazed with excited interest on the shores of the first Greek island of which they had a "close-up" view. The beautiful bay was landlocked, with plenty of deep water inside. Two protecting booms with guns at the ends lay across the entrance, and torpedo-boat destroyers were constantly moving about outside.

"Look at those slopes," said one of the lads of Ngati-Kahungunu; "isn't it like the back-country of Hawke's

Bay?" "It reminds me of Poukawa," said another. As the troopship steamed into the harbour she passed British warships to port and starboard, and the crews were very anxious to know who the new arrivals were.

"Who are you?" yelled a sailor from one of the ships.

A Maori wag shouted:

"The Mah-oh-rees!"

Instantly the reply came, "Oh, the Mah-oh-rees! Three cheers for the Mah-oh-rees!"

The sailors cheered as only Navy men can, and our lads returned the compliment at the call of "Three cheers for the Jackey tars!"

There were four other troopships in the harbour. The Maoris' ship anchored in the inner part of the port. Two or three villages were in view, but the New Zealanders had no chance then of a closer inspection.

Next day the Contingent transhipped to the steamer "Prince Abbas," and sailed for Gallipoli Peninsula at 5 p.m. All was expectancy and excitement among the Maoris; the boys were in great fettle and they slept little that night. In the early hours of the morning the ship anchored off Anzac Cove.

The troops were paraded on deck fully armed and with full marching kit and the disembarkation began. Boats were waiting; one slipped up to the gangway and some of B Company entered it and were rowed off. Another took its place, and as fast as one was filled another moved up, quietly and expeditiously. Now the Maoris could hear the soul-thrilling sounds of warfare ashore, the cracking of rifles up on the heights. The boats landed the men at a small wharf and with tense elation they stepped ashore on the famous sands of the foeman's land. On the shore they saw piles of boxes, supplies of all kinds, ammunition, and everywhere were shelters and dug-outs, for this beach was often under shellfire. Above rose in the gloom the steep face of the clay cliffs where the Anzacs had won their glorious name on April 25th.

The Maoris mustered on the sands in the early dawn and were marched straight up along the deep sap which led into the hills, the "Big Sap," which was to be their main thoroughfare for many a day and night. It led them up to No. 1 Post, where they were to camp. Here they found a squadron (dismounted, of course) of the 10th Light Horse (West Australian) under Major Tom Todd, an old Auckland boy, who served in the New Zealand Mounted Rifles in the South African War). The Maoris were posted to No. 4 Section of Defence, under Brigadier-General A. H. Russell, New Zealand Mounted Rifles Brigade. The Brigadier came out to see the Maoris, and the word was passed that they were to set to work getting their hillside camp into terraces and get themselves comfortably fixed—as comfortably as was possible in such a place—before doing any fighting.

The boom of artillery that was to be a familiar sound for the next three years first startled and delighted the Maoris' ears this July morning. "At last," they said, "here is the real thing!" They saw an aeroplane flying over the Turkish lines on the trench-scored shell-pitted heights above. The enemy shelled it without effect. Turkish shells, bursting, made white puffs of smoke around the flyer, but it was not touched. That evening was a lively one. Our side made a demonstration to draw the Turkish fire, and judging by the rattle of rifle and machine-gun fire they succeeded very well. General Godley visited the Contingent's camp, with Captain the Hon. Herbert, M.P., and Captain Malcolm Ross, the New Zealand official war correspondent, also came out and greeted his newly-come compatriots.

Some days were spent in sapping, forming the terraces and getting the camp into order. Water, it was found, was one of the most precious things here. All the water had to be carried up in 2-gallon milk cans; one gallon per man per day was the allowance.

The Maoris quickly came to recognise the morning and evening roar of the enemy big guns over at Anafarta, way on the left. "Gentle Annie" sent her shells screeching over the gully in which the Maoris lay, and bursting on the beach of Anzac Cove. The usual reply of the British was delivered by a torpedo-boat destroyer, which stood off and shelled the Turkish trenches. Then our machine-guns in the advanced positions got busily to work.

The first casualty among the Maoris was Pte. Rangi Ellers, who was wounded in the shoulder by a shrapnel bullet while working in a sap on Walker's Ridge (July 7th). A number of the Contingent were now employed on various fatigues.

The Turkish big gun at Anafarta sent her usual shells along morning and afternoon. On July 9th Pte. Taupaki, assistant to the Q.M.S., and another Maori, with four *pakehas,* had a very narrow escape from death. A shell burst near them, and the four whites were wounded but the Maoris were unhurt.

Bathing in the sea at night was one of the very few luxuries at Anzac. The British torpedo-boat destroyers, steaming confidently along, were a great comfort to the land forces. Every now and again they would pitch a few shells into the Turkish positions and pass on. Their searchlights, too, playing on the enemy's area, were appreciated by our outposts. The beams directed on the hills on the night of July 9th enabled the men in No. 2 Outpost to shoot several Turks.

On the afternoon of July 10th a battleship, looking like H.M.S. "Agamemnon," but said to be the "Prince George," steamed up, accompanied by a host of destroyers, stopped south of Anzac Cove, and shelled the enemy with her 12-inch guns. She fired a number of shells while the destroyers circled round her looking for submarines. All the time she was firing the Turkish shells were bursting round her, and it seemed marvellous that none of the destroyers was hit. The big ship steamed off; a little later a cruiser appeared. A French biplane—with brown wings and an almost noiseless engine—sailed over the Turkish positions. Every now and again the biplane signalled, and the cruiser instantly opened fire. The Turks shelled the aircraft but without success. Every now and again a blob of white smoke high in the air showed where a shell had burst, the watchers counted eighteen puffs in the air at the one time. The Turks must have wasted fifty shells on the biplane that afternoon. The French craft, looking like a great brown moth, moved serenely on in wide circles over the Turks, and when her work was done flew off to the south. The troops could not observe the effect of the warship's shells as she was firing at the Turks in from Gaba Tepe. A balloon ship, too,

THE MAORI CAMP AT GHAIN TUFFHIA, MALTA.

OFFICERS "DOING THEIR BIT."

In a Trench-digging Competition with British Reinforcements at Malta, the Maoris easily beat all the Pakeha diggers. In the trench—Captain Roger Dansey, Captain Buck. On the right—Captain Hiroti, Lt. Tikao.

THE MAORIS' FIRST MAIL FROM NEW ZEALAND, AT MALTA.

AFTER SKIRMISHING PRACTICE, MALTA.

was standing off that lively Saturday afternoon, out of Turkish gun-range, and a sausage-like captive balloon went up from her; in the evening, hauling the observers' sausage down, she went off. After dark the night was broken for a while by a fusilade of musketry and the bursting of bombs.

Late in the afternoon of July 11th (Sunday), the British cruiser "Talbot" came in and shelled Snipers' Ridge. Some of the shells took the face of the hill a bit low, but others struck the edge and ploughed great furrows through it. Nothing there, wrote a Maori watcher, could possibly live under the shellfire. It was a splendid sight to watch the "Talbot" firing broadsides. A flash of flame along the ship, then almost immediately afterwards the flash of bursting shells along the ridge the sound of whizzing fragments of shell amongst the columns of dust. The machine-gun on Todd's Peak turned on her stuttering bark at any signs of movements on the opposite height. Observers at the post signalled the results of the cruiser's shells, and beyond the "Talbot" the sausage-shaped balloon rode high in the sky, watching the progress of the cannonade.

An incident of the afternoon of July 11th was an urgent summons for Captain Peter Buck, the medical officer of the Contingent, to Todd's Peak. On going up there he found that a man of the 10th Light Horse (Australian) had been shot dead by a sniper; the bullet went through the inner angle of the right eye and emerged at the back of the head. He had been shot from Snipers' Ridge opposite. They had seen the sniper's post and had exchanged shots. After the fatality four or five men with periscope rifles lay in wait, and when they saw the enemy sharpshooter they fired all together. The sniper fell backwards and his rifle went up in the air. So there was at least the satisfaction of knowing that the L.H. man's death was avenged. In the evening Captain Buck and his party, with Major Todd, carried down the dead trooper to the aid post and thence along the beach to the cemetery at the point. The Anzacs who had been there for months took but little notice, the New Zealand Maori surgeon noted; they had become inured to the sight of stretchers bearing down the wounded and the dead. The Maoris presently were to become similarly accustomed to the daily toll of war. Hardly had the Australian padre ended his service, repeated from memory in the darkness, with a glimpse at the words of the last prayer by electric torch, when the party came under enemy fire. "Bullets," wrote the Maoris' surgeon in his diary, "began to whistle and hum like angry bees around us, and the padre shouted, 'Take cover, boys!' In a twinkling we were behind the sandhills under safe cover, with the exception of Major Todd, who says he did not hear the padre, and our own padre, who from feelings of courtesy did not like to leave the Major by himself."

So the great days of stress went on. By mid-July the Maoris were well at home in their camp, and were beginning to feel like veterans, but longing to come to grips with the foes whose shells they heard screaming over them. In the evenings heavy firing was often heard over towards Cape Helles on the right. No. 1 Platoon (Ngapuhi, under Lieut. Coupar, of Southland) were up at Walker's Top, and one night there was a heavy fusilade up that direction. A colonel had asked our men to make a noise so as to draw the Turkish fire. They shouted a stentorian *haka,* and the alarming sound set the Turks wildly replying with rifle fire, bombs and machine-guns. The foe must have used up thousands of rounds of ammunition in reply to the Ngapuhi war-song. There was supposed to be an attack at Cape Helles, and the authorities wanted to keep the Turks on the heights near Anzac fully occupied.

On July 13th Pte. F. R. Rewa, No. 6 Platoon, on guard at No. 4 Depot, was wounded by a rifle bullet in the foot—the Maoris' second casualty.

During July the Maoris toiled splendidly on their chief job in the No. 4 Defence section, the widening of the chief communication trench known as the "Big Sap." This work was the main avenue from Anzac to the outposts and to the steep gullies up which the attacking forces must approach the foe. Pack mules were taken up the trench and it was an exceedingly busy highway of traffic. It was necessary to widen it to five feet all the way, and this was difficult on the hard clay parts. Here and there a recess was made so that troops could stand aside to let urgent traffic pass.*

The excellent Indian Transport Corps aroused the admiration of the Maoris. These Indians carried provisions, water and ammunition on their pack mules, which looked sleek and well-groomed. The Indians camped near No. 4 Depot, had a pet goat, which quickly learned to dive into the nearest dug-out when the Anafarta gun began its fell work.

Some of the Maoris' officers visited the Otago Mounted Rifles (Colonel Bauchop) at No. 2 Post, inspected the trenches, and saw the Rifles' water supply, a spring of beautiful cold water in an old river-bed.

In the middle of July Captain Buck commenced the inoculation of the men against cholera. On July 16th two casualties occurred: Pte. Kennedy, B Company, wounded, while being instructed in bomb-throwing near No. 4 Depot, by a bullet from the Turkish trenches, going through both thighs, and Pte. T. Te Whare, A Company, shot through left thigh while lying down in his bivouac; femur fractured. Both cases were sent to the Field Ambulance quarters.

The Maoris, with their *pakeha* comrades, admired the smart gunnery work of their naval guardian angels the torpedo-boat-destroyers. The "Chelmer" generally started in the evening, steaming up and down using her searchlight and threw her shells on to the Turkish trenches, with great accuracy. There was also a three-funnel destroyer, the "Rattlesnake," whose range-finding and shooting were beautifully precise.

Pte. K. Mehaere was accidentally shot (July 17th) by a comrade who was unloading his rifle. The bullet went through a knee and left forearm, fracturing both bones. A very severe

---

*Major Waite, in his war history, "The New Zealanders at Gallipoli," described the men of the Maori Contingent as "the best workers of all" in the herculean toil on the "Big Sap."

"The Maori soldier, picked man that he was, wished to justify before the world that his claim to be a front-line soldier was not an idle one. Many a proud *rangatira* served his country in the ranks, an example to some of his *pakeha* brothers. Their discipline was superb, and when their turn came for working-party, the long-handled shovels swung without ceasing until, just before the dawn, the signal came to pack up and get home."

wound. Sergt. Te Hau and Pte. Kainga put a field torniquet on the arm immediately after the accident and did it very well. The injured man was sent out to the hospital ship.

The plague of flies in this burning mid-summer bothered the Maoris greatly, and the infection of food was inevitable. A number of men were soon down with diarrhoea.

The boys were now eagerly awaiting the expected order for a general assault on the Turkish positions. It was reported that the enemy had received 100,000 reinforcements and would soon try to drive the British off the peninsula. There was also dread of a gas attack, and the men in the trenches were all served out with gas helmets.

Up at Walker's Ridge the Ngapuhi stood target for artillery, rifle and bomb fire. On the night of July 20th, Pte. H. Rewha (Ngapuhi), when in a trench, was struck by a fragment of a bomb. He staggered to a comrade and handed him his field dressing and when it was applied he collapsed. While he was being carried down he was asked by a sympathiser what had happened to him. "I tunno," he murmured, "but somet'ing hit me on te prurry head."

All hands were on the alert now for the expected Turkish attack (as it happened this was forestalled by the carefully planned British attack), and the troops stood to arms about midnight, at moon-set and also in the early morning. B Company was sent round to No. 2 Post to strengthen it. A curious casualty happened on the night of July 21st-22nd. A man of B Company—while asleep with his reserve—was hit in the side by a stray bullet. It passed through the fleshy part and did not touch a rib or lung. Extraordinary to say, it never woke the man. He was awakened later by the cold, and felt his side wet with blood. The wound was slight. Pte. H. Tokara (6th Platoon) was wounded on the 22nd.

On July 24th, Captain Ennis, Dr. Buck and Padre Wainohu went up to Walker's Top and then through the trenches to Courtney's Gully. It was wonderful to see the various posts—Quinn's, Steele's, Courtney's and the others—hanging on to the sides of the hills, or the edge of the cliff. They were really defended by the trenches on the hither or seaward side of the gully, and the Turkish trenches were only about 15 yards away

OFFICERS COMPARING NOTES—A FIELD DAY AT MALTA.

GENERAL CHAYTOR, AT MALTA,
AFTER BEING WOUNDED AT GALLIPOLI, 1915.

[*Photo by Captain Tahiwi.*

IN THE TRAINING CAMP AT MALTA. PRACTICING THE CHARGE.

FOOT INSPECTION, MALTA CAMP.

from the advanced line. Wire netting had been put up as protection against the bombs.

On July 28th, when a working party of 50 men under Lieut. Stainton was on the way to Reserve Gully, a Turk shell burst overhead. The flying shrapnel wounded three—Petita, through the lungs; Poata, lumbar region, and Wirepa, hand; another man had a slight wound on a hand.

On July 29th, an aeroplane (which proved to be a German) appeared above the beach and dropped a bomb, which fell into the sea. Flying over Walker's Ridge a burst of smoke was seen around it, and it volplaned down beyond the ridge at a very sharp angle; probably engine trouble. Pte. Hauiti, B Company, was wounded this day by a bullet which passed along the front of his neck and through a shoulder. He lost a lot of blood but the wound was not bad.

So went on the hot laborious days, with occasional casualties, until the force was called upon for the supreme effort of the campaign.

CHAPTER IV.

THE BATTLE OF SARI BAIR.
(Gallipoli, August, 1915.)

The beginning of August saw the completion of the commanders' plans of battle for a great general assault on the Turkish positions. The enemy had been sapping forward and gradually establishing themselves in advanced lines, and with the arrival of their reinforcements it was expected that they would launch an attack. A supreme effort was therefore to be made by our combined forces, all along the line. Huge supplies of ammunition had been collected at Anzac Cove, additional guns were landed, fresh British (13th Division) and Indian troops were landed. A great store of water was brought from the ships. The Maoris, with other troops carried out a very large amount of laborious preparation for the big offensive. They made new roads, improved the old ones, dug communication trenches and made terraced bivouacs for the new troops. Practically all this heavy toil had to be done at night. Describing those preparations General Sir Ian Hamilton wrote in his despatch:—

"The local preparations [Anzac] reflect the greatest credit not only on General Birdwood and his staff but on the troops, who toiled like slaves to accumulate food, drink and munitions. The accommodation of the extra troops to be landed entailed immense work in repairing concealed bivouacs and making interior communications. The Australians and New Zealanders worked entirely at night without complaint. The efforts of these much tried troops are as much to their credit as their heroism in the following battles."

The reinforcing troops, to quote Sir Ian Hamilton's report, were shipped into Anzac Cove very quietly. "They were tucked away from the enemy aeroplanes and observatories in prepared hiding places.... I much doubt whether a more difficult enterprise than landing so large a force under the very eyes of the enemy and keeping it concealed for three days is recorded in the annals of war." General Birdwood's troops at Anzac, 37,000 rifles and 72 guns, were supported by two cruisers, four monitors (these monitors mounted 14-inch guns) and two destroyers. The enemy's left and centre were slowly bombarded for three days and then the assault on the Lone Pine entrenchment was ordered for August the 6th, with the object of withdrawing the Turkish reserves from the grand attack.

On August 5th orders were issued for the grand attack. The Maori Contingent was in the right covering force under Brigadier-General A. H. Russell, with the N.Z.M.R. Brigade (four regiments), and N.Z. Field Engineers. The duty of this force was to commence the attack and seize the lower slopes, Big Table Top, Old No. 3 Post, and Bauchop's Hill, with the object of covering the initial advance of the assaulting column. The Maori Contingent, which was the strongest and freshest of the five regiments, instead of being given a section of work as the men desired, was broken up to reinforce the four M.R. regiments; these, owing to losses through sickness and casualties in the field, were barely half strength. These regiments were reinforced by platoons from A Company, while B Company was kept in reserve between No. 2 and No. 3 Posts. There were two platoons of Maoris with the Wellington M.R. regiment, one with Otago, one with Auckland, and one with Canterbury. The orders included the following instructions:—

"By night the bayonet only will be used by troops attacking the enemy. Magazines will not be charged by troops of the assaulting columns, they will only be charged by troops left as pickets and garrisons of posts.

"As soon as the main objectives are reached troops will dig in. Trenches will be traversed and communication trenches made. Heavy hostile artillery fire is to be expected when it becomes light.

"No officer, n.c.o. or man is to fall out to rush to the rear to wounded men; to do this is a serious military offence. Stretcher parties will follow all columns and will attend to the wounded."

The terrain which was the scene of the great attack has been described in detail by many writers, but none gives so lucid a picture of Sari Bair as Mr. John Masefield in his epic "Gallipoli." He explains that Sari Bair begins at Gaba Tepe, to the south of the Anzac position, and stretches thence north-easterly towards Great Anafarta in a rolling and confused mass of hills, with peaks ranging from about 250ft. to 600ft., its chief peak, Koja Chemen Tepe, is a little more than 900ft. Nearly all of it was trackless, waterless, and confused, with brushwood and forest trees in places, a rough savage country. The south-western part of it made the Anzac position; the north-eastern and higher half was the prize to be fought for. It is the watershed; the deep deres or gullies on its south side go down to the Helles point; those on the north to the flat land south of Suvla Bay. The three northern gullies nearer to the Anzac position were rugged defiles, dry water courses (subject to floods in the rainy seasons) running west or north-west from the hill bottoms. The three gullies, nearest to the northern end of the Anzac positions were Sazlia Beit Dere, Chailak Dere, and Aghyl Dere (the New Zealanders saw much, too much of the ravines of death in the August fighting). They led up into the hills, up to the summits of Sari Bair; and up there it would be possible to look down on the whole Turkish position facing Anzac.

"One can see," Mr. Masefield wrote, describing the strategic picture from Sari Bair top, "only three miles away, the only road to Constantinople, and, five miles away, the little port of Maidos, near the Narrows. To us the taking of Sari Bair meant the closing of that road to the passing of Turkish reinforcements and the opening of the Narrows to the fleet. It meant victory and the beginning of the end of the Great war, with home and leisure for life again, and all that peace means. Knowing this, our soldiers made a great struggle for Sari Bair, but fate turned the lot against them."

Of Sari Bair's several peaks and knolls the small plateau of Pine, and Lonesome Pine (400 ft.), were held by the Anzacs. The Turks held the heights called Baby 700 and Battleship Hill, and the difficult peak of Chunuk Bair (about 750ft.).

The plan of the attack was that a strong force at Anzac should attack the right wing of the Turks, seize the heights and drive the enemy south towards Kibr Bahr, so capturing a dominating position on the narrow part of the Peninsula. At the same time there was to be a landing of British troops

AT OLD NO. 3 POST, ANZAC.

Coast view looking towards Suvla. At this post was the only well in the British lines on the Peninsula.

THE BATTLEFIELD OF AUGUST, 1915.

Scene near Walker's Ridge, Anzac, Gallipoli, during the battle of Sari Bair. Shell bursting over the ridge on the right. This photo was taken from the Maori Camp.

No. 1 Outpost Dressing Station, Anzac, Gallipoli.
Medical Officer removing a bullet from a Maori's arm.

One of the Wounded: Private Kainga, Anzac, Gallipoli, August, 1915.

[*Photo by Major Buck.*

The Battle of Sari Bair, Gallipoli.

in great force at Suvla Bay to attack the Turks on the hills behind Anafarta, and then to go in from the north and west in the great assault on Sari Bair. As we know now, the much-discussed failure of the British troops under General Stopford at Suvla—a failure due to faulty staff work, not to the poor brave Tommies—lost us the key of the position, and lost Gallipoli and the campaign.

The operations began at nine o'clock on the night of Friday, August 6th, with a bombardment of Old No. 3 Post by a destroyer. This shelling lasted for half-an-hour and then the attack began. Some of the Maoris were sent out ahead to destroy barbed-wire entanglements. At 9.30 o'clock the destroyer opened fire on Table Top to prepare the way for the Wellington Mounted Rifles.

When night came on the Maoris, like the old Scottish Covenanters and Cromwell's soldiers, gathered for a religious service on the eve of battle. They mustered silently at the "Maori Pa," as their camp at No. 2 was called, and there Captain Henare Wainohu, chaplain, addressed them. His brief earnest exhortation breathed the spirit of the warrior chief quite as strongly as that of the spiritual leader.

"Whatever you do," said the Padre, "remember you have the *mana*, the honour and the good name of the Maori people in your keeping this night. Remember, our people far away in our native land are watching you, waiting eagerly, anxiously to hear how you have behaved yourselves in battle. In a few minutes perhaps many of us may be dead. But go forward fearlessly, with but one thought. Do your duty to the last, and whatever comes never turn your backs on the enemy. Go through with what you have to do, to the very utmost of your powers. Do your duty, uphold the ancient warrior name of the Maori."

The reverberating thump and crash of artillery, the noise of shells overhead, the bursting of shrapnel, gave the touch of deadly realism to the Padre's speech. And it was with full hearts, thrilling to the call of imminent action, that the soldiers sang their favourite hymn,

"*Au, e Ihu, tirohia,*
Arohaina iho ra"

(the Maori version of "Jesu, Lover of my Soul"). Many "Tommy" soldiers gathered around to hear the New Zealanders.

"*Hipokina iho au*
Raro i ou parirau."
("Cover my defenceless head
With the shadow of Thy wing.")

The sweet and solemn beauty of the Maori singing pleased the listening *pakehas*. They thought it was a native "sing-song," perhaps, for they applauded when the hymn ended.

The task before the Maoris was to advance with empty rifles against a foe entrenched in seemingly impregnable positions on the grim dark heights above. The work had to be done with the point of the bayonet. The orders were that not a shot was to be fired; the enemy trenches must be taken by surprise attack. Officers as well as men carried rifle and fixed bayonet. They had no steel helmets; those came later, in France. They wore shirt and trousers only; tunics were an encumbrance.

The 1st Australian Infantry Brigade with desperate gallantry captured the Lone Pine entrenchments. The great assault from Anzac Cove by the Anzacs and the 13th Division and the Indian troops, was up the three deres leading to the peak of the Sari Bair.

Sir Ian Hamilton, in his graphic reports of the Gallipoli operations, described succinctly thus the opening of the grand attack:—

"...the real push...was the night attack on the summits of Sari Bair. Our object was to effect a lodgment along the crest of the main ridge with two columns of troops. We planned that two assaulting columns should work up three ravines, to storm the high ridge. These were preceded by two covering columns, of which the first was to capture the enemy's positions covering the foothills, and the other was to strike out northwards, until from Damakjelik Bair it could guard its left flank of the column assaulting Sari Bair from the enemy on Anafarta valley. The whole of this big attack was made under General Godley. A warship had been educating the Turks how to lose a redoubt near Table Top. Every night at 9 o'clock, the warship threw a searchlight and bombarded the redoubt for ten minutes. Then followed a ten minutes interval and a second illumination, the bombardment concluding precisely at 9.30. The idea was that the enemy should take the searchlight as a hint to clear out until the shelling was ended.

"On the night of the 6th the searchlight was switched off at 9.30, and instantly our men poured out through the scrub and jungle into an empty redoubt at Table Top, a whole series of entanglements being carried by 11 o'clock.

"Simultaneously the attack on the Table Top was launched under cover of the warship's heavy bombardment. The banks are so steep that the Table Top gives the impression of a mushroom summit bulging over the stem, but as faith moves mountains so valour carries them. The Turks fought bravely. The angle of the Table Top's ascent is recognised in the regulations as impracticable for infantry, but neither Turks nor angles of ascent were destined to stop Brigadier-General Russell and his New Zealanders that night. There are moments in battle when men become super-men, and this was one of those moments. The scarped heights were scaled, and the plateau was carried at midnight.

"With this brilliant feat the task of the right covering force ended. The attacks were made with bayonet and bomb only. The magazine being empty by order. No words can do justice to the achievements of General Russell, and the New Zealand Rifles, especially the Otago Rifles, the Maoris, and the New Zealand Field Troop."

The Maoris indeed went into that splendid attack, their first battle with the bayonet, in a mood of savage determination and delight. This was their chance for fame. They went grimly for those Turks, bayoneted them in their lines, they burst into a tremendous *haka* when they had cleared the trenches—"*Ka mate, ka mate, ka ora, ka ora!*"—then silence as they pressed on to the next point.

At Chailak Dere its attackers had had a very difficult task. They were held up by barbed wire of uncommon height, width, and intricacy, closing up the ravine. "Here, a splendid body of men," wrote Sir Ian Hamilton,"—the Otago Mounted Rifles —lost some of their bravest and best, but when things were desperate a passage was forced with most conspicuous cool courage by Captain Shera and a party of New Zealand Engineers, supported by Maoris, who are descendants of the warriors of the 'Gate Pa.'"

When the order to advance was given the Maoris, in their several companies and platoons, some with the various *pakeha* units, moved silently off towards their objective on the dark ridges above.

A Company's great adventure may be followed in most detail. The Company was not attached to any *pakeha* body. There were 70 men under Captain Roger Dansey and Captain Pirimí Tahiwi. They started at 9 p.m., with a *pakeha* captain guiding them. They had not gone far up the gully towards No. 3 Post when they came under Turkish shell fire, and had to return and shelter awhile. After waiting under cover for some time, they went forward again, in single file. The shell fire increased in intensity; the hills shook with it. The Maoris pressed up a steep ridge until they came to the first enemy barbed-wire entanglements at Old No. 3 Post. The wire-cutters sent out in advance had not got through this formidable obstruction, and it held the attackers up for some time. Here one of Tahiwi's lads, Pte. Ropata (of Otaki), batman to Captain Ennis, the Adjutant, was caught in the wire, shot through the body and killed. By this time the Maoris were under a very heavy rifle fire as well as shrapnel shells and machine-guns. Charging on, A Company came to a section of trench and were proceeding to clear out its inmates when they found that it had just been taken by the Auckland Mounted Rifles. Further on the trench was still held by the Turks and Captain Dansey offered to clean up the position if Major Chapman, the officer in command of the Aucklanders, would give him some men. Chapman could not spare him any, so Dansey and Tahiwi pushed on to do the job. About a hundred yards further on up the difficult slope of the ridge they were confronted by a long crescent-shaped trench. Captain Dansey, Captain Tahiwi, Lieut. Hiroti, and one or two men (including the bugler, Corporal H. Tahiwi) jumped into this trench and worked down it in advance of their men; it was impossible to keep closely in touch in the darkness. The Turks still held this trench further on, and the Maoris could hear their voices. The advance party worked towards them, and Captain Dansey said, "Let's charge them!" This the little party did. They yelled as they went, with bayonets at the charge,

> "*Ka mate, ka mate!*
> *Ka ora, ka ora!*"

the ancient Maori battle-song. It was taken up with tremendous voice by the men following them. On they went for those Turks; there was no breath to finish the chant; they needed it to push the bayonet home. The lads hurled themselves at the foe like a band of destroying angels; with bayonet and rifle butt they cleared the trench; only the dead and dying remained. Some Maoris fell, but the victory was with them.

> "*Ka mate, ka mate!*"

the Maoris shouted like mad when the terrible work was done. "*Hupane, kaupane! Whiti te ra!*" they yelled. And from their unseen comrades away along the range they heard the same war-cry above the crackling of Turkish rifles.

That first dash of Dansey and Tahiwi and their companions into the Turkish nest was a daring bit of work. The enemy fired at them at a distance of only two or three yards but strangely, the only one hit, a Taupo man, Pte. Whatu, was behind the others. Many stories have been told in the *kaingas* about that famous war-shout on the Gallipoli hills; it was Dansey and Tahiwi who started it, and it was with a fierce wild delight that the New Zealanders, *pakeha* as well as Maori, heard it taken up all along the line as Turk trench after trench was rushed.

After clearing the Turks out of the trench A Company consolidated the position, sandbagged it wherever needful and held on till the morning. When daylight came they found that from their position they could see the operations at Suvla Bay, and they watched the whole movement of the British troops there, after the tardy landing. It was a beautiful bright morning, and the battle for Chocolate Hill, the hopeless advance of the British under the heaviest of artillery and rifle fire, was clearly visible.

The crash of battle for the Gallipoli summits was now at its terrible zenith. The Maoris, as they crouched in their captured trenches, saw the cruisers all bombarding the ridges, heard British and Turkish shells scream overhead; shrapnel burst over them; rifles and machine-guns maintained a continuous crackling fire. They had but slight shelter, those Anzacs who held the broken slopes and ridges, for the ultimate summits of Sari Bair and Table Top were still above them.

At 10 o'clock in the morning the Maoris received orders to go on to Table Top. A Company and those near them had to cross an intervening gully and ascend a sharp razorback ridge to gain their objective. Under rifle fire they ran down into the valley, singly, and began to climb to the formidable summit; up the way was very steep over rock and hard clay, with low bushes. Many dead Turks lay in the valley and about the slopes. The Maoris reached this top and lay low hanging on to scrub about the precipitous hill-brow. They watched a new "Tommy" regiment working its way up to Little Table Top under heavy fire.

Presently orders came to return to the foot of the hill and reassemble. The Maoris descended, and found comparative shelter behind a small hill. There the men greeted their comrades, and compared notes of the great night's work. The cover here was scant; the place was under rifle fire, as a remarkable casualty proved. Captain Pirimi Tahiwi was in the act of drinking from his water-bottle when a bullet fired from the hill above went through the upraised bottle, entered his neck, just missing the jugular vein, and passed down through the right side of his body, close to the spine. Tahiwi's brother Henare caught him as he was falling, paralysed with the shock. That ended the young Ngati-Raukawa captain's service on Gallipoli: but he made a good recovery in hospital, and joined his comrades in France.

Captain Buck (later Major, with the decoration of the D.S.O.) had a most strenuous time, in the thick of it as medical officer. The following are extracts from his diary:—

"August 6th (Friday)—The Wellington Mounted Rifles moved in here to Major Todd's old camp to attack Table Top. Happy Valley on our left, is full of troops; and men have been moving all night round to No. 2. Our men are distributed out with other regiments of Russell's brigade—two platoons with Wellington, one with Otago, one with Auckland, and so on.

The Battle of Sari Bair, Gallipoli.

In the evening at 7 o'clock, we moved round between No. 2 and 3 outposts. Other troops were there thick. Divisional and Brigade Headquarters moved round, also the A.P.M.S.; Major Holmes is using Otago's aid post. Otago and Canterbury moved out, and some of our men with them. A destroyer commenced the bombardment of Old No. 3 Post at 9 p.m. for about 30 minutes, and the general attack commenced then. Lieut. Coupar and No. 1 Platoon were sent out to destroy barb-wire entanglements. At 9.30 the destroyer shelled Table Top to prepare the way for the Wellington Regiment. B Company of the Maori Regiment was held in reserve. News came through that Colonel Findlay, of the Canterbury's, was wounded, I offered for service and went out with my stretcher-bearers. We met Findlay on the way, shot through the thigh. I sent him in and went on to pick up the Canterbury wounded on the left of our position (Walden's Point). Saw the Australian infantry passing through in the valley near Canterbury Ridge. They had captured half-a-dozen Turks who had been left behind and had them ringed round with bayonets. We passed to the foot of Walden's Ridge and picked up several Canterbury wounded. Some were very bad, shot through the lungs, some with broken legs. We did our best for them and sent some in with our stretcher-bearers. Saw five or six dead lying about, including a Turk. We went up the ridge to the Turkish trench captured and saw two wounded and two killed; did what we could. There was a captured machine-gun in the trench. Came down, saw the Canterbury stretcher-bearers, and located Captain Guthrie, who had established an aid post in the same gully but had been working the other ridge. Meanwhile Ghurkas and other troops were passing through the valley and passing inland. We went thoroughly over the ridge that we had partly done, and whilst exploring it for wounded we were nearly shot at by the Ghurkas; the General considered there was nobody on their left.

"Before this we could hear our men doing splendidly. Rattle of musketry, then silence, and the loud English cheer, followed by a Maori *haka*. Owing to the Maoris being distributed, the *hakas* came from every ridge. Everybody is pleased with our men.

"Handed over wounded C.Y.C. to Captain Guthrie and went back to join the Contingent in the early morning of the 7th. All along troops were pushing on, and over to the left the transports were thick landing on the Salt Lake section (Suvla). All along the track the wounded lay thick, and in many places the dead also. I found B Company reduced to two platoons, the rest having gone out to reinforce the other regiments."

Summarising the results of the first great attack, Captain Buck wrote:—

"The Auckland Mounted Rifles took Old No. 3 but dug-in without cleaning it out. Captain Dansey, with 70 Maoris, asked Major Chapman (Auckland Mounted Rifles) to give him another 50 men and he would clean up the position. This was refused, and Dansey did it with his 70 men, losing only seven killed and several wounded. Major Chapman was killed. The Wellington Mounted Rifles, under Colonel Meldrum, took Big Table Top, but Rhododendron, a little further on, delayed the infantry who were advancing while these operations were going on. The Otago Mounted Rifles, under Colonel Bauchop, with the Canterbury Regiment, under Colonel Findlay, cleared up Bauchop's Hill. Colonel Bauchop was mortally wounded through the chest whilst leading his men; he died the next day. One of the last things he said in the clearing station [to Lieut.-Col. Herbert, O.C. Maori Contingent] was: "Herbert, the Maoris have done splendidly."

There were innumerable incidents of daring in that terrible and glorious night's work. Captain Roger Dansey, whose dash has already been mentioned, himself killed three Turks with the bayonet. An anecdote of his alertness and dash in those August days and nights was narrated in New Zealand by one of his men long afterwards. "Captain Dansey," he said, "is as good a fighter as he was a footballer. Once a big Turk jumps up ahead of him and levels a rifle at his head. But Dansey just ducks and goes for that Turk low down; the bullet goes over his head and the Turk goes to heaven."

"We got our blood up that night," said the same soldier, describing the Friday night assault. "We went right up and

MAJOR PETER H. BUCK (TE RANGIHIROA), D.S.O., M.D.
Served with the First Maori Contingent, Gallipoli, 1915; Pioneer Battalion, Western Front, 1916-1918; New Zealand Medical Staff, 1918.

REV. HENARE WEPIHA TE WAINOHU.
CHAPLAIN, MAORI BATTALION.
Served on Gallipoli and in France. Died in New Zealand, 1924.

into it with the steel. Hand-to-hand fighting was the thing. It was like the days of our forefathers."*

August 7th was a day of exhaustion, the troops lying on the hills, in scant cover, under terrible artillery, bomb and rifle-fire, holding on, gratified with their advance and preparing for a still more desperate advance that night. Captain Buck wrote in his diary of his day's work:—

"August 7th (Saturday).—Set to work to help wounded, who were lying thick between Nos. 2 and 3 Posts, and giving the few men under Major Holmes all they could do. Several of our men came in wounded, and I helped to dress some and label them. Could hardly get away from them. Then collected as many as possible of our stretcher-bearers and set off up the gully. Camped in the afternoon under a small spur leading down on the left of Old No. 3. Near us was an old Turkish bivouac. Went up into the trenches and got three of our wounded; buried seven of our dead. One man was wounded badly through the stomach. They had been seen by Dr. McCormac. Five of our men were wounded here, including Captain Tahiwi (in the neck) and my orderly, A. Simeon. Captain Tahiwi was in the act of having a drink out of his water-bottle; the bullet skidded down into the neck, otherwise it would have gone through his head. A lieutenant sent down as guide was also hit before we moved out at 2 a.m. I sent the wounded back to the Australian Light Horse First Aid Post. We were short of stretchers, owing to congestion in the evacuation on the beach, or rather at No. 2. This was due to the fact that the wharf erected in front of No. 2 for the evacuation of wounded had to be abandoned because of Turkish machine-gun fire dominating it. The men had to be carried round to Walker's Ridge wharf, and the congestion of wounded led to the stretchers being kept on the beach."

---

*"A platoon of Maoris, led by a Wellington officer, also crept quietly up the Chailak Dere in order to get round the back of Table Top to co-operate with the Wellingtons. In the gully between Bauchop's Hill and Old No. 3 a party of Turks fired on the Maoris, who saw red and slew the Turks to a man. Chasing the enemy up the gully the Maoris never stopped until they were round the back of Table Top, and were only with great difficulty restrained from tackling Sari Bair by themselves!"—Major F. Waite, in "The New Zealanders at Gallipoli."
—p. 210.

The Capture and Loss of Chunuk Bair.

Sunday, August 8th, saw the Maoris in the fiercest fighting of all, the desperate attack on Chunuk Bair, as a preliminary to the general assault of Koja Chemen Tepe, the apex of the range held by the Turks. The attacking force was organised in three columns. The Maoris were in the column on the right, under Brigadier-General F. E. Johnston; which was timed to assault Chunuk Bair at dawn. With them in the right column were the 26th Indian Mountain Battery, the New Zealand Infantry Brigade, the Auckland Mounted Rifles, and two British regiments, the 8th Welsh Pioneers, and the 7th Gloucesters (from the 13th Division, in reserve). The centre and left columns, under Major-General H. V. Cox, was comprised of an Indian Mounted Battery, the 4th Australian Infantry Brigade, the 29th Indian Infantry Brigade, and portions of four British regiments, Warwicks, Worcesters, North Staffords and South Lancashires. The troops moved out in the grey dawn, and with splendid dash gained a footing on the ridge and started to dig in. The Maoris were in the thick of it here, and in common with their *pakeha* comrades lost heavily. It was the most deadly yet the most glorious day of the campaign, glorious because of the countless deeds of valour and self-sacrifice that attended the splendid lost-endeavour. The episode of the Maori machine-gun taken up the ridge is worthy of record on canvas by some great artist; it is a subject for an understanding battle painter like the artist of "Rorke's Drift" and "The Roll Call." Lieut. Waldren, a *pakeha* officer of the Contingent, had a machine-gun taken up the hill with great difficulty. When it was set up a heavy fire was concentrated on it by the Turks, higher up the range, and one after another of the crew was shot down. Lieut. Waldren was shot dead while working the gun. Corporal Ferris took his place and he also was shot down. A bullet was the certain fate of any man who attempted to use the gun, and Maori after Maori was hit until seven men were wounded. Then anyone operating the machine-gun had to crawl cautiously up and work it lying down. At last the gun, the only one on this flank, had to be withdrawn.

The troops who gained the top won a deathless name that day. Time and again they repelled Turk assaults. They suffered heavily under artillery, bomb, machine-gun and rifle fire, but they held on, and they repelled repeated attacks with the bayonet. Many a gallant New Zealander fell there; most gallant of them all was that fine soldier from Taranaki, Lieut.-Colonel Malone, who was mortally wounded while he was marking out the line to be entrenched on the crest of the knoll. All that day of terrific fire, suffering from heat, thirst, and the effects of great physical effort, the Maoris (sent out more to the left) and their splendid comrades retained the positions gained, and entrenched themselves as well as they could in the hard, stony soil.

Captain Peter Buck, describing the day's work as he experienced it, wrote in his diary:—

"August 8th (Sunday).—Snatched a few winks of sleep and moved up the valley at 2 a.m. The infantry had passed Table Top and Rhododendron Hill and on to the region of Chunuk Bair. Went up gully and rested for a while at the foot of the hill. A Turkish overcoat came in very handy, as it was very cold. Went up the hill in the early morning. Passed the Otago Aid Post, then an Indian mountain battery, getting busy. We established an aid post in a watercourse at the side of the track. Our men were a little higher up, waiting to go into the firing line. One machine-gun section with us was put on the ridge, and the Turks got on to it. European officer, Waldren, and Ferris were killed and seven were wounded Dressed most of them at our station. Some were wounded by shrapnel. Saw Frank Statham (Major) waiting with Otagos to go into action. Did up several men at our post, including a man hit on the shoulder with a shrapnel case; it only bruised him. Our men were sent into section on the left of Auckland with ammunition for the Gloucesters. Several were shot going across the ridge, including H. Tahiwi, badly in the leg. He was carried in by an Otago man under fire. There was trouble through lack of stretchers, and I sent all who could walk down the hill. Had to make a stretcher for Tahiwi with a Turkish coat and two rifles. R. Morgan came back over the ridge to the left, saying some wounded were there in a gully. Went up the hill and saw Brigadier-General Johnston, who said the Maoris had gone into the firing line on the left. I left the Chaplain at the dressing station, and guided by Morgan and accompanied by Rangi Otene went over the ridge to the left below our aid post. We ran down the hill into the creek bed and worked up to a little flat at the convergence of two small watercourses. There we found heaps of wounded, who had come down the watercourse to the right—Maoris, *pakeha* New Zealanders, and Gloucesters. Adjusted bandages, gave them water, and those who could walk were directed over the hill to the left. One New Zealander was very bad, leg shot off by a shell; so with others, wounds severe. Was assisted by Q.M.S. Mete Kingi; he came over to see his brother, but he was dead; also Cpl. Geary, L.-Cpl. Manuel and Pte. Tuite higher up the creek, very bad abdomenal wounds. The Padre and others came over, and after doing what we could and sending word to the F.A., went over the ridge to the left again, to our men; and found them there next to the 10th Ghurkas. We had come too far to the left, evidently, and so as not to interfere with the Ghurkas' lines we had to go on into the next small gully, where we dug out an aid post. We had three wounded, whom we sent off in the evening under stretcher-bearer escort, as they could walk.

"This is Sunday night, and we have had to rely on the food we brought with us on Friday, and we are still in our shirt sleeves. We have had a severe strain on the water supply for the wounded. The Padre took a tin of water from a unit beside our first-aid post; he took it by force and asked them to report him. To-night we got some water, and also a ration of rum, which was very acceptable.

"The Ghurkas keep flitting about in twos, and one cannot but admire their neat appearance and fit condition. They stop or sit down for a moment, and then blend with the scrub and the shadows as they flit away. One smuggled into our first-aid post during the night and had a good sleep.

"The Infantry Brigade at this period of the battle held the trenches on the slopes of Chunuk Bair to the right of the highest point. To the New Zealanders' left were the Gloucester and Warwick regiments and then the 5th Ghurkas

THE CAPTURE AND LOSS OF CHUNUK BAIR.

The Maoris were to the left again just under the "Farm," where they occupied trenches dug with their entrenching tools. The machine-gun and shrapnel fire was very severe all day. The Royal Irish Rifles, the East Lancashire, Wilts, and Hants regiments came up beside us. To the left again was Cox's Indian Brigade.

"August 9th (Monday).—Shifted our aid post about 10yds. lower down in the gully, and dug in a little as it was liable to shrapnel from the left. A whole lot of Tommies were advancing up into the firing line, but owing to taking the wrong gully they arrived three hours late and started their attack in the daytime. It was slaughter. The regiments passing up were the Royal Irish Rifles, East Lancs., Wilts, Hants, and others. The Royal Irish lost heavily and they came scrambling down the gully to our post. We had the place crowded, and plenty of work. I could not locate the aid posts of these regiments, or get hold of their stretcher-bearers. Had East Lancashires, one abdomenal and broken arm and another with a broken thigh, with us all day. All the wounded came down asking for water. Had some of our own wounded, and fortunately they were able to get away down the gully. Sergeant-Major Hill, of A Company Maoris, was carried over by Sergeant Jacob, but was practically dead when he arrived, shot through the spine with shrapnel. Rawhiti, an East Coast man, carried several wounded men down to us on his back. [Rawhiti received the Military Medal for his fine deeds.] My men worked very hard. We had a very bad time with shrapnel, which burst all about our gully. Only the fact that we were dug in saved us. Even then we were afraid of our projecting feet, as the shrapnel bursts were only a few feet beyond us. Once, while I was dressing a wounded Ghurka, I had to lie down beside him as the shrapnel was striking the ground just beyond us. We had half a dozen Ghurkas in our aid post, but they were the only people who had stretcher-bearers constantly moving about, and we never had to keep a Ghurka long. One of them, hit in three places, came up the gully minus putties, hat and equipment but with a naked khukri knife in his hand; evidently looking for anyone in the way. Another, shot through the abdomen, asked for 'pani'—

water—but on my pointing to the wound and shaking my head he laid his head back with an air of resignation. When I offered him a little to moisten his mouth, he pushed the bottle away, but finally, when I rubbed my lips, he understood, and took just enough to moisten his mouth and voluntarily withdrew his lips from the bottle. The Tommies, through ignorance, drew fire on us several times by exposing themselves. They are strange to this kind of country, and wandered round a good deal. Some of their officers had swords and leather trappings that would delight the snipers. Up here we had a good view of the sea, and could hear the warships sending shells into the hill above us. The roar of bursting shells and the rattle of musketry and machine-guns went on incessantly. The pressure slackened off in the afternoon. A subaltern of the Royal Irish Rifles came into our aid post and had a yarn. He said he was waiting for a cup of tea before going up on duty. Both the Padre and I turned on him simultaneously.—'What! A cup of tea! We haven't had one since Friday.' "

"We had a terrible job to get rid of the Tommy wounded. A R.I.R. man, wounded in the back, whom we had had all the morning, was at last carried off by two of his regiment on a hand seat The only two stretcher-bearers I had seen never came back for the other wounded man of their regiment. I kept asking the officers and men of the Tommy regiments where their stretcher-bearers were, and they all united in cursing them. Finally, I was left with two Lancashire men, and after sending out innumerable men of that regiment to hunt up their stretcher-bearers, I put a Lancs. on guard over them to await arrival of a party to carry the men away. We were without stretchers, and I had sent our own bearers away with our own cases. The one or two who were left were absolutely exhausted after three days' hard work.

"In the evening we got word to move out with B Company, as the Wilts were to take over our trenches. We were to go out and have a spell; and we heard the *pakeha* New Zealanders were doing likewise. They had been badly cut up. Colonel Malone, Major Statham and others killed. A Company were to remain until the Wilts men took over the trenches. We moved off to the right, and passed Lieut. Hiroti waiting to take the Wilts over to our trenches. Captain Pitt had been very sick, and I had sent him away with one of the men in the early evening. Lieut. Ferris was commanding B Company. We moved down the hill and went down Aghyl Dere (where dead men were lying about in several places) and back to No. 1 Post.''

Chunuk Bair was won but for a short space. Under an awful fire, the troops hung on with desperate tenacity, until the night of August 9th, when it became absolutely necessary to withdraw the defenders for rest and food. Their places were taken by two fresh battalions, the 6th North Lancashires and the 5th Wiltshires; there was only space for these two corps in the limited shallow trench line. The Turks made a tremendous assault on these Englishmen at daybreak on August 10th, and drove them off the ridge, or rather wiped most of them out. So Chunuk Bair was lost, and never again did our troops set foot on it.

General Sir Ian Hamilton's despatch must be quoted here, for its vivid summary of the Chunuk Bair battle. Describing the fighting on the hill on the 9th—after the troops had gained a portion of Chunuk Bair—he wrote:—

"The Turks were now lining the whole crest in overwhelming numbers. The enemy, much encouraged, turned their attention to the New Zealand troops and the other battalions holding the south-west of Chunuk Bair. Their constant attacks, urged with fanatical persistence, were met with sterner resolution, and, although our troops were greatly exhausted, at the end of the day they still kept their footing on the summit, which covered the Narrows themselves and the roads leading to Bulair and Constantinople. Eight hundred men held the crest of Chunuk Bair in slight trenches hastily dug, but the fatigue of the New Zealanders and the fire of the enemy prevented solid work, the trenches being only a few inches deep and unprotected from fire.

"The First Australian Brigade were now reduced from two thousand to one thousand. The total casualties to the evening of the 9th were 8500. The troops, however, were still in extraordinarily good heart, and nothing could damp the keenness of the New Zealanders. The new army of Chunuk Bair was relieved after a night and a half. They were dead with fatigue, and Chunuk Bair, which they had so magnificently held, was handed to the 6th North Lancashires and the 5th Wiltshires.

"The Turks delivered a grand assault at daybreak on the 10th, and the North Lancashires were simply overwhelmed in the shallow trenches by sheer weight of numbers, whilst the Wilts, who fought in the open, were literally almost annihilated. The assaulting column consisted of a full division, plus three battalions, and it swept over the crest and swarmed over General Baldwin's column, which only extricated itself after the heaviest of losses. Now it was our turn. The warships and New Zealand and Australian artillery got the chance of a lifetime, and an iron rain fell on the successive solid lines of the Turks, while ten machine-guns of the New Zealand infantry played on their serried ranks at close range until the barrels were red-hot. Only a handful of the enemy straggled back to their own side of Chunuk Bair. By the evening of the 10th General Birdwood's casualties were twelve thousand, including the largest proportion of his officers. The grand coup had failed to come off, as the Narrows were beyond field-gun range.

"It was not General Birdwood's fault or the fault of any of the officers and men under his command. General Birdwood had done all that mortal man could. General Godley also handled his two divisions with conspicuous ability. His troops faced death with joyous alacrity, as if it were some form of exciting recreation, which even astonished an old campaigner like myself."

The casualties among the Maoris were heavy, and Captain Buck and his lads had their hands literally very full. The following are extracts from the M.O.'s diary:—

"August 10th (Tuesday).—This morning we shifted higher up the hill to where the Wellington M.R. had been. We had two wounded here. Curiously, one was wounded in the cheek with the tip of the bullet sticking out and no other wound. I found he had been hit while asleep with his mouth open! The wound of entrance was on the inside of the cheek. It was a spent bullet. The arrangements for the despatch of sick and wounded were much better. There were a British staff and R.A.M.C. at No. 2. The jetty in front had been abandoned for shipping wounded, owing to snipers' and machine-gun fire. The wounded were now being taken to No. 4 Supply Depot and shipped from the wharf opposite. Colonel Maunder, A.D.M.S., was killed by a stray bullet while standing outside his dug-out.

"On the morning of the 10th the Turks made a vigorous counter-attack with bombs, etc., and drove the Tommies out of the trenches and they fell back, leaving all the country under the Farm clear. The attack on the left, which was to take Hill 971, having failed, the trenches on Chunuk Bair offered too great a salient and the men had to be withdrawn, and the position at the Apex straightened. This was very bitter (to us), as the New Zealand Infantry Brigade had held the slopes of Chunuk Bair for 48 hours. However, the Apex was strengthened with machine-guns, and when the Turks attacked in force they were slaughtered. The warships also got on to them with their big guns. A watercourse down the side of the highest point of Chunuk Bair, just above the Farm, was absolutely choked with Turkish dead."

The Maori casualties were severe in the four days' fighting —the first battle in Europe in which Maoris were ever engaged. During August 6th-10th, they had 17 killed, 89 wounded, and two missing, out of 400 men, total strength.

Major J. H. Wallingford, who distinguished himself in command of the New Zealand machine-gun section, wrote to Sir Maui Pomare as follows:—

"As regards the Maoris, two of the machine-guns under my command were manned by them. On August 8th, one of them lost in less than twenty minutes, nine men out of sixteen, and still they fought on. I have seen them lie in the open at the foot of Chunuk Bair, mixed with Ghurkas, for two days and nights, when at least thirty per cent. were either killed or wounded. On sentry at night, when the safety of the army depended on their vigilance, at general fatigue work, and in the digging of trenches—in fact I have seen them under all conditions of warfare, except the actual charge, and I am satisfied that better troops do not exist in all the world."

Captain F. M. Twisleton (of the Legion of Frontiersmen, Gisborne) also wrote from the Front as follows:—

"Twice I had Maoris under me, and in ticklish places. I have also seen a lot of them in action, and I must say they are good stuff. A man need not wish to lead better material into action, no matter how desperate the fighting may be. I should say they are amongst the best bayonet fighters in the world. They are perfect sentries. As trench fighters you cannot beat them. I have not seen them under shellfire in the open, but with a leader they trusted, I am quite sure they would stand anything. As soldiers, officers and men, they are a credit to the race and to their country, and I, for one, hope to see a strong unit kept at fighting strength till the end of the job."

Lieut.-Colonel J. G. Hughes, commanding the Canterbury Battalion, wrote from the Apex, Gallipoli Peninsula, regarding the Maoris, 40 of whom had been attached to his battalion:

"General Godley was here and asked how they were getting on. I told him that I was very pleased indeed to have the Maoris in my battalion, as they are always cheerful, keen to be taught, wonderfully alert in the trenches, willing workers when on fatigue (and God knows there are fatigues in plenty), in fact they were an object lesson to us white Maoris. The General said, write and tell them in New Zealand. Sir James, I am glad of the permission, and hope you will let the New Zealand people, particularly their Maori people, know how splendidly these gallant fellows are doing their bit for King and Empire."

Official Correspondent's Narrative.

The following message from the New Zealand official correspondent, Captain Malcolm Ross, was received in the Dominion on August 26th, 1915:—

"THE HOUR—AND THE MEN."

" .... The Australians and New Zealanders braced themselves for a desperate night attack. They had long been waiting for this hour, marking the end of monotonous days of sitting in the trenches. They were confident they would carry the enemy's works on their immediate front. Strict orders were issued that not a shot was to be fired; they were to rely on the bayonet alone.

"Exactly at 10 o'clock on the night of August 7th the brigade of New Zealanders clambered out of their trenches and charged furiously on the Turkish lines with loud cheers, bayoneting all who came in their way.

"The Turks were apparently taken unawares and fired wildly, being quite unable to check the New Zealanders' advance. In a few minutes all the enemy's positions nearest the sea were in our hands, and the way was thus cleared for the main advance.

"The New Zealanders only stopped for a 'breather'; then they pursued their victorious career, and rushed successively the old No. 3 Outpost, Bauchop's Hill and other Turkish positions.

"The Maoris entered upon the charge with great dash, making the darkness hideous with their wild war cries, and striking terror into the Turks. With the awful vigour of their onslaught, using bayonets and rifle butts with equal effect, the Maoris forged another link in the chain of the Empire.

"The darkness of the night, the broken nature of the ground, and the skill with which the enemy had smothered every available bit of dead ground with deadly snipers, delayed the main advance. After these preliminary positions had been rushed successfully, every hill and spur had to be picketed to keep down the fire of marksmen remaining in the rear of our advancing columns.

"Fighting was continuous throughout the night. In the gloomy ravines the Turks were resisting courageously but despairingly, and many bloody encounters, the details of which will never be known, filled the dark hours preceding the more eventful dawn.

"Throughout the 8th the struggle continued without intermission. The New Zealanders gained some ground, but were finally held up by its enemy's machine-guns and rifle-fire.

"Our men began a renewed advance on the 9th, up the steep slopes. The Turks then gallantly charged from both ends. Many Turks fell, but the survivors closed with the intrepid colonials, bayonets and rifle butts being used. This was just the form of fighting the colonials liked, and their magnificent physique proved its value. Although numerically few they closed with the Turks, and, furiously using their rifles as clubs, they swung them round their heads, laying out several Turks at each sweep. The Turks could not stand this rough treatment, and all those not killed or wounded fled.

"The New Zealanders then began hastily to dig themselves in.

"So far this was the finest feat of fighting and the highest point any troops had yet gained on the Peninsula. The Turks fought with the utmost bravery, but their efforts were in vain. Soon not a single Turk remained.

"Our artillery, assisted by the cruisers and monitors offshore, checked Turkish counter-attacks, inflicting losses.

"Upon the left of the New Zealand advance the Australians, assisted by Indian units, fought splendidly and achieved splendid successes.

"The New Zealand advance resulted in the capture of a Nordenfeldt and two machine-guns, with many trench-mortars, and 600 prisoners were taken."

Sir Ian Hamilton's Praise.

General Sir Ian Hamilton, in a special order, September 7th, 1915, said, regarding the fine feat of arms by Lieut.-General Birdwood's troops during the battle of Sari Bair:—

"The fervent desire of all ranks to close with the enemy, the impetuosity of their onset, and the steadfast valour with which they maintained the long struggle, these will surely make appeal to their fellow-countrymen all over the world. The troops under the command of Major-General Sir A. J. Godley, and particularly the N.Z. and Australian Division, were called upon to carry out one of the most difficult military operations that has ever been attempted.—A night march and assault by several columns in intricate mountainous country,

Sir Ian Hamilton's Praise.

strongly entrenched, and held by a numerous and determined enemy. Their brilliant conduct during this operation and the success they achieved have won for them a reputation as soldiers of whom any country must be proud. To the Australian and N.Z. Army Corps, therefore, and to those who were associated with that famous Corps in the battle of Sari Bair—the Maoris, Sikhs, Ghurkas, and the other troops of the 10th and 13th Divisions from the Old Country—Sir Ian Hamilton tenders his appreciation of their efforts, his admiration of their gallantry and his thanks for their achievements. It is an honour to command a force which numbers such men as these in its ranks."

The following appreciation (by the present writer) of the Maoris' share in the first battle appeared in a New Zealand paper on arrival of the news of the Sari Bair battle:—

"The casualty lists show that the Maori Contingent took its fair share of the Turkish bullets on the Gallopili hills in this month's fighting, and it is not difficult to picture the pride and elation with which the news would be received in the Native villages throughout the Dominion, for the Maori has always gloried in the honourable scars of war. The little Native force certainly appears to have fully justified the hopes of those who expressed the opinion that four decades of peace and more had by no means extinguished the fighting fire of the race, and the people who have long laid down the gun and tomahawk and who are one now with the *pakeha* will feel that their ancient warrior mana is safe in the hands of the young men fighting by the side of their white brothers in the country of the Turk. How thoroughly the Native race is represented in the Contingent may be gathered from the casualty lists. Among the wounded Maoris there are young fellows from the Ngapuhi and Rarawa tribes, in the far north of the Auckland province, and one came from Colac Bay, on the shore of Foveaux Strait. Taranaki has one or two wounded men, one from the shores of Lake Taupo has died of wounds, and a number of Rotorua and East Coast soldiers have also been set down in the roll of honour. There are famous names among them too. Two of the wounded are descendants of the King Country chief Wahanui, who was the power behind the throne in the disaffected districts of the Upper Waikato forty years ago, and who strenuously opposed the white Government up to as late a date as 1880. He was wounded in the Waikato war by a *pakeha* bullet, and now the young King Country soldiers who carry his noted name will bring back to their Rohepotae homes, if they ever return, the marks of wounds received in Britain's cause. If anything was needed to heal for ever the old racial animosities in the Dominion this war in which our white and brown New Zealanders are fighting and dying together against a common foe will furnish it.''

CHAPTER V.

THE LAST WEEKS AT GALLIPOLI.

The crucial battle of the Gallipoli—Dardanelles campaign was over; the grand effort had failed—a glorious effort which would have been crowned with success had not the new English troops at Suvla Bay disappointed their comrades desperately holding the right of the line. After the Sari Bair fighting the Maoris spent about another eight weeks at Anzac and early in October were sent across to the island of Lemnos for a rest, anticipating the final evacuation of Gallipoli by eleven weeks. During the further fighting in August, when Sir Ian Hamilton made a final great effort with his reorganised troops, the Maoris shared with the *pakeha* troops, Imperial and Colonial, the attack on the hill of Kaiajik Aghala (Hill 60), and suffered heavy losses, in company with the Canterbury and Otago Mounted Rifles.

On August 20th, Captain Buck and the Padre, Captain Wainohu, saw General Godley, who congratulated the Maoris on their conduct in the operations of the 6th-9th. He said also that the Colonel of the Ghurkas and British officers, had spoken highly of them. The General said that, in order to give them better opportunities, the Maoris would be distributed and attached to the four infantry battalions, but that they would not lose their identity as they would be kept as distinct platoons. This temporary eclipse of the battalion as a body was not at all to the liking of the Maoris' officers; still there was some comfort in the knowledge that the platoons would remain distinct in each *pakeha* battalion. The breaking-up of the Battalion in this way brought strong protests from its members, and later on, as the result of united action by Sir Maui Pomare, Sir James Carroll and the other members of the Maori Recruiting Committee in New Zealand, the whole body was again united, and was in the end reconstructed as a Pioneer Battalion.*

---

*For correspondence on the subject of the splitting-up of the Contingent and the Maori protests, see Appendices.

The Doctor and the Padre were ordered to report to the Infantry Brigade Headquarters. Brigadier-General Johnston told them that he had watched the Maoris go into action on the Monday. There was no hesitation about them and they did splendidly. He was very pleased with them and considered that the Ghurkas "were children compared with them." He was very pleased to have them in his command.

In the evening of the 20th the O.C., Lieut.-Col. Herbert (who had been warmly praised by the G.O.C. for his services in command of the Contingent) mustered the Maoris and bade them farewell. He said he was going as Colonel to the Worcesters and Captain Ennis was going with him as his adjutant. Captain Buck gave the men the General's message.

On August 21st orders were received for 100 men to report to the Canterbury and Otago Mounted Rifles, for an attack on the left front. Capt. Buck went with them with one hospital orderly and four stretcher-bearers. At 2.30 that afternoon the warships began a heavy bombardment of the Turkish trenches, and the shore howitzer batteries joined in. Our men were waiting behind the South Wales Borderers' trenches. Captain Buck, describing the operations, wrote in his diary:—

"At the end I was on, there were about 25 Maoris. They were to form part of the third line, and were put under Lieut. Blackett. Lieuts. Walker and Stainton of the Maoris were further up. Our attack was launched as the bombardment ceased. Looking over the trenches I could see our men running across the ridges like deer, then resting in a slight gully, and on again. Our men soon caught up to the others. On the flat on our left Australians and Tommies were advancing line on line under a hail of shrapnel. It was like a picture battle. Afterwards I learned that all the hills and ridges near Walker's and stretching back were crowded with our men watching the battle. The firing slackened, and I slipped over the trench and dropped into an oblique little gully running down into the main one. Here I was almost on top of a wounded Canterbury man. I lay beside him and put on his first field dressing. He was wounded in the muscles of his back, not badly. He kept saying, 'I'd be much happier if you would keep your head down a little; I've been watching the bullets pitch alongside.'

"A little lower was young Warakihi lying on his face stone dead. I took his identity disc and passed on down to three wounded. Called for my orderly who hopped over the trench with haversack. Fixed up the wounded and carried one—a sergeant—down into the gully, where we found Captain Guthrie and others. Captain Guthrie himself had a wound through the fleshy part of the back of the neck. I went on and could see wounded men able to walk getting over the trenches into the South Wales lines. The firing was fairly frequent on the table lands, so I worked down the gully and struck a sap in a gully running towards the trenches taken by our people. The Connaught Rangers were widening the sap. Met several of our men (wounded) coming down, and labelled them, including Sergeant Ngamoko Kingi and others. Went on and came to a raised bank behind the trenches, where several wounded were lying, also some of our men in reserve (under Sergeant Te Hau), as the trenches were too crowded. I fixed up the wounded, including Sergeant Wihapi, fractured femur, and Skipper, shot through the hip. Skipper apologized for not securing me a pair of Turkish field-glasses. He said, 'I get hit too —— quick.' Guthrie turned up and carried on, in spite of his wound, until we got most away. Captain Cave, of the Australian Field Ambulance (Light Horse) came and helped get the remaining ones out. Got Corporal Paraone out of the trenches, badly wounded. The Connaught Rangers were digging a communication trench. The Padre and I dug a bivvy in the bank, where we stayed all night. The Turks seemed to make a counter attack every two hours, when there would be a heavy fusilade, with bombs exploding, and the Rangers stood to arms. Once we heard loud cries from the Turks and then a desperate fusilade.

"The trench which our men helped to take is called Kaiajik Aghala, and the gully with the sap running up to the right is Kaiajik Dere. Our men were praised by the General for the good work done in these trenches.

"Lieut. Walker was struck in the side of the face and neck by a splashed bullet from the edge of a machine-gun loop-hole.

This was a Turkish machine-gun captured in the trenches, which Walker fixed up and turned on the enemy. I sent him back to No. 1 Post. Walker was pleased with his men in the charge across the table lands. As he found they were getting too low down to the left he gave them 'Half right form.' They did it perfectly, under rifle, machine-gun and big gun fire."

On August 23rd, Dr. Buck and Padre Wainohu took a party of six men and a sergeant to bury the Maori dead, but were told by Brigadier-General Russell not to attempt it, as the table lands traversed by the forces in the attack were swept by machine-gun and rifle fire. The officers were told that most of the dead had been buried by a party the previous night. The total Maori casualties were believed to be 48 or 49.

The remainder of our men in the Kaiajik Aghala trenches only got out on the 24th. On that day the Maori Contingent paraded for the last time as a separate unit. The men left camp and joined the various battalions of the infantry brigade. Dr. Buck and Padre Wainohu joined the Auckland Regiment (Major Alderman in command) on Rhododendron Spur as the most central. Sergeant-Major Tingey received a commission as 2nd Lieutenant, and joined the Wellington Mounted Rifles as machine-gun officer.

On the afternoon of August 27th, the bombardment of the Turkish positions was renewed by the warships and land batteries. Huge columns of dust rose at Kaiajik Aghala where the shells struck. When the big guns ceased firing machine-gun and rifle fire commenced and continued till early next morning. It was learned in the morning that the infantry in the night attack, had taken two lines of trenches but failed to take the third. The greater part of Hill 60 was now held by our men. The Connaught Rangers did well but had to give up one trench. Next night the attack was renewed, and the hills rattled with heavy rifle fire and bombing.

On August 29th, General Russell delivered another attack on the Kaiajik Aghala trenches. The 10th Australian Light Horse took the third line of trenches and held it against bombs and rifle fire. Our men had now complete possession of Hill

60 and consolidated the position and also established communications across Kaiajik Dere with the 4th Australian Infantry Brigade.

An entry, in a Maori officer's diary, on September 9th read: "Life here is very quiet and there is no excitement." What the humorist implied, no doubt, was that no shell dropped into his bivouac that day.

The British now held the line from Anzac to Suvla securely, but neither side was in a position to launch another great attack. There was considerable shelling on both sides daily, but the hostilities on shore were restricted to trench warfare, with its intermittent machine-gun and rifle firing and bombing. There was much sickness; dysentery was very prevalent.

On September 14th, Captain Buck, noting in his diary the progress of events, wrote that he went up to the Apex to report to Major Alderman, who was in command of the Maoris, and of various New Zealand Details, with Captain Ennis as his adjutant. All the lower slopes of the hills were occupied by Australians; and the Apex by the 28th Australian Infantry. There was intermittent shelling on both sides daily. On the 18th, the Turks started shelling the Apex with 75's, and made it very hot. Then they started to fire on our trenches. The firing spread along to the left, where the flat was under heavy shell bombardment. All hands stood to arms and there was great excitement, for it was thought that another strong Turkish attack was impending. However, it fizzled out; only two of our men were wounded. The warships and our howitzers replied to the enemy fire for some hours. The 19th —Sunday—was "a quiet peaceful day"; just a few shells in the morning, and the Turks "plunked in a few in the afternoon." One Australian at the Apex was killed. The Maoris held a church service in the evening, and the Australians was interested listeners because of the novelty of it.

On September 20th, a burst of shrapnel caught one of the Maoris (Pte. Herewini) in the chest. The enemy still shelled the Apex, sending in single shots at irregular intervals. A warship shelled the enemy trenches at 6 p.m. and put two shots into a blockhouse. The batteries on the beach also sent over several rounds.

On September 21st, in the afternoon, after a quiet morning, the Turks threw some bombs fairly close to the Maoris but fortunately on the uninhabited slopes of their gully. Some of the Maoris gave the alarm when they saw a bomb with a long tail coming down, and everybody dived into the dug-outs. Later, the Turks sprayed shrapnel on the slope below, half-way down the sap. There was an immediate call for stretcher-bearers and Captain Buck went down and found three Australians hit. He went into a dug-out to attend to them, and while there shrapnel frequently burst close by. This slope was in full view of the enemy and there was no protection whatever except in the dug-outs. Thus, when cooking or other work was going on and a few men were collected together, the Turks burst shrapnel over the spot, having the range exactly. More men had been wounded in this place—bad wounds, too, in chest and abdomen, often mortal—than anywhere else about. Five Australians were wounded here this day.

Early in the morning of September 22nd, the Turks started shelling with a seventy-five from the west hills, firing shrapnel accurately on "Mafish Slope," as the Australians' exposed position was christened. Five men were wounded in the early morning bombardment. After breakfast, Captain Buck was half-way through his sick parade when the gun started again. The cries from below for stretcher-bearers, then for another stretcher, and next for a doctor. On going down he found a case at the end of the sap on the exposed slope facing the west hills. Seeing a stretcher-bearer near, he called to him to take cover. An Australian was lying in the open shot through the back of the neck, dead. Buck dived into a shallow bivouac near, but as it already had three occupants he got out and ran to another dug-out. He had only just got down into cover when a shrapnel shell burst over the shelter. Hearing a groan next door, he looked over and saw a stretcher-bearer lying in the dug-out bleeding. The man had been looking out to see what he could do and a shrapnel bullet penetrated the top of his head. His condition was hopeless; he was just breathing when Buck put a dressing on, and left. Immediately afterwards there was another burst of shrapnel. Going down the road the surgeon came on two more wounded men, hit in the legs. He carried one out to a safer place. A breathing spell and a smoke with the Australians, the cool and plucky doctor clambered back to the top of the hill. He stopped to pass the word to the Padre about the wounded men below, and dropped down into his dug-out just as another burst of shrapnel swished along outside the shelter. Again the cry came from below for a doctor. Descending the hill again he found a man dying with a wound in the throat. That made three killed and six wounded to be chalked up against that gun for the morning. Later in the day the '75' got some more Australians, including one mortally wounded in the head. So the wastage tally of these people, the 28th Australian Infantry Brigade, was fairly heavy.

About 11 o'clock that morning, some 40 Maoris and some 60 New Zealand Details were sent down the gully to the Canterburys' old camp; the rest were to follow next day. The Turks sent over this day, among other souvenirs, a bomb at the end of a stick about six feet long, fired out of some gun or other. They were also firing rifle grenades.

The Australians on "Mafish Slope" shifted out of it this day, and the sap was deepened.

On the 23rd, in the evening, the Turks shelled the Canterbury Ridge, and then vigorously bombarded the flat towards Suvla Bay. The flashes of the guns could be seen on the far range of hills. The enemy sent some shells close to the warships at Suvla, and the cruiser there shifted out further. A mortar was used in the Anzac trenches, throwing bombs at the Turk blockhouse. The enemy sent another stick bomb over. It could be seen whirling through the air as it came and landed in our trenches;—nobody was in its way.

Occasional night "demonstrations," with rifle fire and machine-guns, and daytime intermittent shelling, went on for some weeks. This was the entry in Captain Buck's diary for Sunday, September 26th :—

"Another beautiful day; the sea looked very calm and placid from here [the Apex]. The cruiser which lies nearly opposite, always looks lazy, and the only active things are the destroyers, which kept up their endless patrol. For morning service, the Turks sent us some bombs, and one caught the end of the sap near the latrines below us. One poor man [Australian] had his leg blown off, the other leg shattered, his bowels were fully exposed, and both arms were broken. Yet his voice was quite strong when he asked for assistance. Another had several wounds, including an abdomenal, and he died on the stretcher. Two others were wounded; a facial artery spouted away. Later we put the howitzers on to the Turks and there were some terrible explosions. Had sick parade below this afternoon. My cold fairly tight; have now given up shorts—too cold.... Vague rumors that the Balkan States are in the war, also the inevitable prognostication that the campaign will end in days now. Meanwhile the New Zealanders and Maoris continue to supply men for trenches, and can only supply the numbers by sending in sick men. These men should be away now. Another bomb went off to-night below us, and we heard a call for stretcher-bearers—but don't know what happened, as the Australian medical officer went down there.

"September 27th.—One man last night slightly concussioned by a bomb. The Australian Army Medical Corps decided to shift half-way down the hill to the water-tanks; I went with them. Had both sick parades in the morning. The A.A.M.C. dug in a dressing station at the bottom of the sap near the tanks in a good place. Captain Kenny and I got a fine dug-out on the side of the hill, just below the fire trenches. We can make it into a real good place. Last night, about 7 o'clock, word came to stand to arms, so I went up the hill. There was a strong attack on the left. The warships, were firing their big guns incessantly. Fires broke out on the lower slopes of the west hills and the far hills. There was also brisk rifle fire, and rockets and star-shells were going. A warship in the Gulf of Saros was using a searchlight well in advance of our position, on the far hills. The firing lasted about an hour and fizzled out.... A bomb went off in the afternoon near the dug-outs at the Apex, wounded a Maori (Pirika) in the thigh and a New Zealander in the arm."

The Last Weeks at Gallipoli.

Departure from Gallipoli. A Rest on Lemnos.

On Sunday evening, October 3rd, the Maoris broke up camp at their various posts and went aboard the mine-sweeper "Partridge," which left next morning for Mudros, the famous haven of Lemnos Island. The British cruiser "Endymion," was passed on the way. On landing at Mudros, the Maoris were broken up in platoons and located with their previous regiments. The camp, at Sarpi, was 3½ miles out from the port. For an account of this camp and the doings of the Maoris there, I give extracts from Captain Buck's diary, in the absence of official regimental diaries for this period:—

"October 5th—We had a good rest; missed the sound of bullets. The Maoris are with various battalions; a good many have been sent to hospital. Went for a walk this afternoon with Major Alderman, Captain Ennis and the Padre to the nearest village, Sarpi. Went to see Lieut.-Col. O'Neill (Major previously) who now commands the New Zealand Medical Corps.

"October 6th.—Review of troops to-day by General Godley. It was a pathetic sight to see the Main Body men, few in number, battered in appearance, with faded uniforms and weary step, as compared with the 6th Reinforcements. They are a likely looking lot. The infantry number about 1000 and the mounteds about 1100.... More of our boys sent to hospital."

A change of food, plenty of rest, cricket and football matches for those well enough to play, and camp-fire concerts, were some of the things that compensated the war-worn soldiers in Sarpi Camp. British officers of high degree came and had a look at the Maoris.

(A Maori diary entry: "A general wearing a monocle rode over; also saw an admiral wearing one. The Padre wanted to know how it is the English get weak in only one eye.")

One or two of the Maori officers were anxiously awaiting word from the steamer "Aragon," lying in Mudros Harbour, as to when they would get the long-expected leave for a run to Alexandria and Cairo. Their impatience found vent in this diary entry, "writ sarcastic," out of a full heart:—

"The 'Aragon' is a vessel that is anchored in Mudros Harbour. The Navy moves in spheres remote and no man knows what they are doing or what they have done, or when or where they may break out in a fresh place. But with regard to the Army, they revolve round the 'Aragon.' All things Military going and coming have to report to the 'Aragon.' The subaltern going away on sick leave or the General coming in with an Army Corps has to report to the 'Aragon.' In fact, reporting to the 'Aragon' is the one thing that is absolutely necessary towards winning the war."

The M.O. and Padre Wainohu went to Alexandria on leave, and looked up several Maoris in hospital. At Suez they found invalided Maoris in camp, waiting to be sent back to New Zealand—A. Simeon, Te Toa, Mason and Woods. Simeon had been the Doctor's orderly; he was disabled by a bullet which lodged behind the knee cap.

Te Toa—right well named!—was a man who had displayed remarkable stoicism after being wounded in the head in the attack on Chunuk Bair (August 8th). He had lost the sight of one eye, and the other was threatened.

On October 26th, the troopship "Waitemata" (Captain Nicholson) arrived at Suez from New Zealand, bringing 300 Maori reinforcements. The officers of the reinforcements were: Captain Rice, Lieut. Ashton, 2nd Lieuts. H. Kohere, H. Dansey, O'Neill, Kepa Ehau, Hall, McGregor, Bush, and Pekama Kaa; Chaplain-Major Hawkins, Captain Duncan, N.Z.M.C. Major McKenzie was in charge of the ship. The Maoris went into camp at Zeitoun.

Captain Buck wrote from Egypt to the New Zealand members of Parliament representing the Maori race:—

"All who have come through the Gallipoli campaign, where *pakeha* and Maori have shared the fatigue, danger, and incessant vigil of the trenches, side by side, recognise that the Maori is a better man than they gave him credit for, and have admitted him to full fellowship and equality. With a separate unit occupying its own trenches, these friendships which will cement mutual respect and esteem between the two races, do not have the same opportunities of being made as where they are working and fighting side by side. One of the finest incidents in the history of the two races took place when the Maoris left the trenches during the Anzac vacation. Their *pakeha* comrades who were remaining behind for a later shipment, carried their packs down into the gullies, and many stood clasping hands when the moment of separation came, with their hearts too full of *aroha* to express themselves in words.''

CHAPTER VI.
FORMATION OF THE PIONEER BATTALION.

By New Zealand Divisional Orders (February 20th, 1916), the formation of a New Zealand Pioneer Battalion was authorised. The Battalion was to consist of officers and other ranks drawn from surplus of N.Z.M.R. From the Otago M.R., and the whole of the Maori Contingents (two) then serving in Egypt with the New Zealand Infantry Brigade. At this time, the remnants of the original Maori Contingent, together with the whole of the 2nd Maoris, were divided up by tribes among the various battalions of the New Zealand Infantry Brigade and were in camp at Moascar, Ismailia. The Otago M.R. were also at Moascar as Divisional mounted troops, but owing to the decision of headquarters that Divisional cavalry were in future to consist of one squadron only, they were equal to the strength of two squadrons and headquarter's details available for transfer to form the nucleus of a *pakeha* half-battalion of the Pioneers. The balance of the *pakeha* officers and other ranks were drawn from the N.Z.M.R. then in camp at Serapeum (Suez Canal). The original Maori Contingent consisted of two companies and headquarters, but during August, 1915, they were divided up at Gallipoli as follows:—

Nos. 1 and 2 Platoons (Ngapuhi and Waikato) to Auckland Battalion; Nos. 3 and 4 Platoons (West Coast of North Island, Wanganui and Wellington) to Wellington Battalion; Nos. 5 and 6 Platoons (Arawa, Bay of Plenty, Ngati-Porou, and East Coast, Taupo and South Island men) to Canterbury Battalion; Nos. 7 and 8 Platoons (Poverty Bay, Wairoa, Hawke's Bay and Wairarapa) to Otago Battalion. The 2nd Maoris who had joined the 1st, on January 19th, 1916, had been divided up as above and attached to the original Contingent. The principle of this tribal distribution was adhered to throughout the organisation of the Pioneers except in a few cases where the numbers would not fit in.

The Pioneer Battalion was organised in accordance with the wishes of the G.O.C. N.Z. Division as follows:—

FORMATION OF THE PIONEER BATTALION.

A Company—Nos. 1 and 2 Platoons Maoris, Nos. 3 and 4 Platoons *pakehas* (7th Squadron).

B Company—Nos. 5 and 6 Platoons, Maoris, Nos. 7 and 8 Platoons, *pakehas* (5th Squadron).

C Company—Nos. 9 and 10 Platoons, Maoris, Nos. 11 and 12 Platoons, *pakehas* (12th Squadron).

D Company—Nos. 13 and 14 Platoons, Maoris, Nos. 15 and 16 Platoons, *pakehas* (N.Z.M.R.)

Officers were appointed as follows:—

C.O.—Major G. A. King, N.Z.S.C. (from Auckland Mounted Rifles).

Second in Command.—Captain P. H. Buck, N.Z.M.C. (from 1st Maoris).

Adjutant.—Captain W. S. Cooper (from Wellington Battalion).

Quarter-master.—Captain G. D. Hamilton (from Wellington Mounted Rifles).

Medical Officer.—Captain H. M. Buchanan, N.Z.M.C. (from Otago Mounted Rifles).

Instructing Machine-gun Officer.—2nd Lieut. J. O'Neil (from 2nd Maoris).

Transport Officer.—2nd Lieut. M. Broughton (1st Maoris).

A Company.—Captain E. G. Saxby (Auckland M.R.); Second in Command, Lieut. R. I. Dansey (1st Maoris). Lieut. S. J. S. Cooper (1st Maoris), 2nd Lieuts. T. Hetet (1st Maoris), H. Wilson (Otago M.R.), P. Kaa (2nd Maoris), L. H. Reid (2nd F.Coy., N.Z.E.), L. G. Ashton (2nd Maoris).

B Company—Captain W. S. Pennycook (Otago M.R.), Second in Command, Captain P. Harris (Canterbury M.R.), Lieut. J. C. MacLean (Otago M.R.), 2nd Lieuts. J. C. Tikao (1st Maoris), T. Hiroti (1st Maoris), H. R. Vercoe (1st Maoris), J. K. A. Ehau (2nd Maoris), G. A. Bush (2nd Maoris).

C Company—Captain F. M. Twisleton, M.C. (from Otago M.R.), Second in Command, Captain R. M. Gairdner (Otago M.R.), Lieuts. J. Short (Otago M.R.), W. H. Stainton (1st Maoris), 2nd Lieuts. W. H. Walker (1st Maoris), H. Kohere (2nd Maoris), G. Masters (2nd F.Coy. N.Z.E.).

D Company—Captain C. E. Clifton (Wellington M.R.), Second in Command, Captain W. O. Ennis (1st Maoris), Lieut.

L. S. Gibbs (Canterbury Battalion), 2nd-Lieuts. H. Dansey (2nd Maoris), J. Hall (2nd Maoris), J. H. Gilmour (Canterbury M.R.), A. P. H. Kaipara (1st Maoris).

The C.O. and Adjutant reported at Divisional Headquarters for duty with the Battalion, and were instructed to lay out a camp south of the aerodrome at Moascar. This was done. The Maoris marched into camp on March 6th, and started the erection of tents and cook-houses. The camp was soon complete and things squared up. Fatigue duties and drill occupied the newly-constituted unit until the 15th, when orders were received to pack up camp and move east of the Canal. Camp was quickly struck and the Battalion marched at 10.30 a.m. with transport, baggage and tents. The Canal was crossed by pontoon bridge at Ferry Post, and after a halt for lunch on the east bank the corps marched on to the Reserve Camp and pitched tents just east of the Second Infantry Brigade camp and on the south side of the road. Here the Battalion was joined next day (March 16th) by the Third Maori Reinforcements, under Lieut. Sutherland, and other officers, 2nd Lieuts. A. L. Melles, S. Moore, A. McDonald, G. R. Fromm, E. Goodwin, and R. Karauria. The reinforcements consisted of 112 Maoris, 125 Niué Islanders, and 45 Rarotongans, total 282. These new-comers landed at Suez, and came on to Ismailia by train; they were met by the C.O. and Lieut. R. J. Dansey and were marched into camp. As there had been an outbreak of measles during the voyage, the recruits were put into isolation camp 400 yards west of the Pioneers' camp. Fifteen Niué Natives had been left behind in hospital at Suez. On the 17th, General Sir A. J. Godley inspected the Battalion at work, and addressed the reinforcements. On the 18th, a very hot day, with a desert gale blowing and the air full of sand, Major Buck, with twelve officers and 447 Maoris of all ranks, marched from camp with camel transport and took over maintenance of a section of the trenches about six miles east of the camp. The C.O. followed with a detachment, and after a very trying march, reached the trenches. Camp was made alongside the 10th Squadron ((Auckland M.R.) who were holding the line. On the 20th, Major Buck was ordered to return to the Reserve camp owing to an alteration in the plans, and with seventy camels for baggage the Maoris marched back again, reaching the camp at noon. It was hard going under the tropical sun trudging those burning sands, but all stuck to it well and no man fell out. Orders were now received for the Battalion to return to Moascar, and on the morning of the 21st, the camp was cleared up, all the other New Zealand infantry units were also moving. At 10 o'clock the Battalion, in hollow square, was inspected by H.R.H. The Prince of Wales, and various other officers. After the inspection the Ngati-Porou, under Lieut. Kohere, entertained the Prince with a rousing *haka*. Soon afterwards the Battalion was on the move, and crossing the canal, marched into Moascar and took over the old camp ground. The tents did not arrive till next day. The 3rd Reinforcements, having now been released from isolation, were allotted to the various Companies.

The Battalion was put through some more solid infantry training, and was inspected on the desert by General Godley.

The question of the suitability of the South Sea Islanders for coming work in a cold climate was discussed, and the G.O.C. instructed that all Niué men unlikely to stand conditions in Europe would be left in Egypt. A very careful inspection was accordingly held (March 30th), and all the more delicate-looking natives were weeded out and sent to the Base Details Camp en route to Gizeh, Cairo.

Steady training was continued during the early part of April. The Pioneers made a good showing in a parade of the whole Division held in the rear of the aerodrome on the 3rd, for inspection by General Sir Archibald Murray. Next day the General inspected the Maoris at their camp, and the customary *hakas* of welcome were performed in his honour. A *haka* party, under Lieut. Kohere, was drawn up in the hollow square formed by the other platoons. The Ngati-Porou and Arawa tribes gave a vociferous song and dance of greeting. This was followed by a dance and chant by the Cook Island Natives, who also sang a lively marching song.

Major Buck, on behalf of the Maoris, addressed a speech of welcome to the General, who replied briefly and expressed satisfaction at the appearance and bearing of the Battalion in the previous day's review. Generals Godley and Russell and the G.H.Q. Corps and Divisional staffs were present at the ceremonial.

The Departure for France.

On April 5th, the long-expected orders were received for the exodus from Egypt to the great theatre of war, and the succeeding two days were spent in preparing for the move. The evening of the 6th, was a lively time in the big camp. All the canteens were raided and burned by the troops. As soon as the disturbance was reported Major King paraded the whole of the Battalion and had the roll called. No one was missing, so that the Pioneers stood clear of any share in the row. On April 7th, the Battalion was on the move on the first stage of the journey to France. Tents were struck, the camp cleared up and all hands, except the baggage guard, went down for a last bathe in Lake Timseh. That night the Battalion, in two train loads, numbering altogether 28 officers and 948 other ranks, travelled to Port Said, where they embarked early next morning on the transport "Canada." This troopship also took the Second Canterbury Battalion of infantry, under Lieut.-Col. H. Stewart, who was O.C. on the ship.

At five o'clock in the morning of April 9th, the "Canada," steamed out of the harbour bound for Marseilles.

For the voyage up the Mediterannean, the usual danger-zone precautions were taken. All hands were told off to boat stations, and were practiced in standing to the boats. All the Lewis machine-guns were mounted in commanding positions and gun crews were told off in 4-hour reliefs by day and 2-hour reliefs by night. Look-out men (50) were told off to watch for submarines and were arranged in reliefs under Captain Twisleton. At 3 o'clock in the afternoon of the 11th, an enemy submarine was sighted, about 800 yards away, on the port side. The ship's course was altered and the steaming rate increased, and nothing more was seen of the raider. The "Canada" carried enough boats to accommodate all on board, but in most cases they were three deep on the davits and there would have been very small chance of launching them all in case of emergency.

Malta was passed at 5 a.m. on April 12th, and next day the coast of Sardinia was in sight. This day gas helmets and pockets were issued to all ranks, two per man, one to be carried in the satchel, and one in the pocket sewn in the skirt of the jacket.

CHAPTER VII.

ARRIVAL OF THE PIONEERS IN FRANCE (1916).

Marseilles was reached on April 9th, 1916, and the troops disembarked that evening and entrained for the seat of war. The transport "Menominee," bringing the transport and pack animals, under charge of a party of men commanded by Captain Gairdner, had left Port Said before the "Canada," but had not yet arrived. All next day, April 15th, the Pioneers were travelling steadily by train through the beautiful country of Southern France, in its spring dress of foliage. The train was very crowded and there was not much chance of a comfortable rest for anyone. All hands were intensely interested in the country through which they were passing. It was a most agreeable change, after the sojourn in the deserts of Egypt, to see so much eye-resting green vegetation.

On the following morning the train passed through Versailles. Very few halts were made on the journey northward. Abbeville was passed at midnight, and at 6.30 a.m. a halt was made at Steenbecque, where the Battalion detrained.

Stores and baggage were unloaded and the men marched to Morbecque, two miles away, where they took up their first billets on French soil, the school and three farms, within a radius of two miles from the Square. The billets were dirty, and the remainder of the day was spent in cleaning them up and getting settled. It was cold, wet weather, and the change from a warm climate was felt severely, especially by the Niué Islanders, most of whom collapsed on the march to the billets and had to be helped along the road.

Late on the night of the 17th, orders were received to move to Cercus. There the Battalion was joined by Captain Gairdner with some of the men and the pack horses; the remainder of the "Menominee" detachment under Lieut. Wilson, had temporarily been detrained at Marseilles. The Cercus billets were very scattered but were found fairly clean and comfortable. Routine work was carried on at Cercus for some days. On April 23rd, Lieut. Maclean and 60 other ranks, marched to

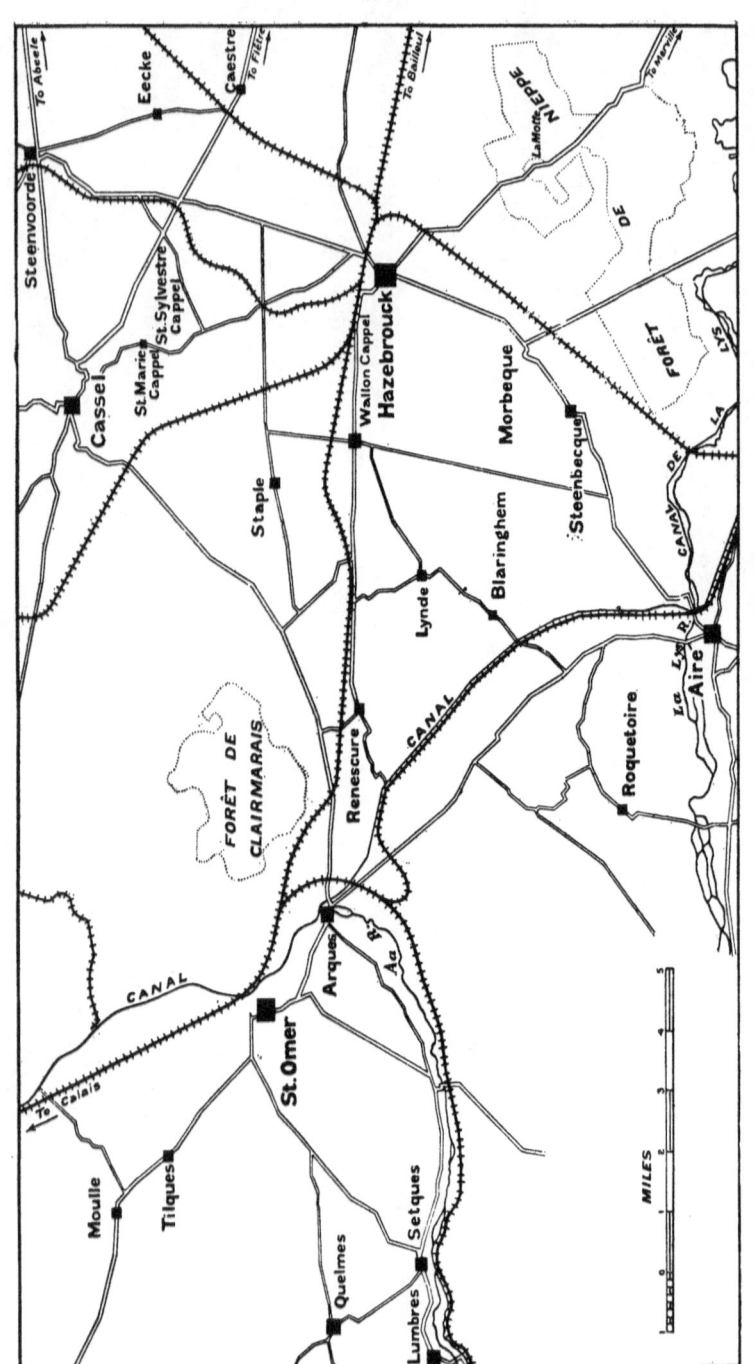

St. Omer and Hazebrouck

Arrival of the Pioneers in France.

La Motte, in the Forêt de Nieppe, to start tree-felling under the official forest control.

Lieut. Wilson, with the transport waggons and horses arrived from Abbeville, having camped at Aire the previous night. Three horses died during the trek, which occupied three days; and the opinion was expressed that it was very foolish to send horses, just landed from a six-days' voyage and 48 hours on a train, right off on a 60-mile road journey, even with empty waggons. The animals were all in very poor condition on arrival, particularly the mules, which seemed to be greatly affected by the cold.

On the 26th, the C.O. and Major Buck rode over to La Motte to see the party of Maori bushmen, who were doing very good work. The Forest Control authorities were very pleased with them. All the trees cut down were felled in the French style, no standing butt was left; the tree was cut level with the ground and the top of the stump showing was carefully trimmed so as to leave a rounded surface, which would not hold water. The forest was mostly composed of oaks, elms and beeches; only beeches were being felled at this time.

In the Cercus camp, the Battalion was kept busy with route marches, bayonet fighting practice and platoon drill.

On the medical side, the inoculation of all ranks for paratyphoid was completed. The men were engaged in putting in order two strong-points on the road south-west of Cercus which had been started by the 10th Hussars the previous year and left in an unfinished state.

Captain Gairdner and Lieuts. Dansey and Hiroti, with a hundred men marched out to Sally-sur-la-Lys, via Estaires, to undertake bridge-head works there.

On April 30th, an interesting forestry competition was held at La Motte, between the Maori bushmen and the French bucherons, a tree-chopping contest, six men a side. Each team had to fell twelve trees, in the French style. The Pioneer team won by three minutes, an excellent performance considering that the men had had to master new methods of bush-falling.

The first of May, 1916, saw another change of scene. The Battalion was moved on to Estaires, a march of seventeen miles, by way of Morbecque, La Motte, and Neuf Berquin, and went into billets previously occupied by the Australians. Various working parties were sent out, and did good work.

On May 8th, the Pioneers had their first taste of the Boches' methods. A German 'plane flew overhead and dropped a large bomb sixty yards from Lieut. Gibbs' party working on defences at Noveau Monde. The explosion made a crater ten feet wide and seven feet deep; no one was hurt.

On May 15th, the Battalion moved on to famous Armentieres, a march of about eleven miles, and was billeted in the cotton factory of Charvel Freres, the Rue de Bizet, just north of the town, on the river Lys. The billets had been left in very good order by the Pioneer Battalion of the 17th Division whom the New Zealanders relieved. With the billets, the Battalion took over the Divisional Trench Warfare School, which used a system of trenches, part of the town defences. Lieut.-Col. King placed Major Pennycook in command of the school, and the Division had arranged to send eight officers and n.c.o.'s from each brigade for each session, three days. The course covered construction and maintenance of trenches of all kinds, machine-gun emplacements, dug-outs and shelters, and the rapid construction of wire entanglements. Any suggested improvements for defensive works were tried in the school before being adopted in the trenches. The several companies were told off for work in the trenches and on communications about the town. These duties were carried out at night only, as it was considered unsafe to move the various parties into and out of the trenches during daylight. On May 21st, the first casualty occurred. 2nd Lieut. L. H. Reid, of A Company, was killed by machine-gun fire early in the morning, Sergeant Moffitt was wounded at the same time.

Meanwhile Maori foresters were doing excellent work. A wood-chopping competition was held in the Foret de Nieppe on May 21st, between teams from the 3rd Canadian Division, two Australian Divisions and the New Zealand Division. The New Zealand axemen were drawn from Lieut. Maclean's party of bush-fellers at La Motte; all were Maoris. The New Zealanders won two out of four contests and were second in the other two—a splendid performance considering some of their opponents were drawn from the ranks of the finest woodsmen in the world.

Trench work was now being carried on under fire and casualties were frequent. During the last few days and nights of May, Lieut. J. Short was severely wounded on the night of the 27th, and died next night at Bailleul. Others wounded were L.-Cpl. J. Danger, Ptes. H. Hirini, T. Matenga and G. Waldron. Several of these casualties were sustained on the evening of the 29th when the billets near the Armentieres railway station and the neighbourhood of the town swimming baths were heavily shelled with high explosive; the Pioneers hit were in the town on leave. On the following day L.-Cpl. N. Toki, and Ptes. R. Elers, H. Kahukiwi, and P. Marunui were wounded.

It was decided to send the Niué Islanders back to their South Sea homes, as they were constitutionally unfitted for work in a cold climate and many had fallen sick. Accordingly, on May 30th (1916), 2nd. Lieut. Fromm and 53 Niué men left Armentieres for Etaples en route for England and New Zealand.

Heavy shelling was now the daily and nightly experience. Once a German 8-inch shell landed in C Company's messroom and "smashed things up a bit," as the C.O. expressed it in his diary.

With the consent of the G.O.C., early in June the Battalion was reorganised into two Maori and two *pakeha* companies; D Company in the meantime to consist of Cook Islanders only, pending the arrival of reinforcements. This company attended to the sawmill work.

The Birthday Honours list issued, showed that Lieut.-Col. G. A. King had been awarded the D.S.O., and Lieut. W. H. Stainton the Military Cross.

Padre Wainohu and Pte. George Gardiner were recommended for the two foreign decorations allocated for service on Gallipoli.

The month of June saw the ranks depleted by numerous casualties inflicted by German shell-fire. On the 5th, Pte. E. B. Brooke was killed. On the 8th the officers' billets and all houses near the main billet were heavily shelled with 8-inch and 5.9-inch H.E. from 7 a.m. till 10 a.m. A hundred and forty-two German shells were fired. All hands were hurried away from the billets into the open, and the horses were sent across the river. Work was carried on as usual after the bombardment. Five Pioneers were killed or died of wounds: Ptes. H. Waru, P. Whitau, E. Kawhia, P. Takauo, and Humphries.

Major Clifton, D Company, was wounded, and Captain Twisleton, B Company, and Captain Cooper, were evacuated sick from Armentieres. Captain Ennis took over command of B Company.

On June 12th, Sergeant Delamere was accidentally killed at the Divisional Bomb School, where he was acting as instructor. There were other casualties incidental to the varied duties of the Pioneers. Lieut. W. H. Walker lost two fingers through an accident at the Divisional sawmills operated by D Company.

On June 13th, all company commanders were taken round the defences of Armentieres and each company was allotted a portion of the defensive line to hold in case of attack.

On the night of the 16th, there was a gas alarm. All the companies paraded and the horses were sent off to Pont de Nieppe. The gas passed west of the town and followed the river to Estaires, causing some casualties among troops, but the Pioneers escaped.

The Divisional authorities having asked for recommendations for Military Medals for good work and bravery in the face of the enemy at Anzac, the following names of Maoris were sent forward for decoration: Sergeants Angel, Rotoatara, Bennett, Corporals Flutey, R. Otene, Sidney, and Pte. Rawhiti.

On June 24th, A Company was severely shelled while on trench work, and a 5.9-inch gun bombarded its billets and surrounding houses. There were eight casualties among the Pioneers, including 2nd. Lieut. H. Hetet (Ngati-Maniapoto). Five days later the same company was the target for another burst of shell-fire, and Lieut. S. J. S. Coupar, from Southland, was killed by a shell. Another South Islander, Lieut. J. C. Tikao, of Rapaki, who was with Coupar at the time, suffered severe shell-shock.

CHAPTER VIII.

MAORI RAIDING PARTIES (1916).

The Pioneers had carried on their trench duties with admirable courage and endurance under harassing conditions but were getting impatient for an opportunity of taking the offensive and having a cut at the Germans. So early in July, the G.O.C. consented to the Battalion making a raid, and there was keen anticipation of an exciting night enterprise. Fifty men were picked from each Maori company, from volunteers, and training was started under Captain R. I. Dansey.

One night (July 3rd), about 9.30 o'clock, Lieut. Dansey saw a man on the roof of a factory in rear of the billets holding a light in the direction of the camp's trenches. He searched the roofs but failed to catch the fellow, so he put all the civilians in the building under arrest and handed them over to the Assistant-Provost Marshal. An enemy bombardment of Armentieres followed immediately the showing of the light. The shelling was particularly heavy and lasted until midnight; the guns used were 5.9-inch, 8-inch, and 11-inch howitzers; incendiary shells were also fired. Several buildings were burned and considerable damage was done, but the casualties in the town were not great. The same night the enemy raided L'Epinette Salient and captured a bombing post of five men. The German barrage de feu which encircled L'Epinette, caused a hundred casualties in the 1st Auckland Regiment, who garrisoned the post.

The Maori raiding party was engaged in bombing practice and physical training, and a model of the section of the enemy's trench to be attacked, was laid out on the ground near the Pont de Nieppe. All ranks were very keen about the coming night adventure, and the volunteers were far in excess of requirements. The C.O. and his officers reconnoitered the ground over which the attack would be made.

At 10.45 o'clock on the night of July 9th, a party, consisting of five officers and 80 other ranks under Captain Dansey, attempted the raid on the German trenches. The raid was to have been made on the 12th, but instructions were received from Divisional Headquarters to get it off on the 9th, so preparations were rushed on. The party, however, found the wire in front of the salient had not been cut, and therefore, was withdrawn. On the return across No Man's Land the men came under a heavy fire of shrapnel from the enemy, and one man (L.-Cpl. Toka) was killed and three were wounded. Trench 84 and the post at Petty Curry were also heavily shelled for about half an hour and four men were wounded in the trenches. The New Zealand artillery put up a counter-barrage fire but were stopped by telephone after ten minutes. The raiding party returned to billets at 4 a.m. It was a bitter disappointment to the Maoris, who had thus lost their longed-for chance of using the bayonet on their foes.

A Raid that Failed.

Next night, July 10th-11th, half an hour before midnight, the Maori raiding party went out again and had a nerve-trying experience in the dark. The wire was cut by trench mortars between 7 and 8 p.m., but scouts found that the fire had not sufficiently destroyed the entanglements, so half an hour's shelling was spent in clearing a track for the raiders. The attacking party, however, were nearly cut off by an enemy force in No Man's Land and had to retire to Petty Curry. There were no casualties. The New Zealand artillery fire was immediately opened and it was hoped caused some casualties among the enemy massed in the open. The Germans' return fire was very poor, and no casualties were caused in the trenches. During the raid the N.Z.F.A. shelled the Railway Salient and put down a barrage fire on the communication trenches in rear of it. Smoke was released from the Pioneer trenches, and drew a heavy fire from the enemy's guns and mortars and a considerable amount of shelling directed on the town.

The following is Lieut.-Col. George A. King's report on the Pioneers' attempted raid of the night July 10th-11th:—

"Scouts under Lieut. Vercoe left the gap south of Petty Curry at 11 p.m. At 11.22 they reported to me that the gap in the enemy's outside wire was not passable owing to the way the artillery had blown it about. The remainder of the raiding party then moved out into No Man's Land and formed up in rear of the scouts. The wire was very difficult and a gap was not cleared until 12.30 a.m. The scouts then moved round the end of the second wire and found a good gap in the third row and so got up to the enemy's parapet, which was about fifteen feet wide on the top. Many Germans were walking about on the parapet to the right of the gap, and as their movements seemed out of place Lieut. Vercoe sent two scouts down inside of the third wire. By this time the whole party was inside the wire and extended ready to rush the trench. Up till now there had not been a shot or a flare fired from any of the enemy's trenches opposite trenches 83 and 84, and this unusual quiet on the part of the enemy caused a general feeling among the raiders that a trap had been set for them.

"At about 12.45 a.m., one of the scouts who had been sent along the wire to the right (south) reported to Lieut. Vercoe that he had counted the heads of 69 Germans crawling along outside the middle row of wire to cut the party off. Captain Dansey immediately swung up the left flank of the raiders to meet the Germans with bombs. The movement was not complete before another scout reported a still larger body of the enemy outside the entanglement nearest our trenches also trying to cut off the raiders. The party was moving in a crescent formation.

"Captain Dansey then decided, as the danger of getting surrounded was too great, to withdraw his raiders. The party withdrew quickly and in good order, the scouts forming the rearguard. The enemy followed up as far as the line of small trees about 75 yards from our post at Petty Curry, throwing bombs.

"As soon as the raiding party got inside our wire I gave a signal for artillery barrage to be formed. The first howitzer shell arrived within 30 seconds of the rocket breaking. The infantry garrison at Petty Curry opened rifle and machine-gun fire on the enemy, who were plainly visible at one time. The 18-pounders' fire covered most of the ground across which the enemy were retiring and the howitzer shells were bursting well along the German parapet. I consider that the fire of rifles and guns must have caused considerable loss to the enemy, as considerable noise and confusion were observed amongst them as they retired, which they did rapidly.

"The Pioneers retired on to the right flank party of the raiders and returned to the trench via south end of Haig's Barrier. The whole party, including raiders, communication post and flank party, were safely in our trenches by 1.30 a.m. without any casualties.

"Lieut. Vercoe is quite satisfied that the gap through the enemy's inside entanglement had been specially made by the enemy to encourage our party to rush the parapet, and I am of the opinion that Captain Dansey undoubtedly saved the party from total loss by withdrawing when he did, and that great credit is due to Lieut. Vercoe and his scouts whose careful work disclosed the trap in time for it to be avoided. All ranks behaved exceptionally well during the retirement under bomb-fire, and there was absolutely no noise or confusion.

"As a raid the operation was a failure, as no information was gained, except that the enemy is very much on the alert and that he had at least 150 men available for a counterstroke."

On the night of the 16th, Lieut. Kaa took a patrol out ready to go into No Man's Land, but was not allowed to make the raid owing to a New Zealand gas attack having been arranged. Next night Lieut. Vercoe took a patrol (A Company) out from Petty Curry but saw nothing of importance.

After this date patrol parties went out frequently at night. One of A Company, led by Lieut. O'Neill, reported having located an enemy listening post and also found a telephone cable running from No Man's Land under the German wire; this they cut.

There was at this time tremendous artillery activity along the front. The Pioneers' O.C. wrote in his diary on July 19th: "There is an awful row going on from our people and the Boches is shelling an oat paddock about 200 yards north of us, with 5.9 h.e."

On July 20th, the Hon. Sir James Carroll arrived with the G.O.C. on a visit to his fellow-countrymen, and received an

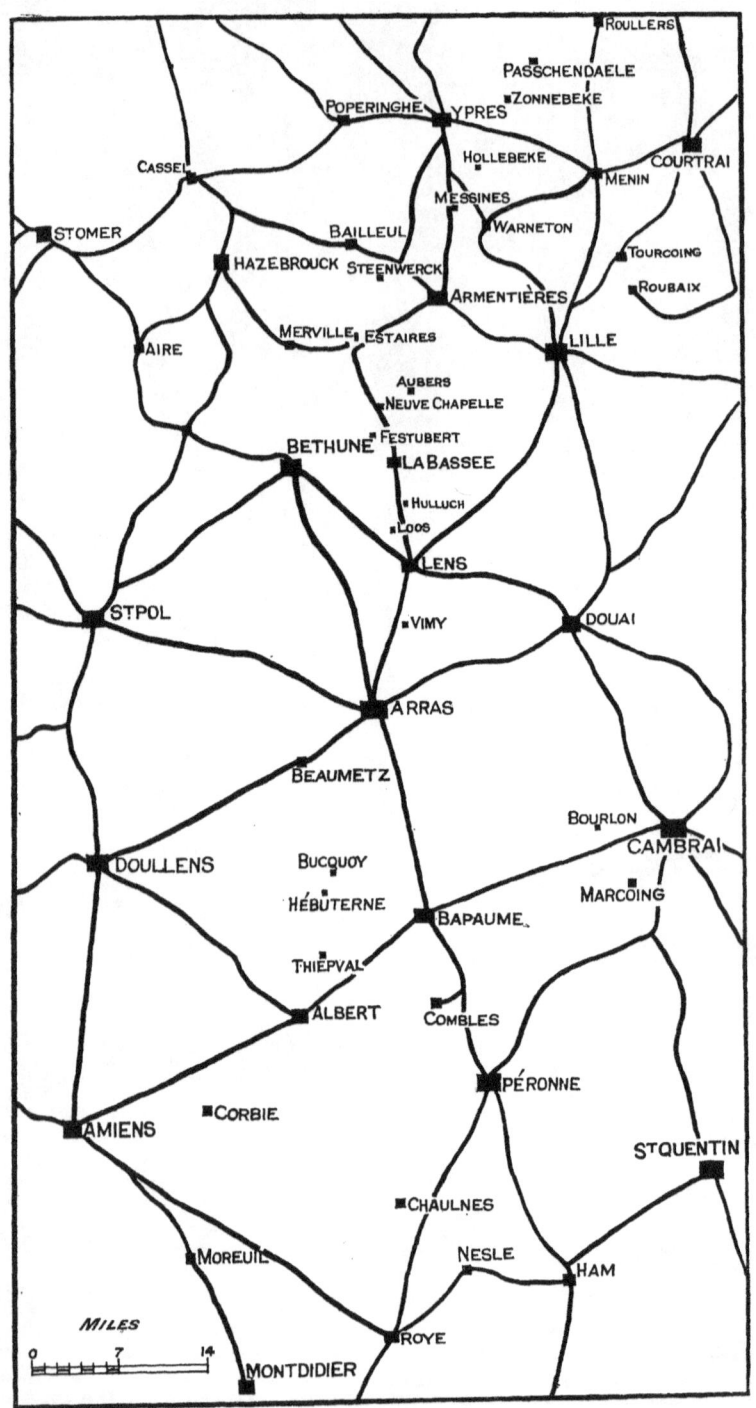

N.W. FRANCE

A Raid that Failed.

exceedingly cordial welcome from the Maori fighting men, with *hakas* and greeting chants after the good old fashion. "Ta Hemi Kara" spent several hours with the Battalion. He was banquetted on pork and *puwha*, the latter gathered from the deserted gardens of Armentieres. The French-grown *puwha* was particularly welcome and served to remind the veteran of the feasts of his homeland.

At this time the duties undertaken by the Pioneers in defence of Armentieres were multifarious and heavy. B Company parties were working on the support and second support lines in the 3rd Brigade sector between La Chappelle and Armentieres and the Bois Grenier; D Company was engaged in the sawmill and on concrete works and R.E. dumps.

NOTES.

The following were the instructions for the N.Z. Pioneer Battalion raid on German trenches:—
(July 8th, 1916.)

BATTALION ORDERS NO. 1.

Armentieres, 8/7/1916.

Orders for Minor Enterprise on Night of July 10th-11th, 1916.

(1) **Attacking Party.**—A party as under, will carry out a raid on German trenches at C. 23.0.8.7. on night July 9th-10th if wire is cut, failing which on night July 10th-11th.
O.C. Scouts.—Lieut. Vercoe, Sergeant Dufaur and 10 other ranks.
Assaulting Party.—Sergeant Heath and 14 o.r.
No. 1 Bombing Party.—Lieut. Vercoe and 8 o.r.
No. 2 Bombing Party.—Sergt. Roto-a-Tara and 4 o.r.
No. 3 Bombing Party.—Cpl. Johnson and 8 o.r.
No. 4 Bombing Party.—Lieut. Kaa and 8 o.r.
No. 5 Bombing Party.—Sergeant Angel and 4 o.r.
Communication Party.—Lieut. Dansey and 2 o.r.
Right Flank Patrol.—Lieut. O'Neill and 6 o.r.
Signallers.—4 o.r.
Stretcher-bearers.—Cpl. Otene and 4 o.r.

(2). **Object.**—(a) To capture machine-guns and trench mortars.
(b) To secure two prisoners for identification.
(c) To kill as many Germans as possible.

(3). **Objective.**—The German salient 500 yards west of Les ?? ?— Hallots and communication trenches within a radius of 50 yards.

(4) **Organisation.**—The O.C. attack will move out from starting point at Petty Curry at zero, preceded by scouts. Assaulting party will accompany the O.C. attack. These parties will move in best formation for ground. Bombing parties will move in rear of assaulting

party in line of parties in single file; No. 1 on the right. Communication party with telephone will move in rear of bombing parties. Cpl. Otene and two stretcher-bearers will accompany communication party. Right flanking party will move at zero from gap south of Petty Curry and get into position at corner of drain at C. 23 C. Centl. One sapper N.Z.E., will accompany Lieut. Vercoe and another will accompany Lieut. Kaa to demolish machine-gun emplacements, etc. Two men from scouts will enter trench after a footing has been gained and act as Intelligence party.

(5) **Preparations.**—All officers concerned in attack will make a special reconnaissance of the position to-night (July 8th-9th). All other ranks will be exercised over specially prepared model of the objective to-night after dark. Identity discs and all maps, papers or other means by which men could be identified will be left at Battalion H.Q. before marching out. No N.Z. buttons will be worn on the jackets. All ranks will be clothed as lightly as possible, and no web equipment will be worn. All ranks will carry 10 Mills bombs in special carrier. No rifles or bayonets will be taken. Officers and sappers will carry revolvers. Other ranks will be armed with *mérés*. Officers will carry luminous watches, which will be carefully checked before starting. Faces will be well blacked. White armlets six inches wide will be worn by all ranks on both arms, but will be covered until enemy's wire is reached. Only Maori will be spoken by all parties after leaving starting point.

(6) **Plan of Action.**—The whole party will leave Petty Curry at zero and will crawl out and take up position as near as possible to the enemy's wire without being seen. Communication party will take up position in large shell hole half-way across No Man's Land and keep touch with starting point by telephone. At 20 minutes past zero (0.20) the artillery will commence diversion on Brume Ruc (1.5B. 4.8). Scouts will examine breach in enemy's wire and if necessary will clear a track through to enemy's parapet, and on completion of the job will report to O.C. attack. O.C attack with assaulting party will then rush point of salient. Nos. 1, 2 and 3 bombing parties under Lieut. Vercoe, will move under cover of enemy's parapet for 50 yards south and will then enter enemy's trench and clear it out. Nos. 4 and 5 bombing parties will enter trench in rear of assaulting party. Scouts, except for two Intelligence men, will not enter the trench but will make all arrangements for a clear get-away for the party. O.C. attack will remain at point of entrance to trench throughout, and will keep up communication with O.C. Communication Post in No Man's Land by means of orderly. A white tape will be run out from gap in our wire by rear man of No. 1 bombing party and will be fastened to end of gap in enemy's wire on arrival, and will serve as a guide for return journey. Gap in enemy's wire will also be marked with white rag by scouts while attackers are in enemy's trench. Prisoners will be handed over to scouts at entrance of trench and they will hand them over to O.C. Communication Post. In the event of a machine-gun being captured, O.C. raid will at once send it with two men to our own trenches. Wounded will be carried back to Communication Post and taken thence to our own trenches on stretchers. Raiders will not remain in enemy's trench longer than 15 minutes, and may be withdrawn earlier at discretion of O.C. raid. Signal to withdraw will be given by whistle by O.C. raid, and on signal sounding it will be passed on by all who hear it, and O.C.'s parties will then withdraw their men to entrance, and get them across No Man's Land as quickly as possible. After satisfying him-

self that all men have left the trench, O.C. raid will form a rear-guard of the scouts, and cover the retirement to our own lines, picking up Communication Post on the way.

(7) **Rolls.**—Will be made out in triplicate and will be checked before men leave billets. The men will be checked into trench on return from the raid, and again by Major Buck at the junction of Wessex Avenue and Subsidiary Line.

(8) **Return.**—On entering our trenches raiders will move straight into support trenches—A Company into S83, C Company into S84 —and will remain until bombardment stops, and will then proceed to billets via Wessex Avenue and "Y" Route.

(9) **Position of Officers.**—During the raid the C.O. and M.O. of the Battalion will remain in Petty Curry locality and keep touch with the raid via Communication Post.

(10) **Artillery Fire.**—The artillery of centre and left groups will make a diversion on 15.b.4.8 from 0.20 until 0.65. If the O.C. raid wishes a barrage de feu put round the section attacked he will put up our S.O.S. rocket, when artillery will switch on to that section and continue until notified to stop by telephone by O.C. Battalion.

(11) **Flank Patrol.**—Lieut. O'Neill's party will leave our trenches at the junction of trenches 82 and 83 and will crawl out and take up position in No Man's Land and prevent enemy patrols or machine-guns from firing on raiders. They will return on seeing signal for barrage fire or on hearing whistle for withdrawal of raid, and will report at S83.

GEORGE A. KING, Lieut.-Col.
Commanding N.Z. Pioneers.

CHAPTER IX.

THE PIONEERS' WORK ON THE WESTERN FRONT.
(1916).

On August 12th, orders came for the New Zealand Division to move to Blaringhem area to rest prior to a move south, presumably for active operations. The Pioneers were alloted to the 3rd Brigade group for the transfer. The Division was being relieved by the 51st (Highland Division), and the Maoris' ground was to be taken up by the 5th Battalion, Royal Scots (Pioneers).

On the 14th, the Battalion with other troops marched to Steenwerck, six miles, and entrained for E'taple, where the Pioneers detrained and found billets waiting, in a very clean little village, surrounded by rich farming land all in crop. Some days were spent here, a pleasant relief from the trench work under shell-fire. Captain Ennis took over the position of Adjutant vice Captain Cooper, evacuated sick from Armentieres.

On the 19th, orders were received to move to the region of the Lower Somme, near Abbeville. Next day the Battalion marched to St. Omer, and there entrained for Longpre, and the Somme. From Longpre the route was an easy march to Hallencourt, where good billets had been made ready. A syllabus of training was laid out, to cover six days, but was not finished, as there was another move in a few days to Fricourt crossroads. Here the Battalion was about five miles behind the front line, but there were big guns all round and there was the continual roar of artillery battle. The Germans were very busy shelling Fricourt Wood, just in front of the Pioneers' position. The traffic on the roads was continuous. There was a continual stream of all kinds of vehicles passing all the time and the never-ceasing procession of infantry and guns.

"I don't care for the position of our bivouac very much," Lieut.-Col. King wrote in his diary, "as it is on the forward slope of a hill running north to Ancre Brook and alongside cross-roads, which seem pretty sure to be shelled sooner or later."

The Pioneers were not long in commencing trench and dugout work. The allotted ground was in Delville Wood, where old trenches were cleared up. The trenches were in a very bad state and mud was everywhere. The road to Montauban was particularly bad. The roads and trenches were under heavy shell-fire and there was much gas from exploding shells, mostly lachrymatory.

On the 31st, one man was killed and five wounded and a sergeant and three men were gassed. Nearly everyone was affected by the tear shells which, as an officer expressed it, "were a damn nuisance, but otherwise pretty futile." About seven o'clock that evening, the Germans shelled the cross-roads beside the camp. There were no casualties, but the O.C. decided to move camp next day to a more comfortable spot.

Various details of trench and road work occupied the force at Fricourt for some days. A number of the men in A Company were feeling the effects of gas, and on September 2nd, Sergeant Duff died of gas poisoning. On the same day Pte. Barton was killed and one man was wounded by a bomb. This occurred when the Corps was sent to fresh ground just west of Fricourt Circus. The C.O. and Company Commanders laid out the lines for new communication trenches, French and Turk Lanes, from Montauban to the front line between High Wood and Delville Wood. There was very heavy fire from our guns (the Australian heavy howitzer battery included) all the afternoon, but not much return fire.

On September 3rd A, B, and C Companies each worked one shift on Turk Lane. DCompany worked one shift on dug-outs for themselves on the ridge behind High Wood. There was very heavy fighting this day all along the front from French Right trench past Bezantin Le Petit. The British flammenwerfen was in action in High Wood, and the C.O. remarked in his diary that he "would not like to be at the wrong end of it." Huge volumes of flame at least 100 feet long and 50 feet high, tore through the wood and must have had a terrible effect on the garrison of the German trenches. Many German prisoners passed through the camp during the evening. At ten o'clock that night, all the companies started on Turk Lane, and full shifts were worked, each platoon being away from camp for 10 hours. Work on Turk Lane went on well for some days, the men digging into it in good style. There was very heavy firing at times towards Poziérés and Givinchy. On September 8th, General Russell came up to see the Battalion's work and expressed his appreciation and that of the Commander of the 15th Corps of what had been done. On the 9th, all the companies were engaged in cleaning up and "duck-walking" Turk Lane, which was now fit for traffic from Montauban Alley to Black Watch Trench, and duckwalks had been constructed to the bottom of Devil's Valley, the junction of Turk and St. George Lanes. No work was done after noon on the 9th, owing to an attack by our British left flank Division on High Wood and Wood Lane. The C.O. and Major Buck went up and watched the attack from Pommiers Redoubt but could not see much, owing to the smoke and dust of the bombardment. The attackers took Wood Lane and held it, but the attack on High Wood was only partly successful; the Germans still held the N.E. corner, where Great Trench starts from. The camp, near the transport lines, was shelled at about 4 p.m., from the direction of Martinpuich, and three men were killed and nine wounded. A horse and a mule were killed and a G.S. waggon was smashed. This damage was caused by the explosion of one shell. Major Buck, describing his observations of the British attack, which was preceded by severe bombardment, wrote:—"We were sitting near a Brigade H.Q., and it was interesting to see an aeroplane fly low over it sounding a horn to attract attention and then dropping a message with a red, white and blue streamer on it. We also saw one of our 'planes come circling down slowly and (then) precipitately with a little flicker of light noticeable. She struck the hillside rather suddenly on the opposite side from us and burst at once into flames. There were two German 'planes up a little while before, but whether they were responsible I do not know."

Twenty reinforcements arrived in camp on September 8th, all for the Maori companies. They included some Samoans.

Orders came through on the night of the 10th, that work could be recommenced after midnight, so Major Buck went out with Lieuts. H. Dansey and Kaa, and set various jobs in hand. A deep dug-out for Brigade H.Q., 20 feet below ground, was finished by D Company, assisted by R.E. miners. Several shells were put on Turk Lane, and there were fears of gas at times. The platoons came off work at 8 a.m. (Sunday, the 10th). One man was killed by H.E.. General Russell went round with Colonel King and the R.E. officer and it was decided to take Turk Lane trench forward to Wood Lane, and the position of assembly trenches for the coming attack was also fixed. This day the 3rd New Zealand (Rifle) Brigade took over the trenches on Bezantin Ridge, and the 2nd Brigade moved up to Fricourt and Mametz Wood.

On September 11th, the Battalion moved up and dug-in east of Pommiers Redoubt, so as to be nearer the work. One platoon from each company was still employed on Turk Lane, making it six feet deep through from Black Watch Trench to Worcester Trench. This day 2nd. Lieut. D. Bruce arrived from the base with forty reinforcements, mostly Maoris. Entry in Major Buck's diary: "Went on to end of Turk Lane into Black Watch Trench and found the work D Company had been shelled out of. Put men on work and explored down trench to the right, the previous front line. Dead men, Germans and English, everywhere in the trench, in the sides of the trench and about in the open, unburied,, and smell fearful. Our artillery started putting in to the German front line stuff like shrapnel but which sprayed out fire like fireworks; it seemed like liquid fire. Fritz sent up distress rockets and the Germans started sending over heavy H.E. We hurried back to our men, who were fairly deep. They went on working, and the bombardment ceased without our men being hit. Captain Harris and I explored to the left and decided on trench to follow on. Everyone thinks highly of our trench, Turk Lane. Got home at 2 a.m."

Next afternoon (September 12th) the C.O. and Majors Saxby and Buck went up and laid off work in advance of Wood Lane ready for the advance, also the line of an assembly trench from Tea Trench to Coffee Lane, which A Company was to dig that night. Heavy shelling started, and hung up the work for about an hour, causing several slight casualties in the 3rd Brigade trenches. The country between Black Watch Trench and the German front line (Great Trench) was in what the C.O. described as "an awful state." The shell craters were so thick that they overlapped one another, and there were men of both sides lying unburied all over the place. Some had been dead since the British cavalry first took High Wood in July.

"The trenches," wrote Colonel King, "are nothing but a wreck, and no one seems to consider it his job to clean them up. Truly the British are a wonderful people. They would rather sit in a busted trench and get shot than do a little work on the end of a pick and shovel. The 3rd Brigade are digging new trenches to live in, which will serve as assembly trenches for the advance."

Of that day's experience under shell-fire, Major Buck wrote:—"While we were looking round the Germans started heavy bombardment with H.E. Saxby and I got into a little bit of old trench about three feet deep and hung it out. It lasted about an hour. The Colonel was over on the left, also in for a hot time. All heartily pleased when it stopped—the severest thing I have experienced and not at all pleasant. Glad to get out.... In the evening we saw some more of the fiery shells [British] going over High Wood. Spirits of men good and we are in for a big push on the 15th."

Next day there was more shelling, but the Maoris kept their work going. On the 14th, work was suspended; all hands had a spell before the offensive of the morrow. Orders for the Battalion's share in it were got out and issued, and in the afternoon all the officers met and talked the whole programme over so that everyone knew what his job was and how to do it. About a dozen tanks, the new armoured caterpillars, passed the camp on their way to Green Dump ready for the next day's work. This diary entry of the C.O. indicates that these engines of warfare had then been seen for the first time by the Battalion:—"They are weird-looking things and ought to scare hell out of Fritz." That evening the camp was shelled from the direction of Morval, and the bombardment while it lasted was severe. Six men were killed, 2nd.-Lieut. Henare Mokena Kohere was severely wounded, and ten other ranks were wounded. The casualties were sustained mostly by C Company.

Lieut. Kohere died of his wound on September 16th at the Casualty Clearing Station, and his Ngati-Porou and other comrades deeply mourned him. He was a grandson of Major Mokena Kohere, who with Major Ropata Wahawaha fought the Hauhaus on the East Coast from 1865 on; the two Ngati-Porou leaders received swords of honour from Queen Victoria. Kohere had command of a full platoon of Ngati-Porou, and his cousin Lieut. Pekama Kaa, commanded a platoon that partly consisted of men of that tribe. He was thus the senior Ngati-Porou officer. His wound was in the groin, but the high explosive fragment had been deflected up into the abdomen. He soon realised the hopeless nature of his injury. Before being removed by the Field Ambulance his last request was that Pekama Kaa should be given command of the Ngati-Porou Platoon. The request was acceded to. Thus on a far-away battlefield in France, there was re-enacted a scene that had occurred on many a Maori chieftain's death-bed in the homeland of Aotearoa. Whether college-bred platoon commander or old-time tattooed chief of a tribe, the warrior's last dying thoughts and instructions were for the welfare of the people he commanded.

The Battle of Bezantin Ridge.
(September 15th, 1916.)

Early in the morning of the 15th, the advance began. Colonel King moved the Battalion headquarters to an old communication trench between the Savoy and Carlton trenches, and just after 5 a.m. the various companies moved to various forward positions. Brigade headquarters watched as much of the advance against the Crest and Switch trenches as was possible from the Savoy Trench. At 10.37 a.m. the C.R.E. issued orders through Captain Shera (liaison officer with 3rd Brigade) to carry on work on various rear portions of communication trenches as detailed in operation orders. A and B Companies moved out at once and marched on to their jobs. At this time things looked fairly quiet along the rear front.

Early in the afternoon casualties began to come back from B Company, mostly slightly wounded, and Captain Harris reported that his company was coming under shell-fire. At 2 p.m. Major Saxby reported that A Company's digging task was well in hand, and that things were comparatively quiet on his side.

Colonel King went off to reconnoitre the road from Longueval towards Flers and found a battalion of English Pioneers working on it just north of Longueval cross-roads. The road towards Flers was under fairly heavy shell-fire, but was passable for waggons so far as the surface was concerned. B Company of Maoris was having a hot time of it. The workers were heavily shelled, and the trench they were at was being blown in as fast as it was done. Captain E. Harris was dangerously wounded and Lieut. Sutherland slightly. Twelve men were killed, and forty wounded. Total Maori casualties for the day's advance, fifty-two—a heavy list. The facts were reported to the Royal Engineers' commanding officer and Colonel King withdrew the company to bivouacs at about 5 p.m. Previous to this B and C Companies had been sent off to work on a road from Caterpillar Road to Longueval in accordance with the C.R.E.'s orders. A Company reported their communication trench work completed, so Colonel King went out and inspected it and found it was rapidly being blown in again by the German shells. All the workers were back in the bivouacs by dark after a day of hard work and many losses. The Battalion diaries naturally are confined to details of trench and road operations in this battle, which is described so well in Colonel H. Stewart's excellent History "The New Zealanders in France" (pages 69-85).

In the operations, the village of Flers was captured by the 41st Division and made secure by the New Zealanders, and other ground was won, which was quickly consolidated and held strongly under severe bombardment.

The battle was renewed on September 16th, and as a part of the general attack by the Fourth Army. Colonel King went out at daylight and made a careful reconnaissance of the ground in front of that won the previous day, and marked the lines for the Pioneer working parties who would go out that night. Most of the trench work done on the 15th had been destroyed by the enemy's shell-fire, more particularly B Company's work, and it was hard to see where they had been

The Battle of Bezantin Ridge.   95

except for the dead who were lying about. A Company's work had escaped more lightly, and it was continued that night towards Flers *via* the line called Coffee Lane. All day C and D Companies were employed working on the roads; D Company later, working under shell-fire, put through the now famous Turk Lane trench from the Crest to the Old Switch Trench. B and C Companies put in eight hours' work on the road between Caterpillar Wood and the top of Bezantin Ridge. The machine-gun section was employed in putting in dug-outs for the 3rd Brigade Headquarters in the Carlton Trench. On the night of the 17th, a lot of hard work was done, following up the further success of the Army (the advance line had been moved a mile forward over a front of six miles). D Company completed Turk Lane to the New Switch, and cleaned up a lot of B Company's old work knocked about by shell-fire. A Company dug the approach trench called Fish Alley, from Switch Trench to Point 41 (Ferret Trench). This was all new work, as the Pioneers found that the old German Fish Alley was simply a line of old pot-holes, mostly filled in and altogether useless. Colonel King and Major Buck, after a visit to the advanced works, were coming back when they were shot at by snipers. The men in the trench said the snipers had killed Captain Jennings and wounded another. The Pioneers picked up another of their dead, Poule, and also a R.F.A. officer, 2nd.-Lieut. Leggat, lying dead in the trench.

Early on the 18th, the Colonel and Major Buck went out to the right. Major Saxby was unable to finish his side owing to shell-fire. New German trenches which were inspected were full of enemy dead and so was the country in front of it. Most of the dead were without equipment, an indication of their complete surprise by the attack; a great many had been killed with the bayonet. Everything now was very wet and muddy, and the work of consolidating the trench positions won was hard and dirty.

Trench work on Bezantin Ridge occupied some days. On the night of September 20th, 1917, the Battalion was much worried by tear-gas shells in the bivouacs, and in the morning every depression seemed full of the stuff. That afternoon, General Russell came up and told Colonel King to ask the

First Infantry Brigade for as many men as he liked; so he obtained the assistance of several hundred men to carry duck-walk material. Turk Lane and Fish Alley were duck-walked over the crest of the ridge.

On September 21st, Major Buck and Lieut. O'Neill had a marvellous escape. They were returning to camp down Fish Alley when a "whizz-bang" grazed O'Neill's right shoulder, knocking him down, and burst in the ground just in front of Buck's feet. O'Neill, who was walking behind the Major, escaped with an abrasion of the shoulder; his tunic, cardigan, shirt and singlet were cut. That day the 1st Canterbury Regiment distinguished itself by taking a portion of the trenches at Flers. They had a stand-up fight with bombs, killed 250 of the enemy and sustained 150 casualties.

On September 24th, operation orders were circulated for the Battalion's share in the new advance on Flers by the 4th Army. The 55th Division was on the right, and the 1st Division on the Left. The objective of the New Zealand Division was to capture Factory Corner and establish a line thence to a spur running N.E., in conjunction with the general advance, and to maintain touch with the 3rd Corps. The Pioneers' special job was to construct various advanced lines of communication trenches. The advance was begun by the 1st Infantry Brigade at 12.35 p.m. on the 25th. At 5 a.m. that day, Colonel King went up to the back of Flers with the Company Commanders and reconnoitred the ground as well as possible for the evening's work; and the officers also went over to Turk Lane and had a look at the country from there. During the morning the companies moved up to their positions of readiness as ordered, each man with his pick and shovel, and the Battalion headquarters moved up to Crest Trench.

The afternoon's attack by the infantry was watched by the Colonel from Switch Trench, and there was a good view of the whole operations, as it was a very clear day. The artillery barrage opened exactly at 12.35 p.m. It was a tremendous afternoon of noise and fire. The thunder of the guns was deafening, and as far as the eye could range there was a line of bursting shrapnel and H.E. The artillery work

was marvellously accurate, and Major Buck noted in his
diary that the shells seemed to be bursting six inches apart.
The watchers saw the infantry leave their trenches and
advance leisurely behind the creeping barrage, travelling at
a rate of 50 yards a minute. Factory Corner, our objective
on the right, was reduced to a mass of ruins, shattered into
fragments which were hurled high into the air by the big
shells. It was soon obscured by smoke, and the advance of
the 1st Canterbury Infantry Battalion could not be followed.
The Auckland men in the centre and Otago on the left could
plainly be seen. The various waves of men were soon formed
into one irregular line. They could be seen hunting about in
the gully and the sections of trenches looking for "Fritz."
The barrage remained stationary for a few moments in order
to allow the infantry to do their work and then went creeping
on again, with the men following steadily behind it.

Now and again a high explosive projectile came over from
the Germans, and the line could be seen to open out or bend to
this side or that to avoid what looked like a shelled area.

The Black Watch Highlanders, who belonged to the 1st
Division on our left, could be seen working along Flers
Trench; some of them ran along the top of the trench to where
they were to junction with the New Zealanders; they then
planted a flag to show that they had reached their objective.
Our men had further to go, having to sweep up-hill and incline
to the left. While they were yet some two hundred yards
away, the Germans in Goose Alley climbed out at the rear of
the trench and fled ignominiously without attempting to put
up a fight. They bunched together, and seemed to hesitate,
as if some officer was endeavouring to rally them. Then
shrapnel burst over them and they ran for the valley beyond.
Our men could not chase them owing to the intervening
artillery barrage. The line advancing up the hill extended
on either flank and went leisurely on. Any bits of trenches
or holes were dealt with on the way. Everything was done
in a most systematic orderly way, splendid to see, quietly
except for the artillery thundering, rocking and crashing.
None of our men seemed to fall, but a wounded man now and
again was seen coming back. Goose Alley was reached but

the Germans had fled, with the exception of a few, and there was no fight in them.

Our troops reached their objective on the left with hardly a casualty, and up went a red flare to announce the victory. This was at 35 minutes after zero. Almost immediately afterwards, through the smoke and dust on the right, up shot two red flares to show that Canterbury had gained the shell-battered Factory Corner. Away to the right again could be seen flags in the advanced trenches. The 4th Army had reached its objective all along the line.

Later a few prisoners came along, carrying stretchers. They were Bavarians and poor specimens of soldiers, being mostly either young or fairly old men. There was some excitement later when British cavalry were seen coming over, but they took up a position somewhere behind Flers, waiting for the right moment. All night the Pioneers laboured with pick and shovel, at the new trenches. Some very deep dug-outs found in sunken roads were utilised by our people. In some parts our artillery interfered with the pushing on of the lines. Some of the 8-inch howitzer shells fell short and made it very uncomfortable for the working parties. The infantry in the firing line immediately in front was very pleased to know the Pioneers were behind them, as the line was very thinly held. King, Saxby and Buck went out in the hope of seeing the cavalry attack, but there was "nothing doing." The news came later that some cavalry went through, and the Germans started a counter-attack, but the artillery crumpled them up. In the evening the report came that Gueudecourt, on the right flank, had been captured by the 55th Division, and also Theipval, and that patrols had entered Combles.

During the night of the September 25th-26th, Lieut. Stainton's party from A Company, completed their digging task to Factory Corner, a standard-size trench 160 yards long. C Company, under Lieut. Dansey, dug 650 yards northwards and joined the North Road up with the outpost line. D Company, under Captain Gibbs, dug in 500 yards of standard-size along Abbey Road connecting up the outpost line on Ridge. Next day all these parties rested, and the rest of A and B Companies carried on with the duck-walks in Fish Alley and

The Battle of Bezantin Ridge.

Turk Lane. On the 27th, the works were pushed on with vigour. C Company were pushing on with Turk Lane when they got shelled off the job, with four casualties. That afternoon the 1st Brigade and 55th Division captured Gird Trench and Gird Support. No work was done by the "Diggers" that night, everyone standing by for orders. At a late hour the orders came from the C.R.E. to return to the bivouacs, as the position of the Gird line was too obscure to carry on work. The following day saw various jobs pushed on well. A party consisting of men from all companies, under Major Buck, after knocking off work on Turk Lane, towards Gird Support, were heavily shelled as far as North Road and had two men mortally wounded (Pte. Ovens, D Coy., and Pte. Pineaha, C Coy.) and seven wounded. Next night 250 men from all companies completed Turk Lane through to Gird Support except for 40 yards in the centre only down three feet. There was heavy German shelling part of the day, from Factory Corner to Abbey Road, and about 450 yards long. but it quietened down, and there were no casualties during the night. The work on hand having been completed, Colonel King, at the C.R.E.'s request, set the Pioneers at a communication trench and assembly trench combined from Turk Lane to the recently captured Goose Alley, parallel with the road via Factory Corner to Abbey Road, and about 450 yards long. 250 men started on the job at 8 p.m. and finished it by early morning. Major Buck made a diary entry: "All worked well, especially the Rarotongans." These men suffered several casualties during the month."

The British push forward was renewed on Sunday, October 1st, and the Colonel and principal officers watched the great attack from Switch Trench. The Pioneers had no part in the action beyond carrying on with Turk Lane and Fish Alley. The attack was very successful along the New Zealand front, but the 47th Division got hung up badly just past Eaucourt L'Abbeye. Our casualties were pretty heavy. Two tanks took part in the operations on the New Zealand left flank, but later went over towards Eaucourt and got bogged out of action. During the battle the Maoris kept steadily at work. Turk Lane was duck-walked as far as Grove Alley, and Fish Alley to within 250 yards of Flers. Turk Lane was completed right through to a depth of five feet in the solid, and four feet wide.

Describing the day's battle, as seen from Switch Trench, Major Buck wrote:—

"We saw plenty of big guns in the gully, including 9.2-inch howitzers. There was not time to form a fixed emplacement, and after each shot the guns worked backwards and forwards on their wheels. The 18-pounders have moved forward, and the valleys round Flers are full of them. At 3.15 p.m., a very intense bombardment began. We have a far larger number of guns than when we started. Saw the infantry leave the trenches and advance in great style behind the creeping barrage. Two tanks going along slowly, crossing trenches, like huge antediluvian monsters nosing round for what they could kill.

"The Tommies went across very thick. Saw 47 prisoners come back from the left. Fritz sent some H.E. on to the ridge behind us, and we had to scale forward. Saw the yellow flares go up, showing that the position was taken. Saw the tanks disappear into the valley near Eaucourt L'Abbeye. Six German aeroplanes came over, and there was much firing in the air. One was hit and fell straight down into Gueudecourt."

On the following day, the shell-fire was very heavy, and some damage was done to the trench work.

Next morning (October 3rd) the Battalion shifted camp *via* Pommiers Redoubt to a site near its first camp at the cross-roads near Fricourt, and on the 5th moved on again, to a reserve camp at Fontaine-sur-Somme, *en route* back to the A.N.Z.A.C.

The trench work done by the Battalion during the strenuous period from August 28th to October 2nd, totalled 13,163 yards. In addition, brigade headquarters had been built at 4 places, dressing stations built at 3 places, and two companies worked 5 days on the roads. The best work was done in Pioneer Lane, where 210 men dug 482 yards of trench 5 ft. x 3 ft. in 5½ hours.

On the morning of October 3rd, Lieut. J. O'Neill, the Battalion's machine-gun officer, who had been lent to the

Brigade, was killed by a shell when coming out of the front trenches and crossing over from Goose Alley to Abbey Road, after having been relieved. "Bad luck, as he was one of the best men we had," wrote Major Buck. O'Neill was hit in the back and had a leg broken. Five other men (No. 2 Machine-gun Coy.) were killed and several wounded. O'Neill had been reported as left dying near a deep dug-out, and on the 5th, Major Buck took out a cross which had been made and made a search for his late comrade. Dead machine-gunners were seen lying on Abbey Road but no sign of O'Neill. The cross was put up at the junction of Abbey Road and North Road near his last resting-place. The Pioneers of the Middlesex Regiment were seen at work near there on the trenches. A machine-gun officer later informed Major Buck that the men had carried Jack O'Neill down to the deep dug-outs in Abbey Road, but as they had so many wounded they left him on the side of the trench and asked the English soldiers to bury him. This was evidently done, and the spot must have been quite close to the cross the New Zealanders set up for him.

General Russell expressed himself very pleased with the Maoris' work. He announced that he was putting the Pioneers on the same footing as an infantry battalion as regarded the number of honour awards, viz., 2 D.C.M.'s and 10 Military Medals.

On October 11th, after a rest of several days at Fontaine-sur-Somme, the Battalion with transport entrained at Longpre for Caestre (west of Armentieres), and from there the men went on by motor lorries to Neuf Berquin. On arrival there, in good clean billets, word was received to prepare to take over from the 5th Australian Pioneers, who were in the Sailly-sur-la-Lys section, as the New Zealand Division was to relieve the 5th Australian Division there. Arrangements accordingly were made for renewed hard work. A, B and C Companies went into billets at Rue de Bruges, and D Company to billets at L'Attargette—Armentieres, as the 2nd N.Z. Brigade was to be attached to Frank's Force now holding the Armentieres section. Each company and platoon were allotted the respective frontages along the subsidiary line which the Battalion took over. Each company had a total frontage of

2,000 yards, and each platoon 500 yards. The total length taken over was 6,000 yards. Each Company had three platoons in the line and one in billets at Rue de Bruges. Of these, one platoon was at the disposal of the C.R.E. and two for drainage jobs under the direction of the Section Drainage Officer (Captain Perrett). The subsidiary line consisted of a series of strong points in fairly good repair, connected by a system of trenches only small patches of which were completed. The rest of the line was dug out to an average depth of 3 feet, without any revetting. The trench system consisted of a traversed fire trench, with a winding traffic trench about 20 feet in rear. From October 16th to October 31st, the Companies each worked one platoon on the subsidiary line and two platoons on winter quarters for themselves in rear of the line. The roads also were put in good order. The men housed themselves comfortably, and a cinema theatre was built at the junction of the Rue de Bruges and Rue de la Lys. Screens for traffic on the road between Sailly and Estaires were constructed. D Company (two platoons) ran a sawmill and burster factory, and one platoon ran the trench tramways and railways; the fourth platoon did emergency work about the town. October 31st was medal decoration day. General Godley arrived with Mr. Massey, Prime Minister of New Zealand, and Sir Joseph Ward, and the Canterbury men and the Pioneers were inspected by them. During November and December the various works were quietly carried on. Among the details a lot of barb-wire entanglements were erected along the 1st Brigade support line.

Christmas was spent peacefully in good winter quarters, and the men enjoyed a bountiful Christmas dinner, consisting chiefly of pigs and fowls bought locally. All the meat and vegetables were steam-cooked in *hangis* in the good old Maori way and were pronounced *tino pai.* "Our guns," wrote the O.C., on Christmas Day, "were very active during last night, and to-day and this evening, especially the 60-pounders."

CHAPTER X.

THE PIONEERS' WORK ON THE WESTERN FRONT.
(1917).

With the New Year, 1917, the Battalion was reorganised. The composition of A, C and D Companies was altered so that they now consisted only of Maoris. Only B Company was composed of *pakehas*, as no *pakeha* reinforcements appeared to be coming forward for it, and Maori reinforcements were accumulating in England. A Company was made up of Ngapuhi and the South Islanders (Ngai-Tahu); C Company of Bay of Plenty Maoris, Ngati-Porou, Hawke's Bay and Wairarapa; D Company of Arawa, Waikato, Wellington, West Coast, Whanganui, and Taranaki men.

Various works along the subsidiary line, digging, screening, roads and wiring, were carried on steadily during January and February, and the specialists were busy training. Many machine-gun dug-outs were constructed.

Lieut. Tingey received his promotion to captain and Sergts.-Major Mete Kingi, Roto-a-Tara and Kemp received commissions as 2nd Lieuts., to complete the establishment. Then on February 6th, twenty cases of *toheroa* bivalves arrived from New Zealand for the Maoris. On February 16th, orders received created a stir in the camp. The Division was to be relieved by the 57th Division, from England, and the New Zealanders were to relieve the 25th Division on the Ploegsteert section. The 57th was a Territorial Division, who had been two years training in England and doing coast and home defence. One officer and one N.C.O. per company were with our men to "get the hang of things."

On February 15th, Major W. S. Pennycook was wounded in the left forearm. On the 19th, D Company marched out from camp for the Oosthove Farm, Belgium, to relieve A Coy., 25th Div. Pioneers; and on the 22nd C Company marched over and relieved C Company of the 6th S.W.B. Pioneers. On the night of February 23rd, one man of C Company was killed by a sniper near the support line. On the 25th, headquarters and

A and B Companies marched out of the comfortable quarters they had occupied so long and took over their new Belgian section, at Oosthove Farm. It was a very good hut camp, each company being self-contained. Next day work was started on the new sector, the whole Battalion working from the Farm, less hutting parties. Most of B Company were employed in shifts carrying out spoil from tunnels which were being worked by the 3rd Canadian Company at St. Yves Hill, and most of C Company were set to on repairs to Toronto Avenue trench and support line. On the 28th, a draft of 53 Maoris and South Sea Islanders arrived from the base; they were mostly old hands returned from hospital. "The trenches in this S.W. sector generally," the O.C. noted in his official diary, "are in a pretty rotten state and full of mud, water and ice—worse than at Armentieres when we first went there. The support line is mostly far too close to the front line and is wholly within minnewerfer range. It wants a great deal of work doing on it. The communication trenches are bad and wet, except in Ploegsteert Wood, where they are simple duck-walk tracks on the surface and in fairly good order."

About 5 o'clock on the morning of the 20th, the enemy raided the Auckland Battalion and killed several men, but were cleared out, leaving one man in the trench. Our casualties were from the bombardment, which was heavy, mostly trench-mortar shells.

In February, 1917, Sir Maui Pomare wrote to Major Buck:

"I agree with you that the training, the influence, and the discipline that the men are receiving at the Front will mean a great awakening for the Maoris, and I agree with your sentiment that 'what matters if we were wiped out, for it is a damned sight better to go out in a big thing than to fritter away in idle security at home.' Your boys have proved beyond a doubt what the race is capable of, and, more than that, in the reshuffling of Empire the Maori will hold a respected place."

Captain S. Nicholson, commander of the transport steamer "Waitemata," wrote as follows to Sir Maui Pomare, on March 27th, 1917:—

"I have the honour to report to you that for the second

time since it has been my privilege to command a transport conveying New Zealand troops to the base, I have again had aboard my vessel a body of Maoris, namely, the 13th Maori Reinforcement Draft, under the command of 2nd Lieut. A. Te W. Gannon, It affords me great pleasure to have to inform you that a better or more well-conducted body of men I could not hope to meet, and, I may add, they have proved invaluable in assisting to keep the ship clean and tidy at all times. They were always alert at early dawn, and, with a bright and cheery demeanour, set about their work as though it were a mere recreation. To their officer, Mr. Gannon, of whom I cannot speak too highly, they were obedience personified. These men, through their Commanding Officer, presented me with a nicely worded address, which I shall always retain as a souvenir of a memorable and pleasurable episode in my life.''

CHAPTER XI.

COOK ISLANDERS IN THE FIELD.
(Egypt, 1916-17.)

In a letter from Egypt to Sir Maui Pomare, under date April 22nd, 1917, Captain G. A. Bush wrote as follows about the Rarotongans and other Islanders composing the Cook Islanders attached to the New Zealand forces:—

"I had half the detachment up with the Mounted Brigade at El Arish and Sheikh Zowaiid from January 22nd until March 9th, when we returned to Moascar. While at El Arish the boys proved themselves expert surf-boatsmen, and were of great assistance to the Naval Detachment in landing stores and supplies.... On April 7th, we received orders to proceed to rail-head, and on arrival there we were attached to Eastern Force Ammunition Column and Depot.

"The Rarotongans have proved themselves invaluable in this work, loading ammunition of all classes up to 8-inch howitzer shells, weighing 300 lbs, and getting waggons away while the Tommies are thinking about it. The other night they loaded 22 G.S. waggons with 18-pounders and 60-pounders, and had the job done in thirteen minutes—and times is everything while this stunt is on.

"I have two parties detached for the same duty at Um Teibig and Sheikh Nebhan, one under Lieut. Fromm—who, by the way, is the making of an exceptionally good officer—and the other under a Sergeant-Major.

"We have 104 of the men on service at present, the other five being in hospital."

The following is an extract from a letter dated May 14th, 1917, written by Captain G. A. Bush, to Sir James Allen, Defence Minister, regarding the Rarotongan unit:—

"You will remember inspecting and farewelling my command in the Drill Hall, Wellington, in November last when you spoke of the peculiar nature of my command.

"I would like you to know that right through the voyage to Suez, these men behaved in a most creditable manner, and

Cook Islanders in the Field—Egypt.

since their arrival at Moascar on December 28th, 1916, till their leaving there for these parts on April 7th, they had the credit of having the neatest and cleanest camp, and also of turning out the smartest guards in the whole of the Australian and New Zealand Training Depots. I received this compliment from the Commandant of the A. and N.Z. Depot, Colonel Arnott (an Australian), on several occasions.

"On August 7th, we came up to the Front and were at once attached to Eastern Force Ammunition Unit. During the fighting from April 16th-20th the Rarotongans were employed on Ammunition Supply, and, if ever men worked, they did, practically day and night. They received much high praise from the several officers of the Eastern Force Staff on their work; the O.C. Depot told me he does not know what he would have done without us. He says they were excellent. What pleases me is the cheerful way they do their work. They are happy in the thought that they are now really helping in the great struggle.

"Though they have not been in the firing line yet they have experienced several day and night air raids by the enemy, and I must say their steadiness and contempt for danger were excellent. Should we ever go into action I feel sure they will give a good account of themselves.

"These men are all Mission boys, and they have a short religious service every evening, which all attend. I encourage them in it, as I think it is a grand thing to keep them together. I have never known them to quarrel or to pilfer from one another since coming under me in Narrow Neck in July, 1916."

CHAPTER XII.

THE PIONEERS IN THE BATTLE OF MESSINES.
(June, 1917.)

Many weeks were occupied by the New Zealanders in the spring and early summer of 1917, with preparations for the great attack on Messines, the object of which was the capture by the 2nd Army of the six miles length of this ridge occupied by the Germans from St. Yves in the south beyond Wytschaete, and the capture of as many as possible of the enemy's guns in the vicinity of Oosttaverne and to the north-east of Messines, to take Messines, to consolidate the line which would give possession of the ridge, and to establish a forward position on which counter-attacks could be met at a safe distance from the crest. General Godley's command for this operation comprised the New Zealanders, the 3rd and 4th Australian Divisions, and the 25th and 57th English Divisions. The Maoris were to have their due part in the operations of consolidating the positions won.

Meanwhile the work of the preceding three months will be summarised.

Oosthove Farm remained the headquarters of the Battalion until the last days of March, when headquarters shifted over to Pioneer Camp. A great deal of hard and useful work was done during the month, including assistance to the Canadian tunnellers, the continuation of the work on Toronto Avenue and St. Yves Avenue trenches, and the digging of a new support line, Prowse Point to St. Yves post office, a new support line on the left, R.E. Farm to Midland Farm. On the 29th, the Pioneer Camp was taken over and Oosthove Farm was handed over to the 2nd Royal Irish Rifles (25th Division). On the 30th, there was heavy German shell-fire, directed on the 60-pounder battery near B Company, working on one of the support lines. On March 31st, Colonel King laid off a system of terraces with deep tunnelled dug-outs in the rear slopes of Hill 63 (which the Germans had been shelling heavily) between Red Lodge and Hyde Park Corner, for the Battalion. A and C Companies started work on these next day, erecting tents in which to live in the meantime. The Germans were still busy shelling the 60-pounder battery on the Neuve Eglise road behind B Company. The work on this big job and on the various trench lines occupied the Battalion during April. One of the tasks given to D Company, was widening and deepening a Canadian trench called Medicine Hat Trail. Another, C Company's job, was Calgary Avenue. On April 13th, Lieut.-Col. King was evacuated sick (measles) from Bailleul to hospital at Wimeneux, Boulogne, and returned well, on April 20th. The enemy artillery was active all the month. Headquarters was shifted to Red Lodge, and in the early part of May, A Company continued the tunnelling job at Hill 63. B Company was employed entirely in operating, constructing and deepening the divisional train system between De Kennebax rail-head and the front line system. C Company kept one platoon (Kaa's) working with B Company on the trains, and the remaining three platoons finished off the repairing of Plum Duff Road and the road from Leeuwerk Farm to Le Rossignol, and also completed the formation of emergency roads west of Plum Duff Road. D Company completed the new portion of Currie Avenue from Plum Duff to the tram-line and from Well Lane to Gabion Farm. The Company also started on repairs to the old portion between those places. Later some men were employed on emergency roads in Kennebax Valley and cutting down trees to clear lines of fire for the New Zealand Divisional Artillery. During the latter part of the month artillery firing on both sides was heavy, and dumps were exploded almost daily on both side of the line. Railway sidings and other works for trains were constructed, roads were formed and metalled, trenches were elaborated, and there was plenty of repair work always going on, as "blow-outs" were frequent occurrences owing to the attentions of the enemy artillery. On the last day of May there was particularly heavy gun firing, and the enemy was throwing gas shells about freely. A large enemy dump was blown up behind Messines early in the morning and the explosion shook the whole place like an earthquake. In the evening a British dump was burning for some hours. "There is a most appalling row going on the whole 24 hours near our headquarters," wrote Lieut.-Col. King, "and we shall be glad to move further forward."

June came in with fine weather, mostly brilliant, cloudless days. Trench work was carried on vigorously and the various other activities of the Corps were kept going, including such jobs as building a ration dump siding on the rail line and putting up name and direction boards on all roads and tracks. Constant and heavy enemy shelling kept the repair gangs working full time on communication trenches and tram-lines. Some very good work was done by these parties working under heavy fire, and at no time were either the trenches or the rails blocked for more than an hour or two. The casualties for June, 1st-6th, were 3 killed and 24 wounded.

On June 1st, Captain Ennis was promoted to major for good service in the field, and took over command of D Company. Captain Young was appointed adjutant in his place.

On the night of June 6th, orders were issued for what was styled the "magnum opus," and all the companies remained in camp ready to start on the "big stunt." The O.C., with Major Buck and the company commanders, and taking runners and telephones, went on the forward slopes of Hill 63 just after dark and dug-in in a position from which they would be able to keep track of the fight. The foe's gas shells were very troublesome during the night.

The orders issued by the O.C. Pioneers are worth giving in full here for their historical military value as a specimen of the very full and clear operation orders given out by the Battalion Commanders during the war:—

[SECRET.]

New Zealand Pioneer Battalion.
Special Order No. 2.
By Lieut.-Col. G. A. King, D.S.O.

(1) The Second Army has been ordered to capture the Messines-Wytschaete ridge.

(2) The frontage of the attack allotted to the Corps extends from St. Yves to the Wulverghem-Wytschaete Road.

The Pioneers in the Battle of Messines.

(3) The attack will be carried out by three divisions disposed side by side:—3rd Australian Division on the right, N.Z. Division in the centre, and 25th Division on the left. 20 tanks will co-operate—12 with the N.Z. Division, 4 with the 25th, and 4 held in reserve.

(4) The boundaries and objectives of the attack area of the N.Z. Division are shown on map to be seen at Battalion H.Q.

(5) The tasks allotted to the Battalion are as follows:—

A Company.—Three platoons will construct a communication trench from the head of Wellington Avenue to German front line at approximately [numbered position on map given] thence [shown].

One platoon will repair road from Stinking Farm to Messines, first making it fit for pack transport throughout and later for waggons.

B Company will operate with Divisional trench tramway system according to programme laid down by the C.R.E.

C Company and such men of B Company who are not required for tram operating work, will extend the present tram system from head of existing line at Well Lane to such a place S.E. of Messines as may be found practicable by reconnaissance after capture of the ridge.

D Company will construct a communication trench from the head of Calgary Avenue to the German front line, at about Oyster Avenue, thence to [numbered positions on map].

(6) Battalion report centre will be at junction of Hughit Support and the Stinking Farm-Messines road.

(7) Companies will remain at their present camp on Z. day until they receive message "Carry on," from Battalion H.Q., when they will move straight to their jobs by nearest and safe route.

(8) Kit and equipment as in Special Order No. 1.

(9) Each man will carry his iron rations and unexpended portion of his day's ration, and Coy. C.O.'s will arrange to have a hot meal ready in camp 6 hours after men start work.

(10) A and D Companies will complete their tasks as far as the German second line at least before leaving work, unless the enemy's fire is too heavy in the opinion of the C.O.

The work of B and C Companies will depend on the nature of the country, but the line will be pushed on as far as possible in the first 9 hours after start, unless shell-fire is too heavy and the work being destroyed.

(11) Each platoon will post a gas-shell picquet of one man while at work.

(12) All tools will be brought back to camp by men using them.

(13) Equipment and arms of all dead and wounded men to be brought back to camp by their own platoon.

(14) Officers and men must stick to work. No hunting for souvenirs to be allowed.

(15) All papers, maps, etc., taken from enemy dead or found lying about must be collected by officers and handed in to Battalion H.Q., immediately on return from work. Anyone found in improper possession of above will be severely dealt with.

(16) As far as practicable all dead of this Battalion will be sent down by trench trams and buried at Le Plus Oouve Farm Cemetery.

(17) On returning from work officers in command of parties will report in person at Battalion Report Centre, and give detailed report of work done during shift.

(18) Company C.O.'s will arrange shifts to keep the work moving as fast as possible after the first day.

(19) All Companies will return to present camps after shifts until further orders.

(20) Transport officers will supply waggons on demand from Battalion H.Q., but will not shift camp without written orders from O.C. Pioneers or O.C. Divisional Train.

(21) Rations will be supplied as at present except on Z.A. and B days, for which they are held by companies.

(22) All trenches to be 3 ft. x 3 ft. at bottom.

(Signed) C. le P. YOUNG, Captain.
Adjutant N.Z. Pioneers.

At 3.10 a.m., on June 7th, the battle opened with the firing of mines on the front and a tremendous burst of fire from artillery of all sorts and sizes, besides machine-guns. For an hour or so it was too dim to see much of what was going on, but after that our infantry could be seen well around Messines, and apparently suffering very few casualties so far. At 8 a.m. the Pioneers moved forward and all parties were started at their big tasks, with the exception of A Company, whose work ground was being very heavily barraged, especially round Petit Douve Farm. A Company continued the Wellington Avenue trench from the old front line to the enemy support line (500 yards) and repaired Stinking Farm-Messines Road as far as the old front line. B and C Companies operated and maintained Well Lane and another trench and extended the Well Lane line 400 yards to the east. D Company carried Calgary Avenue as far forward as the enemy support line. The day's casualties among the Pioneers were:—

	A Coy.	B Coy.	C Coy.	D Coy.	H.Q.
Killed	—	2	—	3	—
Wounded	—	2	2	16	4

Total: 5 killed, 24 wounded.

On the following day, June 8th, all companies carried on with the jobs. A Company dug a further 225 yards in Welling-

SCENE IN THE BATTLE OF MESSINES RIDGE.
A shell bursting on the front line, June 14th, 1917.

AN EXAMPLE OF THE GERMANS' WORK.
Wreck of a church shelled at La Creche. Photo in June, 1917.

OPENING A COMMUNICATION TRENCH, NEAR THE FAMOUS BUTTES, YPRES.

THE MARKET-WOMAN.
A picture somewhere in France.

ton Avenue and laid duck-walks throughout the new position. B and C Companies kept the Divisional trams running and completed lines on the 400 yards of formation done the previous day. They completed 190 yards of formation eastward and also maintained and operated Shrine and Hill 63 lines, which were blown in badly by the shell-fire. D Company dug and duck-walked a further 200 yards of Calgary Avenue trench, still in very bad ground. One man was killed and five were wounded this day.

On June 9th, A Company completed Wellington Avenue and laid duck-walks. B and C Companies worked on the tram lines, and also finished off the extension of Well Lane line, making 1,500 yards of new line open for traffic.

D Company carried on Calgary Avenue, making 1,200 yards new trench. A Company also worked one platoon on the Stinking Farm-Messines Road, and finished 1,400 yards of formation. The casualties for the day were two wounded.

On the morning of June 10th, the Battalion, less B Company, marched to a point on the road south of Neuve Eglise for a rest. B Company continued to operate and maintain the tram lines for 24 hours. News now came that the Division had been relieved by the 4th Australian Division and we handed over to the 4th Australian Pioneers (Colonel Sturdee). Everyone was very tired and the Maoris were all heartily glad to get out for a rest after the most strenuous toil under shell-fire. Red Lodge and Hill 63 had been heavily shelled every day since the 7th, and pelted with gas shells every night, so that no one had much sleep. All next day the Battalion rested. B Company handed over to the Australians and rejoined the other companies.

On June 12th, the Battalion moved on to Nieppe Chateau and took over from the 3rd Australian Pioneers. Headquarters and A Company were in the chateau, and the other companies in the neighbouring farms. Orders came to start work in the Ploegsteert area next day.

On the 13th, B Company took over the trench trams in Ploegsteert Wood from the 3rd Australian Pioneers. C and D Companies moved from the farms into the chateau as they had been shelled at night, when two men were wounded. The O.C.

and Company Commanders went over the new area on the 14th and found that the Australians, had done very little work since the advance on the 7th, and what there was done was of poor value. On the 15th, the Pioneers started work in shifts. A and C Companies set to at Anton's Farm communication trench. B Company extended the tram line and D Company continued on the road repairs east of Le Cheer. The roar of artillery was unending, and as the whole area was heavily shelled very little work was done. Two men were wounded. Trench work and other details were carried on. One job was the digging of Ultra Lane from the old front line to the German old front line, and the cleaning out of a considerable portion of German trenches.

On the 17th, A and C Companies dug a further 400 yards of Anton's Farm communication trench and other tasks were done. In the evening the Battalion moved back to the old quarters at Red Lodge. All the parties were heavily shelled this day. Twelve men were wounded and nine were gassed.

On June 18th, A and C Companies did further work on Anton's Farm communication trench near the Potteries. The ground was very bad and wet and heavy shell-fire interfered with the work. B Company operated and maintained the Divisional trench trams and extended the Prowse Point road formation 160 yards. D Company dug a further 150 yards of Ultra Lane trench and laid duck-walks throughout. Red Lodge and the Camp were shelled with high explosive and gas most of the night. The casualties for day and night were one man killed and eight wounded. A heavy thunderstorm in the afternoon added its artillery to the guns of man. Similar work was carried on for some days, and every day had its casualties from the almost constant shell-fire. On the 19th, three Maoris were killed and 12 wounded. The shelling at night was particularly troublesome; one man was wounded on the 20th. Three were killed and three wounded on the 21st; amongst the wounded was Captain Bruce; he was but slightly injured and remained on duty. Trench extension, constructing tram lines, repairing and the revetting of the trenches, and laying the wooden duck-walks were continued each day. Some of the trench was blown in on the night of the 22nd by heavy H.E.

fire from Lille. Lieut. Vercoe sustained a slight wound but remained on duty. On the 23rd, three men were wounded and one gassed. Red Lodge's garrison had the night's sleep interfered with by gas and H.E. shelling. One man was killed, three were wounded and seven were gassed on the 23rd-24th. A man was killed by shell-fire and 15 were gassed on the 25th, when the fire was so heavy that no working parties were sent out. On the previous night gas shells were showered for six hours on and about Red Lodge. The casualties for the 26th and 27th June were two wounded and seven gassed. On the night of the 27th, the Battalion, less B Company, moved on to De Seule. B Company remained at Underhill Farm until the night of the 28th to hand over to the 4th Australian Pioneers, who were only taking over the trams and not tackling the communication trenches. It was announced that the New Zealand Division was being relieved by the 4th Australian Division, but the New Zealand 4th Brigade remained holding the right flank to the River Lys. The Maoris were heartily glad to get away from Red Lodge, where they had been shelled regularly every night from 10.15 until 2 a.m. with gas and H.E., and no one had had any sleep worth mentioning. One man was wounded this day.

The Battalion's casualties from June 7th to June 28th (1917) were:—Killed 17, wounded 88, gassed 45, N.Y.D. 5; total 155.

The work done in the fortnight from June 14th totalled 5,000 yards of trench digging and the construction of considerable lengths of tram lines.

On the morning of June 29th, the Battalion packed up and complete with transport, marched for Vieux Berquin, where it halted at 10 a.m. Very good though rather scattered billets were found to the N.W. of the town. Next day the Battalion rested ("No work for anyone," the O.C. noted in his official diary, "and a damn good job.") So ended the strenuous month of June, 1917.

CHAPTER XIII.

THE PIONEERS' WORK IN FLANDERS.
(July—September, 1917.)

The Battalion's tasks on the war-torn soil of Belgium for the month of July, shifted back and forth along complicated lines of trenches.

After several days' needful rest, the Maoris received orders very early on July 3rd, to march with the 3rd Brigade group to join the First French Army under General Antoine in the area north of Woesten. The route of march was *via* Strazeele Fletre to Eecke, camping at the latter place for the night. General Godley addressed the officers and N.C.O.'s on the roadside and told them what "a fine crowd" they were. He informed them that they were going to help the French in their big north offensive, because their people were tired after the heavy fighting in the Champagne. Lieut.-Col. King left the Battalion to Major Buck for the march, and the force arrived at its destination at noon and went into bivouac. The O.C., in the meantime, went by car with 3rd Brigade representatives to report to Colonel Cavendish at the British Mission with the First French Army at Rexpoede Nord. The New Zealanders saw General Anthoine and were sent round the French front by cars to see the places were the Brigade was to camp and to visit the French Artillery Brigades for whom they were to work.

Coppernolle Hock was the headquarters for the next few days. The 3rd Brigade Group was divided by the G.O.C. 3rd Brigade into four groups, as follow:—

A Group.—1st Battalion N.Z. Rifle Brigade and A Company New Zealand Pioneers; camp at Hoogstade (Lieut.-Col. Austin).

B Group.—2nd Battalion N.Z. Rifle Brigade and B Company New Zealand Pioneers; camp at Eykhock (Lieut.-Col. Stewart).

C Group.—3rd Battalion N.Z. Rifle Brigade and C Company New Zealand Pioneers and half 2nd. Field Company, N.Z. Engineers; camp at Eykhock (Major Bell).

D Group.—4th Battalion N.Z. Rifle Brigade, D Company New Zealand Pioneers, half 2nd F. Coy., N.Z. Engineers, and section 3, Field Ambulance; near Coppernolle Hock (Lieut.-Col. King).

Each group was attached for work to a group of French artillery and was to be employed in building dug-outs, gun-pits and shelters and in burying cable.

All the groups arrived at their camp grounds before noon on July 4th, and drew camp equipment (tents and shelters) from G.H.Q. lorries which came in from Calais. The rationing was by G.H.Q. direct. "The men," wrote the O.C. Pioneers, "growled like hell at losing their well-earned rest, having to march yesterday, but to-day's ride and the novel surroundings have cheered them up wonderfully, and they are settling down quite happily. We are on the south edge of the French area and have the Guards Division (British Left Division) on our immediate right; the French north to the Yser, north of which are Belgians."

July 5th, was a quiet day, allowing the Group to get settled down in camp.

Lieut.-Col. King went with Major Pow, 4th Battalion, Rifle Brigade, and met the staff officer of Cole Jaquemann; commanding the French 1st Division Artillery, and arranged the tasks for the various parties of Pioneers, who would be working for four regiments of artillery. One party would work for each regiment, in two shifts, half the party from 5 a.m. till noon and the rest from noon till 7 p.m.

In the afternoon the O.C. Pioneers and Major Pow arranged the rendezvous for the parties and guides at the cross-roads south of Woesten, and scouted up the routes from camp to work. "It seems a nice quiet sector," Lieut.-Col. King wrote; "with good crops of potatoes and grain, well up in front of the subsidiary line."

A week thereafter was spent on the various jobs allotted to the Pioneers, and on July 13th, orders came for another shift of operations. General Anthoine inspected the Pioneers' camp that day, and spoke to the officers. He said he was very pleased with the work done for him. The Battalion's casualties for the period were: A Company, nil; B Company, nil;

C Company, one wounded; D Company, one killed and one wounded. General Anthoine promised the Croix de Guerre for the wounded.

A Company had been employed during the week in burying 8,600 yards of cable and in building stations for wireless and telephones and digging forward control stations. B Company dug 900 yards of travel trenches, excavated 16 ammunition dug-outs and two telephone dug-outs, and also dug and camouflaged eight heavy gun positions. C Company did similar work for its artillery and carried aerial torpedoes to the trench-mortar forward positions.

On July 14th, the Pioneers, with the other units of the Group, marched for a new area of work. The route taken was *via* International Corner, Poperinghe and Abeele, 14½ miles to Eecke. The road from Poperinghe to Beauvouze was full of field-artillery brigades, moving N.E., with scarcely an interval between them. On the following day the march was resumed, to Vieux Berquin, in the New Zealand Divisional area (a six-miles march at the usual pace, three miles an hour). Another shift was made on the 19th, when the Battalion marched for De Seule and the old jobs were taken over. On the 23rd, the Battalion was moved to the old 4th Australian Pioneers, camp, because the distance from De Seule to the work was too great and because also, if the men went to work by train the danger of moving them through the shell-ridden Ploegsteert Wood from the terminus would be greater than the jobs were worth. The camp was on Leeuwert Farm, and the site was a good one, although a trifle far to walk to the working area; it seemed to be outside the radius of the enemy's gas shells and there were no guns in the immediate neighbourhood. Two platoons of each company were worked daily on trench and other jobs. The other two platoons did platoon and company drill under the Regimental Sergeant-Major, who was also taking all N.C.O.'s for two hours daily. No new work was done on the communication trenches, the Battalion simply keeping them open for traffic. Shelling was rather heavy, directed on all communication trenches, tram lines and roads; and there was plenty to do. Half the Battalion was employed every morning for several hours.

The Pioneers' Work in Flanders. 119

It took about an hour and a quarter to walk from camp to jobs. All hands practised gas-helmet drill daily.

August set in wet, and all the trenches were in an awful mess. The drill and trench platoons alternated their day's work, so that no party had two days' continuous work with the shovels.

On August 2nd, Lieut.-Col. King conferred with General Braithwaite regarding a scheme of wiring the posts in front of La Basseville. It was decided that the Pioneers should construct wire entanglements in front of the posts from Le Rossignol-Warneton Road to the River Lys, east of La Basseville on the night of August 3rd. Headquarters and A and D Companies had to be moved as the camp was shelled on the night of August 1st. At one o'clock on the morning of the 3rd, the O.C., with Captain Tingey and Lieuts. Leef, Ehau, Roto-a-Tara, Kaipara and Hetet, went out to reconnoitre the ground in front of La Basseville. The party had a good look round, each officer taking the sector allotted to him for the tasks, and got back to camp about 6 a.m. It was raining hard nearly all the time, and there was a good deal of enemy artillery fire.

At eight o'clock that night, the wiring parties went out—under Captain Tingey's command—A Company, sixty men under Lieuts. Leef and McNicol; C Company, 110 men, under Lieuts. Kaipara and Roto-a-Tara; D Company, 80 men, under Lieuts. Hetet and Ehau; also 45 men from A Company, under Lieut. Cameron to carry material for Leef's party, and an officer and 32 other ranks from 2nd Battalion, Canterbury Regiment, to carry for C Company. It rained hard all night and the ground was sodden and very rough; moreover, there was much enemy shell-fire and the Maori workers had a bad time. Most of the wire-entanglements (which were 875 yards in all) were constructed successfully and all the parties returned to their quarters about 6.30 next morning. Two gaps were left, owing to the heavy shelling which prevented Lieuts. Hetet and Cameron from carrying out the orders given them. The Maoris' casualties were heavy, but all except one man wounded occurred while the parties were going to and from the job. 2nd Lieut. Kaipara was killed, 2nd Lieut. McNicol was mortally wounded, Lieut. Ehau was wounded in both legs. Four other ranks were killed, one was missing and 29 wounded. 2nd Lieut. McNicol died after being carried to the Australians' camp. "This is a most unfortunate loss," the O.C. Pioneers wrote, "as he was a very promising officer."

Duncan B. McNicol had come as Quartermaster-Sergeant with the Second Maori Reinforcements. He got his commission in France and for a time was acting-Quartermaster. Though a *pakeha*, he spoke Maori like a native. His business in North Auckland as agent and auctioneer for the farmers' organisation had taken him constantly among the Maoris, for whom he had a great affection. When A Company (North Auckland) was short of platoon officers he begged to be transferred from the administrative branch to the combatant side, and this was done. McNicol looked forward to the days of peace when he would be able to assist the men of his company with advice in farming pursuits and so use the splendid qualities that the war had brought out in them. But it was not to be.

Wiring parties went out again on the night of the 6th-7th to complete the jobs. A Company's party returned at 3.30 a.m. and reported that while going up the tram line from Prowse Point they were heavily shelled and 2nd Lieut. Cameron and two men were killed, and one sergeant wounded. They tried to get on to the wiring job but were blocked by machine-gun fire. Lieuts. Hetet and Roto-a-Tara completed their jobs, and Lieut. Hetet filled in the gap where A Company should have been working. The O.C. recommended Lieut. Leef and Ptes. T. Brown and J. McAndrew for honours in recognition of their fine work in the wiring. Lieut. Leef a few days later received the Military Cross and the two privates the Military Medal.

On the night of the 8th, D Company had an officer and 19 other ranks doing some additions to the wire-entanglements. Their casualties, from shell-fire, were three men wounded (one each from A, C and D Companies).

An entry in the Battalion Diary for the 11th, ran: "Twelve men skinning Machine-Gun Company's horses which had been killed by bombs." The enemy's aeroplanes were very active at this time. During the night of the 10th-11th two or three bombs

AROUND THE HANGI.   COOKING THE CHRISTMAS DINNER.

MEAT FOR THE FIGHTING MEN.

CHAPLAIN WAINOHU WITH SOME OF THE BOYS, AT THE WATER-CART.
Somewhere in France.

were dropped in A Company's billeting area. There were no casualties in camp, but one man was killed and two were wounded at work. Casualties were fairly frequent during the following days.

On the 14th the German artillery paid particular attention to Ultimo Avenue, where the Maoris had nine casualties. Lieut. Kaa was killed by a shell near the entrance of St. Yves-Ultimo Avenue, while assisting to get wounded men to the dressing station. He had been with the Battalion since its formation and was a most reliable officer. Kaa's death was a real loss to the Battalion. He was buried at Kandahar Camp. The other casualties were four other ranks killed and four wounded.

On August 15th, Lieut.-Col. King went away on leave, and Major Ennis took over the duties of second in command from Major Buck. The latter officer had been acting as O.C. of D Company since Major Pennycock was wounded at Fleurbaix. Major Buck helped to build up the company to a high state of efficiency, and voluntarily relinquished his position as second in command to retain the more active duties of Company Commander.

Pte. J. Newton, reported missing on August 4th, was now (August 15th) reported killed.

Work was carried on vigorously on keeping clear and repairing trenches, repairing and maintaining trench tram line, salvaging material, and so on. One man of D Company was wounded on the 15th, and on the 17th two were wounded—one was Pte. Rini, who had suffered a previous wound (August 14th). On the 20th D Company commenced shifting material to Gunners' Farm line, the extension of which was pegged out. The 9-lb. rails were to be lifted and replaced with 16-lb. rails, to carry tractors. Two men were attached to the Light Railway Operating Company to learn the work on the tractors. Otherwise this day the work was as usual. Casualties—four men wounded, one remaining on duty. On the 21st Pte. Pira was wounded by an aeroplane bomb.

Lieut.-Col. King, D.S.O., was now transferred to the Canterbury Regiment, Major Saxby, later promoted to Lieut.-Col., was left in command of the Pioneers.

On August 23rd, the North Brigade Area work was handed over to the 4th Australian Pioneers. On the 24th, some final work was carried out on the rail lines. The day's casualties were six men wounded, of whom two remained on duty. On the 26th, the Battalion moved on from Leeuwerck Farm to Tahuna Camp, D Company, owing to lack of accommodation, remaining temporarily at the Farm. Leeuwerck was shelled 15 minutes after the other companies were clear of it, the shells landing in the headquarters cook-house and the R.Q.M. store. The 4th Australian Pioneers, who were shifting in, suffered a few casualties.

At Tahuna Camp the Battalion was under the Commander Royal Engineers, 8th Division. He arranged that the Pioneers should concentrate their work on trench tramways, pushing ahead the formation on the Gunners' Farm and La Basseville lines, replacing certain portions with heavier rails, and repairing the light railway parallel to and east of Ploegsteert Road, and salvaging material on the Lancaster line. Arrangements were made with the light railways to convey the men to and from work and to run up ballast. On the 27th, the Battalion paraded for Lieut.-Col. King, who left on transfer to the infantry (1st Battalion, Canterbury Regiment). It was this fine officer who formed the Pioneer Battalion and commanded it up to this date, and the foregoing pages of the War Diary used in this History are a record of his untiring energy and industry.

On September 1st (1917), the Battalion was on the march again, this time a longer trek, to Bournonville. There for several days the Battalion put in five hours a day in squad, platoon, company and battalion drill. The *Pakeha* company, B, was disbanded and detachments were sent to the various infantry battalions. Maori reinforcements had arrived in England in such numbers that the Maori Companies were over strength. The *Pakeha* battalions, on the other hand, were in urgent need of reinforcements, and it was therefore decided by headquarters that the tried *Pakeha* veterans of B Company should be sent to *Pakeha* battalions, the surplus Maoris in England taking their place in the Company. Now with the conversion of this company into a Maori company, the Pioneer

Battalion became a full Maori unit, and the old name was restored —the New Zealand (Maori) Pioneer Battalion, and the proud badge was re-adopted, "Te Hokowhitu a Tu."

On the 9th the Battalion was visited by the G.O.C. the Division, who was accompanied by Sir Thomas MacKenzie, New Zealand High Commissioner in London. Several days more were spent in drill in preparation for the expected visit of the Commander-in-Chief.

On September 14th, the inspection was held. Twenty officers and 580 other ranks of the Battalion marched nine miles to the parade ground. The New Zealand Division marched past in column of platoons and then straight back to billets.

The camp was changed again. The Battalion arrived at Hazebrouck on the 26th, after a 25-miles march from Harletts, with all transport. A spell of a day there and then a move on to Watou No. 3 Area. Once more a trek, and the Pioneers found themselves in famous war-battered Ypres. C and D Companies had quarters in cellars in the town; headquarters and A and B Companies camped just west of the town and south of the Poperinghe Road. C Company commenced repairing work the same night on Bridge Farm Road. A and B Companies (on the 30th) began the tram extension from Bridge Farm, but were taken off after doing one shift. C and D Companies were on night work, Bridge Farm to Spree Farm Road.

CHAPTER XIV.

THE THIRD BATTLE OF YPRES.
(October, 1917.)

The New Zealand Division was now preparing for its part in the new offensive around Ypres. The Anzac troops under General Godley relieved the Fifth Army Corps in the northern sector of the extended Second Army front, and the Pioneers had a very busy time preparing the way for the artillery's movements and the passage of troops and transport. At 6 a.m. on October 4th, our guns opened a tremendous barrage fire on the German defences. Those who heard that artillery fire say it was the heaviest of the war. Besides the big howitzers, the New Zealanders were supported by one hundred and eighty 18-pounders and sixty 4.5-inch howitzers, and there was also a machine-gun barrage to take the assaulting columns forward, break up counter-attacks, and protect the infantry on the captured objectives. As it proved, our attack only just anticipated an intended enemy attack. The Anzac infantry moved out in splendid order, covered by the splendidly accurate barrage and soon were closely engaged with the Germans, capturing trenches and "pill-boxes," shooting, bayoneting and taking prisoners.*

The day's work resulted in the establishment by our men of a new line beyond Gravenstafel and Abraham Heights, and the capture of over 1,000 prisoners. The enemy's shelling was not heavy west of Kansas Cross, and at 11 a.m. B Coy., and later A Coy. Pioneers commenced repairs on the road forward to Kansas Cross. The Maoris did excellent work on the roads and artillery tracks, but wet weather on the 6th and several days afterwards, and the trains of pack mules along the newly formed earth road turned it into a quagmire. For several days it was a steady fight with mud. All available men were set to work carrying fascines. Guns and horses were bogged

---

*See Colonel H. Stewart's history, "The New Zealand Division, 1916-1919," pp. 250–293, for an excellent detailed account of these operations, known as the Third Battle of Ypres. The present narrative is necessarily restricted to the Maoris' share in the great offensive.

The Third Battle of Ypres. 125

everywhere. The Maoris pulled many guns out and into position but the road was in a fearful condition. The O.C. noted: "The trains of pack mules, with their small feet and incompetent drivers, are our worst trouble, as they play havoc with our work." Rain every day (7th-10th). On October 11th all possible assistance was given to the R.F.A. who were trying to get their batteries into position. D Company took three platoons over to assist the N.Z.F.A., who were getting their guns forward on the St. Julian Road.

On the 12th, the New Zealand Division renewed the attack but were held up by machine-guns and wire on Bellevue and suffered heavily. "It was the Division's one failure on a large scale," wrote Colonel Stewart. The casualties included Lieut.-Col. King, D.S.O., late C.O. of the Pioneers, also Captain A. E. M. Jones, Lieuts. French and Watson, late of the Pioneers, all of whom were killed.

It was with great sorrow that the Battalion heard the sad news that its late Commander had been killed in the assembly trenches before moving out with his Battalion. Lieut.-Col. Saxby went out with a party and brought in Lieut.-Col. King's body, and the funeral took place on the 14th (Sunday) in the Military Cemetery in Ypres. General Russell was present.

Work on the roads was continued with great energy under heavy shell-fire. By the 20th, the road had been improved greatly, and the guns and transport had a good hard bottom as far as Deuce Farm. The Canadian Pioneers then arrived to relieve the Maoris. The Pioneers' casualties during the heavy operations were comparatively slight, totalling four men killed or died of wounds, and one officer and 30 men wounded.

On October 21st, the Battalion moved on by 'bus to billets at Bournonville, where training and musketry were carried on. A Foden disinfecting lorry spent two days there treating the men's clothing and blankets. Captains Tahiwi and Stainton and 2nd Lieut. Pohio arrived from the base on the 24th.

On October 22nd, it was announced in orders that Military Medals had been awarded by the Army Corps Commander to Corporals T. W. Nicholls (D Coy.) and A. Sparks (A Coy.).

Ptes. A. Conway (H.Q.), W. Tangatake (B Coy.) and T.-Cpl. J. Apa (B Coy.).

The month of November, 1917, carried varied work for the Battalion, and although not without casualties the losses were light. For the first ten days training, route marching, musketry, and recreational exercises were carried on, and a sports meeting came as an agreeable change. These sports were held at Bournonville on the 6th and 7th. The mules in the "New Zealand Pioneer Grand National Steeplechase" were the best fun of the meeting. No spurs or whips were allowed. C Company's "Pioneer Stew," led the field to the turn, where he was challenged by D Company's crack mule "Pork and Beans," which after a desperate finish, won by a head.

The following soldiers of the Battalion were awarded the Military Medal for work at Ypres:—Sergeants W. Barclay and A. Rogers, T.-Cpl. J. Munn, L.-Cpl. A. Hughes, Ptes. H. T. Leefe, R. Ngapo, G. Maxwell, J. Panoho and P. Te Amo.

Captain Ferris and 2nd Lieuts. Paku and Parakuka now joined the Battalion from the base. Lieut. T. R. Overton was seconded for duty with the N.Z. Light Railway Operating Coy. The bandmaster of 1st Canterbury took charge of the Maori buglers and drummers for a fortnight, and they were soon able, the O.C. noted, "to make a most joyful noise to cheer us on the march."

On the 12th, the Battalion was on the move again, bound to Dickebusch, a two-days' journey on foot and in train.

Lieut.-Col. Saxby met the O.C. 14th Northumberland Fusiliers (Pioneers) and arranged to take over the maintenance of the Chateau Road, otherwise the work that the Englishmen had been doing was out of the New Zealanders' area. A Company began work on that road and Glencorse Lane. After moving to Ridge Wood Camp, Lieut.-Col. Saxby went round with the Commander of the Royal Engineers and Captain Bruce and arranged to lay off a new tram system as far as Crucifix, also to take over the road forward from Westhoek. Captain Bruce found a good grade for the tram line and 100 men started work on it. On the 21st A and D Company, working on the roads, were heavily shelled and had three killed and ten wounded. Next day A Company commenced to double the duck-walk track from Polygonveld to Black Watch Corner and also kept maintenance going on Glencorse Road. The O.C. arranged with the C.R.E. to shift the Battalion gradually to Ypres. Among other works C Company and a platoon from D Company started work on a new communication trench required from Butte to the neighbourhood of Jolting Houses. Captain Tingey had charge of the job. The water here was very close to the surface, so the trench was not dug very deep. It was duck-walked as the digging proceeded. The weather was now getting colder, and leather jerkins were issued.

The New Zealand Division was now holding the front covering Polygon Wood to Reutlebeck. From here the front line cut away in a S.W. direction. The divisional area was a long narrow strip, the northern boundary of which just intersected the south part of Ypres. This meant that instead of running back at right angles to our front the area lay at an angle of of 45°. The effect was that the Germans' barrage lines lay diagonally across the New Zealanders' communications and therefore covered a great deal more of our ground than they would have done had our area been at right angles to the line. Consequently the country between Birr Cross Roads and the Westhoek Ridge, a distance of over 2,000 yards, was all subject to the enemy's heaviest barrage. The piles of derelict waggons and dead animals showed very plainly the effect of this diagonal and therefore deeper barrage line. The Pioneers found the quietest time for work here to be between daylight and 11 a.m. The working parties were only once fairly caught in this shell-fire, which was particularly heavy that day. Intelligence reported that 15,000 enemy shells fell in the Chateau Woods area alone. The month's casualties were:—Killed, six men; wounded, one officer and 22 men. Most of the wounds were slight. The health of the Battalion had on the whole been good, and the evacuations per thousand were well below the average of the Division.

Early in December the Battalion headquarters, A Company and one platoon of B Company moved to new billets in Ypres. The Corps Commander's certificates for meritorious service were allotted to Sergeant A. Anderson, L.-Cpl. S. M. Hodge, L.-Cpl. S. G. Karetai, and Pte. G. A. Moore. D Company on the night of the 4th dug 240 yards of support line by Polderhoek Chateau; other work was as usual. Permission was obtained to build stables for the horses east of Ypres-Comines Canal, and the Rarotonga natives' platoon, which was awaiting orders to join the Rarotonga Company in Egypt, moved to billets near the site and was employed on the construction of the stables. The remainder of B Company moved into new billets in Ypres, and D Company returned to their work on Westhoek Road.

On the 7th, two shells caught B Company on the way to work. Two men were killed, one died of wounds and six were wounded. On the whole, though, the Germans' shelling had eased up considerably and had interfered little with the works. Padre Wainohu left for England that day on duty.

By the 12th material was coming up to the Maoris' work by the light railway, which greatly facilitated the laying of the Westhoek plank road. The weather now became very cold and it was freezing steadily, making the ground hard to work. On the night of the 20th, a number of shells were thrown into the Pioneers' camp but did no damage. Next night German 'planes came over just after dark and dropped several bombs in the Battalion's area. The men in billets were all right, but some who were out loading a waggon which had just come in were caught. Three were killed and two wounded. One bomb burst on the roof of a bivouac, but thanks to its instantaneous fuse the men inside were unharmed, though the roof was smashed in. Another bomb was apparently after the Adjutant and succeeded in knocking his house in almost on top of him. The chief anxiety was for the safety of the pigs which had been collected for Christmas, but the excitement cooled down when it was found that neither these nor the beer had suffered.

Christmas Day was devoted to the serious business of disposing of the extra food collected. The porkers and potatoes were steam-cooked in *hangis* after the good old Maori style. The O.C. noted officially of the festival:—

"Although one poor soldier is reported to have written to his friends that he had received only a few extra carrots to mark Christmas Day, the next sick parade showed that the

Mr. Massey (Prime Minister of New Zealand) and Sir Joseph Ward inspecting the Pioneers at the Bois de Warnimont, June 30th, 1918.
Lieut.-Colonel Saxby, O.C.

NEW ZEALAND'S PRIME MINISTER ADDRESSING THE PIONEERS,
BOIS DE WARNIMONT, JUNE 30TH, 1918.

A HAKA FOR THE CHIEFS, AT THE BOIS DE WARNIMONT, JUNE 30TH, 1918.

THE THIRD BATTLE OF YPRES. 129

rest had managed to do themselves pretty well. Every man received most acceptable parcels from Lady Liverpool's Fund, while the Y.M.C.A. most kindly sent cases of chocolate, etc., for distribution. The mid-day meal was a dreadful exhibition, but luckily Lord Rhondda [the British Food Controller] did not appear on the scene, and the Battalion relapsed into a more or less comatose state for the rest of the day, waking up somewhat towards evening to polish off the remainder of the feast."

Twenty reinforcements arrived on Christmas Day to fill up wastage. Work was resumed next day, and one of the stables was finished and was occupied by 48 horses. On December 28th-30th the enemy's artillery became more active, and on the 30th A Company had to leave their digging job for Fritz to play with. He threw over between 400 and 500 shells, and the Battalion was fortunate in having only one man slightly wounded. On the 31st, Lieut. Paku's platoon of C Company was caught by a shell in the early morning at the junction of Saville and Zouvebeke roads. The losses were six men killed and Lieut. Paku and 14 men wounded, two of whom died. A most unhappy ending to 1917.

The Lessons of the Push.

The Battalion's experience of the last three weeks, Major Ennis noted in his official diary, had demonstrated the vital necessity when an advance was made of pushing roads, light railways and tram lines forward with all possible speed. When the 2nd Anzac Corps took over this sector practically nothing forward of Wieltje had been done. No attempt had been made to make the road to Steenbeck fit for heavy traffic; the light railway was only laid as far as Wieltje, and nothing had been done in the way of tram lines. The front line was only 4,000 yards from Wieltje and our Division had to attack on the 4th October, the day after coming into the sector. The various corps at once commenced laying a plank road from Wieltje to Steenbeck, while the New Zealand Pioneers had to carry the road from Steenbeck as far forward as possible, and commence laying tram lines from Brigade Farm forward. The Light Railways were expected to have their line to Bridge Farm by

J

the 3rd, but did not actually get there until about the 5th. They were therefore of no use in our first advance, and later were only used for their own construction and ammunition for the heavy artillery.

The Maoris made a start at once on road and tram line. For the latter they were at first promised three miles of 20-lb. track; this was altered to 1,500 yards of 9-lb., and finally, after labour had been wasted on formation it was found that only 500 yards of bare 20-lb. rails were available at Abeele, without sleepers, fish-plates and dog-spikes. Tram lines were at once stopped and the Pioneers never laid a rail. Attention was therefore concentrated on the roads. From Steenbeck to Spree Farm was a shaking bog, and it had to be fascined. Sufficient material was not available, so only a single track could be laid. Some guns got past this; many more were bogged. However, the weather kept fine until the night of the 3rd, and the attack of the 4th was well covered by the artillery. After the 4th the Battalion took over the road as far as Spree Farm, and with practically no material we had to make the road forward passable for guns. This could easily have been done in fine weather, but in the wet weather that followed, and hampered by the continual and increasing trains of pack animals the Pioneers had no chance. No further attempt could be made to push forward the tram lines owing to the lack of material. Even had this been available the congested state of traffic on the road from Ypres to Steenbeck made it almost impossible to get waggons with material forward.

The 47th Division relieved our infantry and were timed to attack on the 8th October. After their failure the New Zealand Division returned to the attack on the 12th. Both these attacks were failures, because—from the Pioneers' point of view —of the failure of roads, light railways and tram lines. With material available, a tram line could have been laid very quickly, at least to the bottom of Gravenstafel Hill, and would have been invaluable, if only for supply of ammunition and evacuation of wounded.

Casualties and Sick, December, 1917.

Though there had been no serious epidemic the Battalion's evacuated sick for December were rather heavy. Besides the wounded, two officers and 80 other ranks had been sent away and although many returned after a few days at the rest camps the wastage was considerable. All things considered, the men were fairly comfortable. The bivvies now in use were warm and dry; firewood was plentiful; the rations were good; and the men got a daily change of socks—a most important item in the field. Footballs had been provided, and platoons commanders were responsible for the use of these by their men, also camphor treatment for the prevention of "trench feet." There had been a steady dribble of casualties, which made a rather heavy total for the month, vix.:—

Killed and died of wounds, 15 men; wounded, five officers and 41 men; total casualties, 61.

The reinforcements nearly balanced the total losses and evacuations.

An opportunity was given the members of the Battalion to subscribe to the New Zealand War Loan, and over £4,500 worth of bonds were taken up.

The total strength of the Battalion in the field at the end of 1917 was 928 of all ranks, consisting of 29 officers and 899 other ranks. A Company numbered 196, B Company 203, C Company 182, and D Company 236; transport 66. In addition there were about 50 men at Etaples ready to come forward, a further contingent at Sling Camp, and 15 N.C.O.'s at the O.T.C.

CHAPTER XV.

WORK ON THE WESTERN FRONT.
(January-May, 1918).

The New Year, 1918, saw the Pioneers hard at work around Ypres. The chief tasks then in hand were:—

A Company.—Revetting and building up the "P. and O." communication trench.

B Company.—Construction of light railway to Crucifix.

C Company.—Working with B Coy. and salvaging material; constructing Wattle Spur Line; doubling plank road from Westhoek to Divisional boundary; building Y.M.C.A. hut at Lille Gate. Each Company worked three platoons a day, Sundays included. This scheme worked well and insured continuity of work. The ground was frozen hard.

On January 6th, A Company dug a deviation in the P. and O. trench at the second support to provide better cover from enfilade fire. This was a wet trench, with difficult drainage. necessitating more building up than digging down. There was a considerable amount of shelling in the forward areas, and the party had to leave the work. Several blow-outs in the tram line and plank roads were repaired. The following New Year honours and awards appeared in Orders: D.S.O., Major W. O. Ennis; M.C., Captain D. Bruce, Captain W. H. Walker; D.C.M., Regimental Sergt.-Major Gustafson, M.S.M., Sergeant Cameron. In writing to congratulate Major Ennis, the G.O.C. added a note, "The Pioneers deserve all they get," a comment which was much appreciated by the Battalion. On the 6th, thirty-seven reinforcements arrived. Work on the various jobs was pushed on with energy. On the 10th a thaw set in, which increased the labours of the Pioneers. A new communication trench from Crucifix to the left of Battalion H.Q. was marked out by Lieut.-Col. Saxby. This was through very wet country badly churned up by shell-fire. The new trench to the support line was intended to lighten the rather heavy casualties incurred by the infantry carrying parties. The shelling on the 11th compelled the tramway gangs to cease work. It was

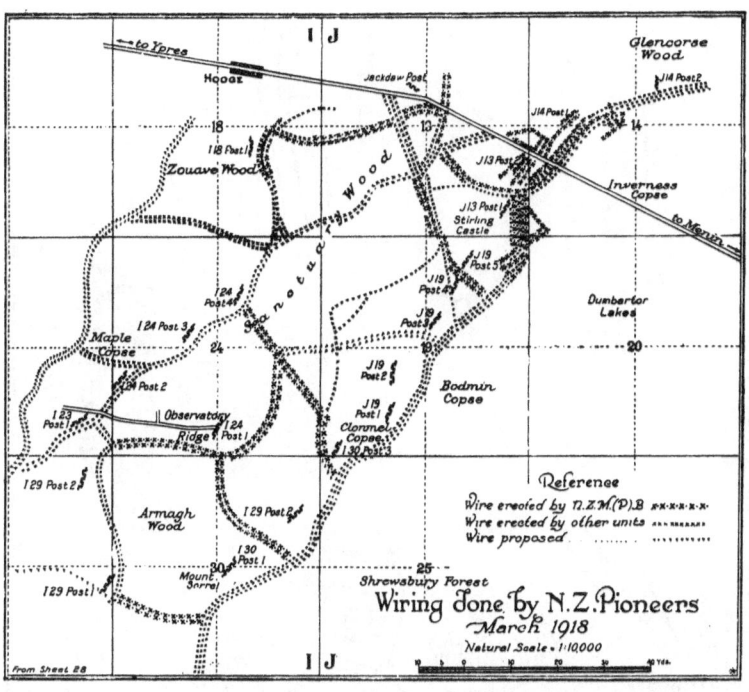

Plan of Barb-wire Defences constructed by the Pioneer Battalion, near Ypres, Western Front, March, 1918.

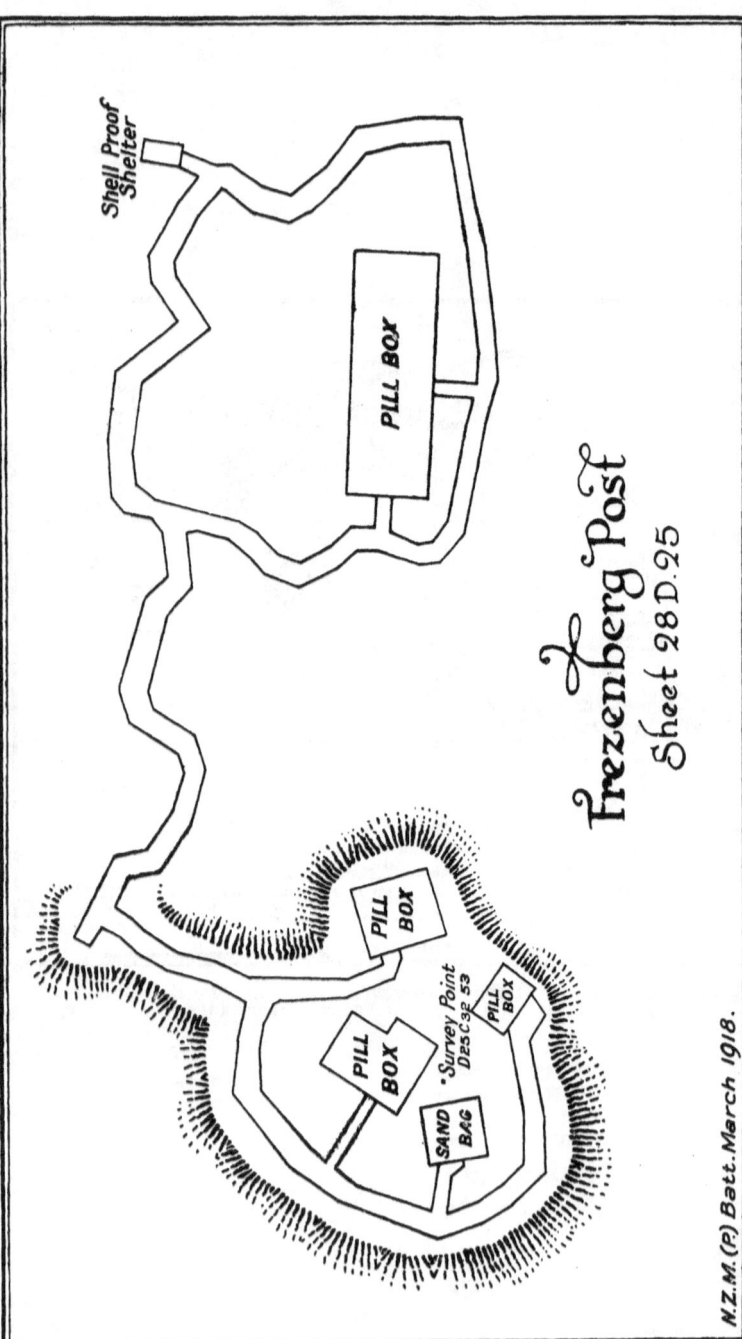

ENTRENCHMENTS BY THE PIONEER BATTALION, FREZENBERG POST, MARCH, 1918.

announced that day that C Company, with an average of £7/12/8 per head, and D Company, with an average of £7/6/9, had won the Divisional 2nd and 3rd prizes in connection with the subscriptions to the New Zealand War Loan.

Thirteen reinforcements arrived on January 13th, and had their taste of a snow fall in Flanders. On the 14th, the Rarotongans and other South Sea Island men, numbering fifty, left to join the Rarotongan Company in Egypt. Lieut. Wilson went in charge as far as Marseilles. A thaw and heavy rain now complicated the toil of the Pioneers and its various jobs. "Rain and slush," the O.C. wrote; "all unrevetted work is flowing in like porridge."

On January 17th, Major Peter Buck left the Battalion on transfer to the New Zealand Medical Corps, after a most useful period of service with the Pioneers. He served through the Gallipoli campaign with his Maoris, as M.O., and in the West Front fighting as a combatant officer. His departure was very deeply regretted by all his fellow-New Zealanders. 34 Maori reinforcements arrived that day. Shelling on both sides was very active during this period. On the 20th, three of the Maoris were hit, but only one was bad enough for hospital.

On the 21st, Lieut.-Col. Saxby went round the artillery positions with the staff Captain, N.Z.F.A., with a view to putting in 9-lb. tram lines to supply them. A scheme was arranged which would take 2,600 yards of line. Next day C Company started on this line formation in front of Westhoek. On the 23rd, two men were wounded, but not seriously, by shell-fire. On the 24th, the O.C. arranged with the Royal Engineer officers to carry a dummy tram formation about 300 yards past Crucifix Dump so that the railhead should not show up too conspicuously in enemy aerial photographs. This day one man was wounded.

The month's work gave the Battalion a good deal of experience in dealing with frozen ground. Formation done while the ground was hard collapsed badly as soon as the thaw commenced, and the trenches and drains were filled with liquid mud. In the new job on the Crucifix communication trench, no more work was done than could be revetted the same day. Plank roads in hard weather were as slippery as glass, and even with frost cogs on the horses could not take an ordinary load. Far better use was being made of the light railways, on which trains now ran through right up to Crucifix Dump. Generally speaking, the Battalion had a quiet month, with casualties far below those of December. One man died of wounds, and one officer and 16 men were wounded. The health of the Battalion had been fairly good; the sick parades much smaller than those of December, but the evacuations were rather heavier—one officer and 80 other ranks. Many of those sent out soon returned from the rest camp and hospital.

February was a fairly quiet month for the Pioneers, but it did not pass without casualties. Two men were killed and and officer and six men were wounded. The fatalities (C Coy.) occurred on February 19th, when the men were at work on the P. and O. communication trench.

Lieut.-Col. Saxby went on 30 days' leave and in his absence Major W. O. Ennis had command of the Battalion.

Pte. H. Kanara, A Company, was awarded the Croix de Guerre by the King of the Belgians, and the decoration was presented by General North on the 12th. About this time the shelling on the forward area was heavy. Work on the 9-lb. artillery line forward of Westhoek, was discontinued owing to the removal of the batteries. A good deal of labour was wasted on this line through the failure of the artillery to advise the Pioneers of their intention to remove guns. 2nd Lieuts. Gannon, Ngatai, and Mete Kingi reported from the Base on the 13th and were posted to D Company. Various heavy works were carried on well including the P. and O. trench, on which 230 men were working. On the 18th shelling in the forward area was above normal, and 2nd Lieut. Dufaur and four men were wounded in the P. and O. trench. There were fifteen "blow-outs" on the Westhoek Road, and the work of repairing was heavy. On the 20th orders were received to arrange exchange of work with the 19th Lancashire Fusiliers (Pioneers, 49th Division). The officers of the two corps went over the Divisional and Company works together, and on the 22nd the

Maori Battalion took over work on No. 9, Potsdam. The P. and O. trench had been completed all but 100 yards of building up on each side just forward of the reserve line. The digging and building of this work was a big task and A and C Companies worked very hard to complete it. A Company specially received high praise for the excellence of the job. The Crucifix trench had been dug, revetted and duck-walked, providing fair cover from Crucifix to the reserve line. D Company did good work on this trench. The light railway from Hannebeke to Crucifix was handed over by B Company in excellent order. On the 24th, the New Zealand Division, less two companies of Engineers, the Maori Battalion, Working Brigade and Artillery were relieved by the British 49th Division.

On the 27th, 2nd Lieuts. Pohio and Te Hau and 19 other ranks reported from the Base.

The first part of March was spent in Ypres carrying on the trench and wire work, wiring south of the Menin Road and strengthening the Frezenberg Post. Work here was the construction of a traversed fire trench to the embankment. The country throughout was marshy and difficult of drainage and badly shaken up with shell-fire. Forward of this line was "Potsdam," a post consisting of four strong German pill-boxes and gun position connection by a traversed trench. A Company was well ahead with a lot of heavy concrete work here, constructing machine-gun positions, but had to leave the job unfinished when the Battalion was withdrawn. In the Frezenberg Post about 80 tons of concrete was put in to strengthen the existing pill-boxes and these were connected with a traversed trench. Wiring south of Menin Road was in charge of Lieut. Leef with three platoons. The type adopted on this front was three parallel lines of double apron fence at about 20 yards interval. The Battalion was also about to start work on Jackdaw Post on the Menin Road, but this with all other work was stopped on March 21st.

Major Ennis, Captain Chapman and Lieut. Pohio fell ill with malaria and were sent out to hospital on the 22nd and 23rd.

Meeting the German Push.

On the 21st, news came through of the German offensive in the Cambrai area, and next evening, after nearly three months' stay in Ypres, the Battalion was on the road to camp near Ouderdom. The Maoris were not disturbed on the march except by a few parting shots as they passed Shrapnel Corner. On the 25th, the Battalion entrained, and went by a loop line round Hazebrouck, and arrived at Amiens about noon next day. Immediate orders were received to move out in fighting kit with 220 rounds S.A.A. per man and all Lewis guns. After a meal the men left by motor lorry for Pont Noyelles, thence on foot to Hedauville, where they spent a very cold night. Many refugees were on the road, and parties of labour troops. Our Division was at first intended to march for a position towards Bray, but events moved quickly, and a gap was found in the line between Puisieux and Hamel through which the Germans were coming without opposition. By the time our infantry came up the enemy was in Hebuterne, Colincamps, and Mailly Maillet. Our people very soon cleared the two last named places and Auchonvillers, and the Australians pushed him out of Hebuterne. A line was established with a slight westerly bulge from east of Hebuterne to west of Hamel. It was a fine quick piece of work for which our Division got great credit. The Battalion moved on on the 27th from Hedauville to Bertrancourt and then to Sailly au Bois. By dark all available men were at work, and by 1 a.m. the Battalion had finished and handed over to the infantry garrison a line of posts from the rear of Colincamps to near Hebuterne. There were no casualties but the enemy's machine-gun fire was decidedly annoying. Next day similar posts were dug from Beaussart to near Forceville. The New Zealand Engineers looked after the country between Colincamps and Beaussart, so that by the night of the 20th there was a line of posts dug right across the New Zealand Divisional area.

On the 28th, A Company commenced digging a continuous trench line from Colincamps north to Hebuterne and had 800 yards of this finished when the work was handed over to the 3rd N.Z.R.B. On the 29th D Company commenced cleaning out and enlarging deep dug-outs for the Left Brigade headquarters, while C Company spent the 29th and 30th digging machine-gun posts all over the Divisional back area.

The casualties during the month were light—one man died of wounds, and one officer and nine other ranks wounded. Three officers and 97 men were evacuated sick.

The month of April at Bertrancourt was spent almost entirely on defensive work digging trenches and wiring, for the most part working on reverse slopes and away from the enemy's observation. The scheme was to provide a defensive system in depth line after line of prepared and wired defences with hidden machine-guns covering every avenue of approach. The Divisions on the Battalion's flanks had also put in an immense amount of work on their rear defences, but while our Divisional scheme had been more a succession of small posts often arranged checkerwise with wire so placed that it could all be enfiladed, they had dug deep solid continuous lines with a belt of wire running in the old style parallel to the front trench. In our case the enemy would have to distribute his fire, while with the continuous line he could concentrate.

Entry by the Battalion Commander in his official diary for April:—

"As Sailly au Bois was just outside our northern country we shifted on the 2nd, to Bertrancourt, and have since been deluged with claims for the frightful excesses our men did not commit in the former village.

"One platoon, though accused of consuming between 2 a.m. and 8 a.m. 10 bags of flour, 2,000 kilos of potatoes, 200 kilos of grain, and all a French gentleman's furniture, did not show any excessive corpulence, while it was a mystery what another platoon had done with 1,000 francs' worth of straw they were accused of annexing for bedding."

The weather was damp and showery and so for once in our favour. There was a gradual increase in shelling until on April 5th the line Hamel-Hebuterne was bombarded in depth, and an infantry attack developed with the probable objective Colincamps or the high ground east of that village. The enemy occupied La Signy Farm, but otherwise failed to improve his position. He harrassed all roads and communication with artillery and paid particular attention to the valley running south from Colincamps towards Mailly Maillet. Some 60-pounders beside C Company billets were heavily shelled with big stuff and so the Company was shifted out into the fields. The casualties were, 2nd Lieut. Thompson, badly wounded and 2nd Lieut. Amohanga slightly wounded; four men killed and seven wounded. Lieut. Thompson was wounded east of Colincamps. L.-Cpl. Tamati Taiapa showed a great deal of pluck in getting him out through the barrage; he was awarded the Military Medal.

On the 6th, C Company and two platoons D Company, dug platoon posts to command the Hedauville Valley in case the right flank Division gave way. A, B, and C Companies then concentrated on wiring until the 20th. On the 11th, the Battalion had 11 men wounded in billets, and as it appeared that the enemy were going to make all villages within range uncomfortable, the Battalion shifted out into bivvies in the paddocks where there was less danger from the German area shoots.

On the 25th, the Battalion side-stepped one Brigade front, handing over the Mailly Maillet sector and taking over the Hebuterne part.

The casualties for the month were:—Killed four, died of wounds two, wounded 41; total 47.

Particularly good work was done by D Company under Captain C. W. Salmon in making the underground headquarters at the Sailly-Colincamps Road.

CHAPTER XVI.

THE SUMMER OF 1918—WESTERN FRONT.

Early in the month of May, work was rearranged amongst the Companies. A Company took on all work at Hebuterne, chiefly cleaning out, and making firesteps, duck-walks in the Hebuterne Switch, and clearing the houses, trees and grass in front to give a fair field of fire, building machine-gun emplacements, wiring strong points, cleaning out Woman Street and communication trench through Fort Hugh to Fort Hector, and cleaning out Cross Street. Nearly all the material was salvaged on the spot, and practically all the duck-walks put in were made in Hebuterne.

A Company also put in four 50-foot drives into the banks at their billets. Cross cuts connected these up in pairs, and sufficient shelter was provided for the Company in case of shelling. These tunnels were afterwards taken over as Brigade Headquarters.

B Company assisted by a platoon from C Company, dug Hay Avenue connecting up Beer Trench with Rum Trench and Hebuterne Switch. This was a standard size trench, fire-stepped for all-round defence and joined the northern face of Fort Herod. The completed trench was 1,500 yards long. It was referred to afterwards in another Division's Orders as an example of how a communication trench should be dug and camouflaged.

C Company took charge of all wiring between Colincamps and Hebuterne. D Company did a lot of wiring. On May 11th they dumped some exposed wiring at One Tree Hill and in front of the Sugar Refinery and suffered only two slight casualties. At Fort Bertha this Company did the best hidden trench work that had yet been carried out by the Battalion.

The enemy's artillery activity during the month was rather below normal, though he was quite spiteful in regard to certain spots, such as the Sugar Refinery and the neighbourhood of Courcelles, and developed an unpleasant habit of throwing over crashes, a concentration of a number of guns on a particular point for about a minute. These crashes came without warning; they were a mixture of shrapnel and H.E. from guns of all calibres up to 8-inch. "The weather," reported Lieut.-Col. Saxby, "has on the whole been fine, with a few wet days in the middle of the month, and it was rather surprising that with so much in his favour he developed no infantry attacks on our front. Still, he was busy elsewhere, and probably knew as well as we did the stack of troops we had behind us."

All the work was carried out in the morning, leaving the afternoon free, and football and even tennis were played, "weapons" for which were supplied by the Y.M.C.A.

Influenza resulted in a good deal of sickness, but casualties were extremely light; only three men were wounded during the month of May.

In the early part of June, trench work was pushed ahead to finish the job and it was nearly all done when the sector was handed over to the Northumberland Fusiliers. The Battalion had done over 40 miles of wire fencing since coming into the sector, making a formidable obstacle. On June 7th, the New Zealand Division was relieved by the British 42nd Division, and the Northumberland Fusiliers (Pioneers) took over the Maoris' work and camp. The Battalion then took over the camp at Coigneux, vacated by the relief. A good deal of work was done here when orders were received to shift to a camping area nearer Souastre. Here, after dragging over an appalling quantity of salvaged iron, timber and other rubbish the Maoris were soon dug-in again. On the 21st, the Battalion was on the move again, and spent the rest of the month in an excellent camp at the Bois de Warinmort. On the 29th, the Maoris were inspected by Mr Massey, Sir Joseph Ward and General Richardson. Altogether it was an easy month. Casualties, only two wounded. Major Ennis returned from hospital on the 19th.

The Battalion's strength on June 30th was 972 of all ranks.

At the beginning of July, 1918, the Division went into the line again, taking up the Corp's centre sector with the northern boundary just above Rossignol Wood, and the southern boundary on the south edge of Hebuterne. Headquarters and horse

INSPECTING THE N.Z. PIONEERS, BOIS DE WARNIMONT, JUNE 30TH, 1918.

RIGHT HON. SIR JOSEPH WARD ADDRESSING THE PIONEERS, AT THE BOIS DE WARNIMONT, JUNE 30TH, 1918.

Cheers for Mr. Massey, at the Bois de Warnimont, June 30th, 1918.

Mr. Massey at Etaples, July 3rd, 1918.

lines were taken over from the 2nd and 5th North Lancashires at Coigneue. A Company went into camp here and B, C, and D Companies went a little farther forward, to Bayencourt and near Chateau de la Haie. The out-going Pioneer Battalion (Northumberlands) handed over piles of papers relating to everything but work. They had just completed the work they had in hand (dug-outs in Beer Trench) and had apparently no programme ahead of them. Company Commanders went out at once to report on their various jobs, and work was put in hand at once. The horse lines had very poor bomb protection, and this was fixed up at once. The communication trenches were for the most part in dry weather order as the Gommecourt village and defences were being kept by the French as a war memorial. The Germans had turned the village into an extremely strong position with numerous deep dug-outs and it was their successful defence of this place and the line to the north that held up the British advance in June, 1916, when they broke in at Fricourt and further south. The defences were therefore noteworthy, and it was the French nation's decision to keep it intact that enabled the Maoris to take over a position which only needed some wiring to make it as strong against attack from the E. and S.E. as it had been from the W. and S.W. Work went on quietly until July 15th. Shelling was normal, and each side seemed content with the "quiet life," until the Rifle Brigade disturbed the harmony by ousting the Bosche from his positions east of Hebuterne, and obtaining a view which made the Germans' line of approach very uncomfortable. About 40 prisoners and 15 machine-guns were taken by the "Dinks." The enemy became very peevish (to quote Saxby's report), and the value of the Brigade's gain was soon known by his withdrawal, partly voluntary and partly forced, from Rossignol Wood. Our infantry followed him up closely, and his heavy shelling of Rossignol Wood and its surroundings showed how much he resented being forced back into the low country.

The advance extended the Pioneers' work, adding 500 yards or more to each of the communication trenches, besides necessitating the wiring of the Forbes-Faith-Welcome-Cod Trench line.

For the month the casualties were light—one killed (a shell splinter), and seven wounded. There had been 93 cases evacuated, mostly influenza, but about 40 of these returned to the Battalion during the month.

The Battalion had an allotment of ten men per fortnight at the Divisional Lewis Gun School, and most of them came back with excellent reports. Every advantage was also taken of the chance to send officers and men to the Corps and Army Schools, particularly the Musketry Schools. Arrangements were being made to get a sufficient number of men trainéd as cooks, in the interests of economy and better feeding.

CHAPTER XVII.

FINAL STAGES OF THE WAR, 1918.

The first part of August, 1918, was spent in getting the lines ready for winter. The Cod Trench-Forbes Trench line was wired by C and D Companies, with only five casualties (all wounded, C Company). A Company worked at the Pasteur communication trench, and C Company on Cross Street, and they gave good well-protected access to the Forbes-Welcome line, while C Company pushed ahead Nameless and Biez Switch to provide good communication forward for the left Brigade front. B Company worked the tram trench, and other communication trenches, and also laid a continuation of the tram line to Biez Switch. This rail-laying work was done at night under an annoying machine-gun fire. Lieut.-Col. Saxby wrote of this line:—"The Bosche had this so well ranged that I do not think any use could be made of it by our infantry."

On the 11th, an officer and 150 men of the United States Army Pioneers were attached to the New Zealanders for duty. They were just newly landed and were very keen. The Americans got on very well with the Maoris, and both parties were sorry when the time came for the new-comers to move on.

When the Maoris went out to their trench and tramway tasks on the 14th, they found the New Zealand infantry patrols pushing forward to occupy positions which the enemy had occupied during the night. They could see their comrades working up to Serre and past La Louverie Farm, and the Pioneer officers therefore put parties on at once repairing the roads forward. D Company succeeded in making the Hebuterne-Crucifix Road passable by 3 p.m., and it was at once used by the artillery. B and D Companies each sent a platoon out at night and repaired the Crucifix-Biez Wood road sufficiently for gun and limber traffic. Next day A Company cut a new dry-weather track—which was named Dead Horse Trail—from Hebuterne towards Serre and on the following day, with the assistance of C Company continued this to the

Puisieux Road. This proved a most useful track and carried a great deal of artillery and rations traffic. D and C Companies carried out a similar track to Luke Copse, but as this route ran into the 42nd Division Area, it was not of so much use to the New Zealanders, though the 42nd Division used it a great deal. B Company repaired the Sixteen Poplars road from Hebuterne to La Louverie Farm and later continued it down the valley to Box Wood. From there D Company carried on through Puisieux as soon as the situation allowed.

The enemy continued to fall back steadily, and on the 22nd C Company went out to work on the forward part of the Puisieux-Achiet-Le Petit road. This was rather premature, however, as the Germans were still holding the Irles Ridge, Miraumont, and the slopes east of the Dovecote, and he gave the working parties a hot reception. They were withdrawn immediately, but one man was killed and two were wounded. The ground about Achiet-Le Petit was heavily shelled during the day.

On the 23rd, infantry patrols were on the Bihucourt-Irles road. The Engineers and Pioneers were left out with orders to stand by, and it was not until the 25th that orders were received to move forward to Achiet-Le Petit. Late at night further orders altered this to Irles. On the 30th the Battalion moved forward to Grevillers, transport remaining at Irles.

When the Pioneers marched into Irles on the 26th, after a muddy tramp, they set to on "bivvies" for themselves, and as was the way with the resourceful colonials, their neighbours were soon levied upon for material. Lieut.-Col. Saxby made a diary note:—"The boys got busy pinching iron from the very irate Tommies, and were soon coming in from all directions with sufficient material to house twice their number."

Our infantry were now pressing close round west and north of Bapaume, but the British 22nd Division on our right never seemed to keep up, and so our right flank was continually in the air and bent right back for our own protection. On the night of the 28th, the enemy left Bapaume, falling back to about the Bancourt-Fremicourt line. A and B Companies repaired the roads right up to Bapaume, and also the Bapaume-

REV. PENI TE UAMAIRANGI HAKIWAI, CHAPLAIN, PIONEER BATTALION.
Served on the Western Front.

Albert road, and on the 30th C Company went on with repairs through Bapaume to 1,000 yards along the Cambrai Road.

On the 30th, Captain Chapman and three other ranks left the Grevillers camp as the Battalion's first detachment for New Zealand duty leave. Lieut. Dansey took over the duties of Adjutant.

The weather during August was on the whole good and helped the British advance considerably. The Germans did very little in the way of demolition, though from the number of prepared but uncharged land mine boxes found at the large dump near Miraumont, it was evident that had they had more time roads and railways would have suffered considerably. As it was, there was not a crater blown in any road in our area either in Bapaume or west of it. In this advance the New Zealanders passed just north of Flers and Gueudecourt, two villages well remembered, from the Somme battles of 1916, when we approached them from the south. The country was still an absolute desert. Dark patches of weeds and thistles covered the remains of demolished dwellings. These, with a very few shattered tree-trunks, were all that remained to mark the sites of what were once prosperous and happy homes. No attempt appeared to have been made after the Bosche fell back in 1917, to renew the occupation of territory.

The losses during the month were two killed and 15 wounded. The total evacuations, sick and wounded, were 98.

In the early part of September the enemy's retirement continued slowly, and on the 3rd the British infantry worked through Haplincourt and on to Bertincourt. Communications were left in good order, and the few hasty attempts made to mine the roads were discovered before any damage was done. The Battalion road patrols followed the infantry closely and the roads were quickly made fit for traffic.

The Maoris moved forward on the 4th, as far as Haplincourt. The water supply was a big problem, as there was none in the stream courses, and the Germans had destroyed pumping plants and many of the wells. Their demolition was not carried out very thoroughly, however. In the attempt to destroy deep bores they simply blew a crater at the top, whereas half the charge lowered fifty feet down the piping and then

K

exploded would have ruined the bore completely. As the Pioneers' transport was in rather an uncomfortable place owing to long-range shelling (which cost the Battalion two wounded horses), it was shifted on to Haplincourt, where good protection was at once built for the horses.

As it appeared the enemy intended making a stand on the Canal Du Nord-Haplincourt Wood line, the Pioneers began a defensive line of trenches on the ridges east of Barastre and Haplincourt . After a day's work had been put in on these our infantry pushed forward through the wood and beyond Metz, establishing themselves on the ridge just east of that village. It was there that the Pioneers found the first thoroughly demolished roads. Large craters had been blown at the cross roads in Metz and on all roads leading from the village. Effectively placed, these delayed transport considerably and the Pioneers had a great deal of hard work ahead of them. Risky work, too, for the German gunners devoted special attention to places where they knew the foe would be at work repairing the damage they had wrought. B Company tackled these craters first, while D Company was moved forward into bivouacs near Ruyaulcourt. D Company took over the work while B Company also shifted camp forward, and the two companies took over the repairs of advanced roads while A and C Companies were employed on back area work and the construction of new quarters for the Division.

The 3rd Brigade delivered a further attack on the German line early on the morning of September 12th, and at 7 a.m. reports showed that they had reached their objective. But neither of the flank Divisions had come up, and this compelled a slight retirement. That evening B and D Companies of Pioneers each sent out two platoons and they spent what was described as "a filthy night," very dark and raining, helping the infantry to consolidate the positions won.

On the 14th, the Division was relieved by the 5th Division, and the Pioneers of the Argyll and Sutherland Highlanders took over from the Maoris, who shifted back from their comparatively comfortable dug-outs to a particularly dirty camp at Sapignies. A Company went into rather better billets at Fremicourt.

On the night of the 16th, the Pioneers were nearly flooded out in a great downpour of rain. Next day some one in high authority found that half the Battalion was camped in the area of the next Corps. Though these warriors had, as the Maori O.C. remarked, most of France available for camping ground, they decided that the spot the Maoris occupied—which with much labour had been made moderately clean and sanitary—was just the very spot they required. So out the Pioneers had to go; but it did not matter very much, as they shifted into clean ground and took most of their salvaged iron with them. The next few days were spent in reorganisation and in training, mostly of a recreational character.

As A, B and C Companies were all under strength and D Company well over strength, the Ngati-Maniapoto and Waikato men were transferred to C Company and the Ngati-Raukawa to B Company, making the four companies fairly equal.

The Germans were now strongly posted in the Old Hindenburg Line on our front, though their positions were being flanked from the North. Preparations were made for another general advance, and as our Corps and that to the north of us were very dependent on the one road through Bertincourt and Metz, the Pioneers were sent forward on the 25th to widen the way in places and make the Ytres-Neuville road fit for two-way lorry traffic. The Maoris camped near Ytres, and Fritz made himself disagreeable by throwing shells at them every night. The work required was quickly done and the road was put in a satisfactory condition. The attack by the 5th and 42nd Divisions on our front was moderately successful on the left but was held up for a time on the right. After Beaucamp and Villers Plouich had been taken the New Zealand Division came in again and took Welsh Ridge and Bonavis Ridge, which put us right through the Hindenburg Line. The left flank Corps secured Marcoing and Masnieres while our Division came up to the line of the Canal, the right Division forming a defensive flank facing Gonnelieu, which for a time held out. The Pioneers moved forward to Trescault, and then (less D Company) to Welsh Ridge, where they dug in in the Hindenburg trench system. The Bosche had been pretty roughly handled here, and his dead were freely scattered about, while many dead horses and abandoned guns showed that he was not at all willing to lose his very strong position.

The Divisional communications forward were very bad, and the artillery had to depend on cross-country routes. Luckily the weather remained passably fine; had it been otherwise, there would have been great difficulty in getting transport forward. A great deal of use was made of the Trescault-Ribecourt road, which was in a very bad state. D Company, with 20 waggons, kept continually patching it with brick and kept it from going altogether to pieces. Our infantry got across the canal, and the enemy fell back on our Divisional front to the Masnieres-Beauvoir line, a shallow but well-wired line which had been constructed as a support to the Hindenburg Line. We were now just south and slightly east of Cambrai, which was gradually being pinched out. Our infantry had a particularly severe time of it at Crevecoeur; the Auckland and Wellington Battalions suffered many casualties. The Pioneers' work still consisted of keeping the roads repaired as close up behind the infantry as possible.

The September casualties among the Maoris were 13 wounded and 45 sent out sick.

During the month of October, the Battalion was for the most part engaged on road work, but before the advance on the 9th a considerable amount of work was also done on approaches to bridges erected by the New Zealand Engineers over the Canal De L'Escaut. On the New Zealand Division taking Welsh Ridge and Bonavis Ridge, the Battalion went forward to Trescault, then to Welsh Ridge, there the Maoris were employed on the repair of roads leading to Crevecoeur and Les Rues des Vignes, and the preparation of bridge approaches thereabouts.

Battalion Headquarters and most of the men were encamped on Welsh Ridge. D Company remained at Trescault and carried on work with 20 waggons in the Trescault-Ribecourt road, which was in a very bad state. A Company laboured on the Villers-Plouich-Marcoing road, B Company on the Ribecourt-Marcoing road and C Company on the formation of

A GERMAN SHELL BURSTING ON A ROAD WHICH THE N.Z. PIONEERS WERE REPAIRING.
Photo taken at Puisieux on the morning of its capture, August 21st, 1918.

A GERMAN ANTI-TANK RIFLE, TAKEN BY THE NEW ZEALANDERS AT COUIN, NEAR HEBUTERNE, AUGUST, 1918.

THE PIONEERS AT TRENCH IMPROVEMENT WORK, NEAR GOMMECOURT, AUGUST 28TH, 1918.

MEAL-TIME WITH A PARTY OF THE MAORIS' PAKEHA COMRADES, AT GREVILLERS, AUGUST 24TH, 1918.

artillery tracks. Most of the roads, however, were not in a very bad state, as no mines had been exploded; all the damage had been done by shell-fire.

On the night of the 5th, the infantry attacked and captured that part of the Masnieres-Beauvoir line opposite the Divisional front. In preparation for this operation B Company made a cross-country track from the Dressing Station at Ribecourt to Brigade headquarters, and on to Masnieres while C Company repaired the road from Masnieres to Crevecoeur. These tasks completed the two Companies prepared the approaches to bridges on the Canal De L'Escaut. Lieut. Wilkinson (B Coy.) was slightly wounded here on the 6th and was evacuated to hospital. Two platoons of C Company were working in conjunction with a Royal Engineers bridging train on approaches to tank bridges at Masnieres. The weather had been fairly good, with very little rain, but at times it was foggy and very cold.

On October 9th, the New Zealand Division again attacked with great success, capturing Lesdain and Esnes, and taking a large number of prisoners. Our casualties were very light. That afternoon the Pioneer Headquarters and B and C Companies moved forward to a position in front of Esnes. There was an encounter with an unexploded shell when part of the transport was returning to the Trescault camp. One of the waggons passed over a "dud" shell stuck in the ground with the nose cap protruding. The shell exploded, wounding the driver, and also a horse which was so badly hurt that it had to be shot. The transport and A and D Companies moved up and joined the Battalion at Esnes on the afternoon of the 10th. A lot of work was done on the surrounding roads. The Germans had blown mine-craters in all important road junctions, and all culverts were demolished. However, had the British advance been delayed a few days the roads would have been in a far worse state, as many mines were being made ready but were not completed when our attack was delivered.

The hard-fighting infantry carried on their brilliant advance on the 11th, reaching the line of the Selle River. That night the New Zealand Division was relieved by the British 42nd Division, and went into reserve for ten days at Beauvois and

Fontaine. The Pioneers moved from Esnes to Beauvois, where the Maoris all found billets in houses. It was a mighty agreeable change for the boys after the rough bivouacs. Another good thing highly appreciated was the abundance of vegetables in the gardens, and the supply of potatoes, cabbages, etc., was very welcome. During the period spent in Beauvois all the work done was on the roads. The enemy had made a good job of his demolition; mines had been blown in all important road junctions, and there were two particularly large craters on the road to Caudry and one at the entrance to Fontaine.

A pleasant incident this month was the inspection of the Battalion by H.R.H. the Prince of Wales. The Prince made a little speech complimenting the Maoris on their smart and soldierly appearance.

There was another change of scene on the 20th, when the Battalion moved on to Viesly, where most of the men were billeted in the village. That morning the 42nd Division renewed the attack on the German lines, and by 4 in the afternoon, had taken their final objective (the Brown Line). The enemy had thrown a lot of gas shells into Viesly in the morning, and when the Pioneers arrived the place was reeking with it. However, it soon cleared and evidently was not thick enough to injure anyone. Next day D Company moved into billets in the village. The Battalion still carried on with road repairs, but most of the roads hereabouts were in fairly good condition, and the only explosions—craters—were small ones near Quievy and one large one at Fontaine au Tertre Farm. A large amount of work was done on the roads and approaches to bridges over the River Selle near Briastre. The country was very wet and boggy here, as the river had been dammed up by the Germans, and the roads near the Selle all had to be fascined.

On October 23rd, the 42nd Division pushed on again, carried their objectives on time, and allowed the New Zealand Division to pass through and carry on the advance. The attack was completely successful, the Division advancing about 1,000 yards past their final objective. That day the Pioneers moved on again, to billets in Solesmes. This was the first village in which civilians were living that the Battalion had yet occupied. The inhabitants gave the Maoris a vociferously hearty welcome. Next day the Pioneers moved on to bivouacs near Vertigneul. Most of the roads here were in pretty good condition. There were very few demolitions except the Pont A'Pierres Bridge. The approaches to this bridge were repaired by B Company under heavy fire from the enemy. There were several British batteries of artillery waiting to get over, and becoming impatient they all opened fire on the foe—9.2-inch and 6-inch guns, and 18-pounders, and of course the Germans got on to them and, as the O.C. Pioneers recorded: "nearly strafed the place off the map." However, the work was completed in good time and on went the gunners. B Company also widened and metalled the Romeries-Beaudignies road from Le Trousse Mimon onward. The other companies repaired the roads between Solesmes and Romeries.

The casualties for October were 10 wounded, besides 41 sent to hospital; 91 men returned from hospital and base.

CHAPTER XVIII.

THE CAPTURE OF LE QUESNOY—THE ARMISTICE.

November, 1918, proved the last month of warfare. At the beginning of the month the New Zealand Division was still holding the line in front of Beaudignies, which was taken on October 23rd, but to our left the advance was still being pushed on well. Even at Valenciennes the enemy was being squeezed slowly out of his positions. At the beginning of the month the Battalion was occupied in repairing the roads round Beaudignies and neighbourhood in preparation for the coming advance.

On November 4th, the Pioneers moved up to Beaudignies, where with the exception of the transport, camped on the outskirts all the men were billeted in the village. That morning saw the memorable offensive preliminary to the capture of Le Quesnoy. The New Zealand Division attacked at 5.35 a.m., in conjunction with the British Divisions on its flanks. The object was to establish a footing in the line Franc a Louer-Herbignies-Tous Vents, and if opportunity offered to continue the advance eastward through the Forest of Mormal. Heavy fighting continued all day and gave the New Zealanders a splendid opportunity, and the last, as it developed, of displaying their dash and their pertinacity. Le Quesnoy was not directly attacked at first, but the troops moved round from north and south and encircled it, the movement involving some hard fighting. The ancient town, with its deep and wide moat and its lofty bastioned ramparts, was a fortress dating from the Middle Ages, and its fortifications showed the additional defences designed by the famous Vauban. Its great ditch and its strong high walls presented an apparently insuperable object, garrisoned as the place was by German artillery and infantry. Our New Zealand infantry, however, were not to be beaten. With scaling ladders a few daring men entered the place, after some rifle and machine-gun fighting, and others followed. It was singular to see at one part of the ramparts our men and the Germans fighting for possession while a few hundred yards away the civilian inhabitants were joyously cheering the New Zealanders on. In the process of cleaning up the town it was found strongly held in places and defended with machine-guns. After some street fighting, however, the whole of the garrison, numbering about 1,500, surrendered. The day's operations were thoroughly successful. Practically the whole of the Foret de Mormal was cleared, and a total of 27 officers and 2,050 other ranks were captured, besides over 40 guns.

That morning, soon after the infantry had advanced, the Battalion commenced to work on the roads in the newly captured territory, and as the town of Le Quesnoy was at the time holding out, they had a very trying time of it. The Maoris were under sharp machine-gun fire most of the day. In spite of this, however, some very good work was done.

One dangerous task well accomplished deserves special mention. A German motor-lorry was lying disabled on the road, where it was blocking traffic. It was noticed that the clear part of the road had lately been disturbed, and on examining it the place was found to be mined. Owing to the position of the lorry the first vehicle to go along the road would have had to pass over the mine, with serious results. However, in a very short time the mine was safely cleared away, and the road was repaired.

On the afternoon of November 5th, the Battalion moved forward from Beaudignies to billets in Le Quesnoy. The roads ahead of the captured town were not in a bad state so far as shelling was concerned, but all important junctions, bridges and culverts had been mined. The most important of these was the bridge over the railway at Pont Billon, which was completey destroyed. This necessitated the making of a deviation over very soft ground, which had to be fascined for the heavy traffic. The Battalion carried on with repairs on the roads forward of Le Quesnoy. These highways were for the most part fairly good, though in many places craters had been blown. In many other places they had been mined, and were ready for exploding, but the rapid advance of the New Zealanders had given the enemy no time to trouble about firing them; he was too busy saving his own skin.

The New Zealanders had pushed on again with the advance on the morning of the 5th, and got well forward of the Foret de Mormal and nearly on the line of the River Sambre. On the night of the 5th-6th, they were relieved by the British 42nd Division.

Then on the morning of November 11th came the joyful news that hostilities were to cease at 11 a.m. The Maoris regretted that owing to their being so far away from what they termed "civilised parts," they could not celebrate the Armistice in a manner befitting the great occasion. However, all hands were pleased at the cessation of the fighting and particularly at the silence of the guns, which had been thundering almost without ceasing for a period that seemed a lifetime.

Road repairs were carried on with until the 15th. Route marching and recreational travelling followed. On the 18th, the O.C., Lieut.-Col. Saxby, D.S.O., went on leave to England. This brave and able officer, unhappily, was destined never to see his Pioneers or the shores of New Zealand again. On the 28th his comrades received the news that he had died of pneumonia in London. The whole Battalion grieved deeply for their gallant leader, who was liked and admired by all for his personal qualities and his soldierly ability.

Orders to move came on the 21st and a billeting party, Y.M.C.A., and the regimental canteen went next day to Bevillers, followed on the 23rd by the Battalion. The Company cookers left ahead of the Battalion and halted at Romeries, where at mid-day the men found a hot lunch awaiting them. At Bevillers the mornings were spent in route marching and ceremonial drill, with a little physical training and bayonet exercise. The afternoons were devoted to recreational training, in the form of inter-platoon football matches, cross-country runs, and wood-chopping competitions. On the 26th the first round of the New Zealand inter-Battalion Rugby football matches was played, the Pioneers beating 1st Auckland by 27 points to 3.

On the 27th orders were received to move to Viesly, but at the last minute these were cancelled and the Maoris were told to hold themselves in readiness to march to Germany.

The Capture of Le Quesnoy—The Armistice. 155

Next day the journey was begun. Before leaving Bevillers, 116 men whom it was thought were unfit to undertake the march were sent to the Base. The Pioneers' blankets on the way eastward were carried in motor lorries, and the Battalion, headed by its drum and bugle band, marched very well. Solesmes was the first halting-place. On the 29th, the force reached Artres, where billets were found for the night. In the morning the march was resumed to Heau-sur-Hon, near Tasnieres, a long day's tramp, broken near Wargnies for midday meal and rest. The weather was very foggy and cold and not at all the sort of weather one would choose for a walking tour; however, it was Peace. That day it was announced that the Corps Commander had awarded the Military Medal to Pte. A. Anderson. On the 15th of the month the IV. Corps, of which the New Zealand Division was a part, came under the command of the Fourth Army.

The Battalion remained at Tasnieres two days, and on December 3rd, moved on to Roncq, on the Sambre, about four kilometres from Maubeuge. Here there was difficulty with the transport, and repairs were necessary to the bridge before the waggons could cross it. From Roncq the Pioneers marched *via* Jeumont and Sol-sur-Sambre to Merbes-le-Chateau. Here, as the Maoris marched into the town headed by their band, they were given a hearty welcome by crowds of the Belgian inhabitants. This was the first Belgian town entered since the route march began. On the 5th, Gozee was reached; from here a few of the Battalion visited Charleroi by steamtram. Charleroi was one of the principal commercial cities of Belgium and was the finest place the Pioneers had yet seen in that country. Couillet, one of the suburbs of Charleroi, was reached on the 7th. When the billeting party started their work they were most warmly greeted by the civilians, who all wished to have soldiers billeted on them; and so practically every one in the Battalion had a bed. Anti-German feeling ran high. On the day the Maoris arrived the inhabitants were going round the town smashing the windows and breaking the furniture in the houses of those who had done more than tolerate the Huns during their occupation of Belgium. Jemeppe-sur-Sambre was the next halting place.

Here the Pioneers were again made very welcome; the people on whom they were billeted treated them with great hospitality. St. Servais, a suburb of Namur, was reached on December 9th. As the Pioneers were doing three days' march and then having a day's spell, the Battalion had nothing more than a foot inspection on the 10th. The men stood the long march very well, especially considering the fact that the weather was very wet. Major Sutherland was now appointed Second in Command of the Battalion, under Lieut.-Col. W. O. Ennis; Captain P. Tahiwi took over the command of D Company and Captain J. H. Hall took over A Company.

Marching on by way of Gelbressee, Couthiun was reached on December 12th. Headquarters there were in a very fine billet, the Chateau d'Envoz. Two companies, A and B, were also quartered in a large chateau. Here the Maoris saw something of the wanton destruction for which the enemy had become so infamous. The Chateau which had been beautifully furnished, was in a shocking condition. Horses had been stabled on the ground floor; mirrors had been broken, pictures ripped from their frame, and furniture of all sorts smashed to pieces.

Everywhere along the line of march the Belgian civilians turned out to welcome the New Zealanders, and everywhere they were hospitable to their Allies quartered on them. On the 16th, at Amay, a football match was played between the officers and the other ranks, resulting in a win for the men, by 9 points to 7; an exciting game.

Angleur, a suburb of Liege, was the halting place on the 17th. On the 18th the Battalion moved to Pepinster, and on the 19th a halt was made at Stembert. That night the billeting party under Lieut. Bevan left on bicycles for Herbesthal, just across the German frontier, where they entrained early next morning for Ehrenfeld, a suburb of Cologne. The Battalion was to move into Germany in three groups, halting at Herbesthal. However, on December 20th, orders were received cancelling the move for Germany and instructing the Pioneers to go to Dunkirk for England, *en route* for home again.

TIMI ENJOYS ONE OF SIR JOSEPH WARD'S CIGARS,
AT THE BOIS DE WARNIMONT.

NEW ZEALAND MINISTERS ADDRESSING THE ENTRENCHING GROUP,
PAS, AUGUST, 1918.

SLINGING A PRESENTATION GUN INTO LIGHTER, AT RAROTONGA, 1919.

SIR JAMES ALLEN ADDRESSING RETURNED SOLDIERS AT RAROTONGA, 1919.

The Capture of Le Quesnoy—The Armistice.

So, on the morning of the 24th, the Battalion left Stembert and marched to Verviers. All Christmas Day was spent in the train, going through Tournai, Lille, Armentieres and Hazebrouck, and by 5 o'clock next morning the Maoris gladly jumped out of their trucks at Dunkirk, their long, long months of campaigning on European soil over.

Dunkirk was a wet and comfortless camp. It was practically under water and all the men were in tents. Major Sutherland, Captain Dansey, and over 60 men went into hospital, most of them with influenza, and Lieut.-Col. Ennis and many others kept to their blankets, sick. On the 28th, the Transport went to Calais and gave over their horses and equipment and returned to Dunkirk on the 30th.

Entry in the O.C.'s Diary:—"During the stay in the camp the men had the day to themselves, and in the evening leave was granted till the night of the 31st. They seemed to take leave of their senses. It appears that there was a bit of indiscriminate shooting going on, and when the piquet appeared on the scene and attempted to arrest one of the offenders he resisted. Lieut. Wickham, one of the officers of the picquet, tried to gain possession of the revolver, but was shot and died of the wound. Lieut. Angel was also slightly wounded."

Early in the month four representatives were picked from the Battalion for a representative football team from the Division, to go to England. The players chosen were, 2nd Lieut. W. Barclay, centre-threequarter; 2nd Lieut. H. Jacob, wing forward; Sergeant F. Barclay, five-eighths, and Pte. S. Gemmell, forward. However, nothing further was heard of the proposed tour.

So ended the ever-memorable year which had seen all the phases of the Great War from the German offensive of March-July, when things looked black for the Allies, to the glorious Allied attack which began on July 18th and never ceased until the enemy had been driven right out of France and out of half of Belgium, pushed so far that recovery was hopeless and acceptance of the Armistice the only alternative to an invasion of Germany.

The Battalion in England.

Major Sutherland and Captain Dansey returned from hospital on January 2nd, 1919, and on the same day orders were issued for embarkation for England on the following morning. Crossing in the steamer "St. George," the Battalion disembarked at Southampton, whence they went by train to Amesbury.

From there they marched to No. 5 Camp, Larkhill, which was to be their home until they embarked for New Zealand. It was a most agreeable change to be quartered in huts with fire-places and bunks and to enjoy the use of bath-houses, recreational halls, and the two dining-halls given over to the Battalion. On January 7th, the Battalion was inspected by the G.O.C., Brigadier-General Stewart, who complimented the Maoris on the work they had done in France, and informed them that they were to march past the King, at Whitehall, before leaving for their homes.

For some time thereafter the Battalion practised ceremonial drill for the Royal review. On the 10th, a draft of 100 men arrived from Germany. This was the billeting party, and the men who had been sent back when the Battalion was on the march across Belgium. Owing to the prevalence of measles in the neighbouring camps it was found necessary to have an inspection by the M.O. every day, but fortunately there were very few cases in the Battalion. It was ordered that before leaving for New Zealand every man must undergo strict medical and dental examinations, and in order that this should not have to be done hurriedly at the last moment the men were put through before embarkation leave was granted. On January 12th, the first batch, 400 men, left on 14 days' leave, and the rest of the Battalion left in parties between that time and the end of the month. On the 13th, the Battalion drummers left for a course of instruction at the Guards' School, London.

Owing to an outbreak of influenza while most of the Maoris were on leave, the camp was put under isolation. The epidemic was severe; seven or eight cases a day were sent to hospital, but very few cases proved fatal.

After leave, the Battalion was kept busy preparing for demobilisation. Clothing cards and demobilisation cards had

The Battalion in England.

to be made out in duplicate for each man, and all shortages in clothing and equipment had to be made up.

When the Battalion left France the O.C. received a message from Lieut.-General Sir A. Godley, complimenting them on their good work done as infantry on Gallipoli and as Pioneers in France, and wishing them a safe and speedy return to New Zealand.

February of 1919, found the Battalion still in No. 5 Camp, Larkhill, anxiously awaiting the day of embarkation for their far-away home. Towards the end of January the epidemic of influenza had abated somewhat, and it was hoped that it would be possible to remove the edict of isolation; however, owing to a fresh outbreak early in February this was found impossible, and the camp remained in isolation until the Pioneers left. The whole of the officers and men were inoculated against influenza.

On Tuesday, February 4th, the Battalion was inspected by Brigadier-General Stewart, G.O.C., who said he was well satisfied with the smart and soldierly appearance of the Maoris. The Battalion was again paraded on the 11th, when the G.O.C. presented decorations as follow for gallantry in the field:—

Distinguished Medal.—Sergeant F. Barclay.

Military Medal.—C.Q.M.S. M. R. Jones; Sergeant J. Munn, Corporals A. Sparks and G. Maxwell, L.-Cpls. T. T. Morgan and R. Ngapo; Ptes. T. Taiapa, P. Te Amo, T. Te Patu, T. Brown and H. T. Leef.

Meritorious Service Medal.—Sergeants H. M. Davies and H. Kerei.

At an investiture in Buckingham Palace, on February 13th, three officers were decorated by His Majesty the King. Lieut.-Col. W. O. Ennis received the D.S.O., and Captains Stainton and Hiroti received the Military Cross.

The *pakehas* remaining with the Battalion were, with a few exceptions, transferred to Sling Camp (four officers and 45 men). Classes were started during the month in general education and elementary agriculture, and the good attendance showed how keen the men were to avail themselves of any opportunity of making themselves more fit for their occupation in civil life.

Football was the men's great sport during the month. The Battalion football team played three matches. The first was against the Royal Naval Depot at Devonport; in this game the Maoris won by 6 points to 3. The second match was played at Swansea against Swansea, and was also won by the Battalion —the score being 9 points to nil. The last match, played against Llanelly, was won by the Welshmen by 6 points to nil.

On the 25th, the final inspection of the Battalion was held by the G.O.C., who wished officers and men a safe and speedy return to their homeland and to all who were waiting for them there.

The final move came on the morning of February 28th; when the Battalion entrained at Amesbury for Liverpool, where the transport for New Zealand, the steamer "Westmoreland," was boarded late in the afternoon. At ten o'clock that night the troopship hove up her anchor in the Mersey and steamed out for sea on the long home voyage to New Zealand.

The Home-Coming.

The "Westmoreland" made the passage direct to Auckland, *via* Panama Canal. The reception of the soldiers on their native shore was a soul-stirring welcome-home after their long heroic adventures at world's-end. *Pakeha* and *Maori* alike, the people delighted to do honour to the returning *Hokowhitu a Tu*. The Battalion, under the command of Lieut.-Colonel Ennis, marched through the flag-decorated city, cheered by thousands, and up to the Auckland Domain, where a grand Maori reception and feast had been prepared. Many hundreds of people, from a score of tribes, were encamped on the Cricket Ground oval, awaiting with intense excitement and overflowing hearts the coming of their young men. It was a scene of old Maoridom revived, the return of the war-party from the fighting trail. The waiting Maoris were assembled by tribes, and after the first tremendous roaring chorus of welcome from all, they sprang up, *iwi* after *iwi*, from Ngapuhi southward, chanted and danced their *powhiri* of greeting, and sang their *waiata* of praise and affection to the warriors. Sir James Allen (Minister for Defence) and Sir James Carroll addressed the soldiers; ''Ta

The Home-Coming.

Hemi Kara's'' speech was poetically eloquent in the true Maori manner.

All the old war-songs were sung, the ancient war-cries were heard again. Chants that inspired the defenders of Orakau and the Gate Pa and many another battlefield came from the grey-beards of the tribes; from the women and girls came songs, composed for this day, and the rhythmic and melodious *poi* enchanted all eyes and ears. And the grand old "Toia Mai" chorus of greeting to the honoured ones was heard again and again: it likened the soldiers to a canoe crew returning to the loved home shores:

> *A-a tōia mai*
> > *Te waka!*
> *Kūmea mai*
> > *Te waka!*
> *Ki te urunga,*
> > *Te waka!*
> *Ki te moenga,*
> > *Te waka;*
> *Ki te takotoranga*
> *I takoto ai*
> > *Te waka.*
> *Toia mai te waka*
> *Ki te urunga!*

[Translation.]

> Oh haul away
> > The war-canoe!
> Oh hither draw
> > Our grand canoe!
> To the resting-place,
> To the sleeping-place,
> To the abiding place—
> > Our great canoe.
> Oh haul away!
> For home comes our canoe!

APPENDICES

THE MAORI ROLL OF HONOUR.

List of Dead, Gallipoli, 1915, France and Flanders, 1916-1918.

The following is a complete list of fatal casualties in the Maori Contingent, Gallipoli, 1915, and the Maori Pioneer Battalion, France and Flanders, 1916-1918, together with other deaths (accidental and disease) on active service. The details are from the Defence Department's official list of total deaths in the New Zealand Expeditionary Force during the War:—

16/1007 Adam, Kiro Luke, Pte. Killed in Action, France, 7/10/17.
16/598 Akena, Rakapa, Pte. Died, United Kingdom ex France, 16/6/18.
19840 Albert, Windy, Pte. Died, New Zealand ex France, 29/5/19.
9/1256 Allison, Wm., Pte. Killed in Action, France, 15/9/16.
16/1392 Anaru, Albert Paul, Pte. Killed in Action, France, 7/6/17.
19460 Andrews, William Wilson, Pte. Accidentally Killed, France, 20/1/18.
16/583 Angel, Edward, L.-Cpl. Died of Wounds, France, 29/12/17.
16/1182 Anthony, Manuel, Cpl. Died, New Zealand ex France, 10/5/17.
16/1365 Apatari, Manu, Pte. Killed in Action, France, 14/9/16.
16/87 Aramataku, Herewini, Pte. Killed in Action, Gallipoli, 6/8/15.
16/1139 Arii, ——, Pte. Died, France, 24/8/16.

16/524 Baker, Whare, Pte. Killed in Action, Gallipoli, 21/8/15.
19236 Banaba, Beni, Pte. Died, New Zealand ex Egypt, 16/9/17.
16/435 Barton, Whare, Pte. Killed in Action, France, 2/9/16.
22759 Bourke, John Joseph, Pte. Killed in Action, France, 15/9/16.
19671 Bristowe, Sam, Pte. Died, France, after Armistice, 5/4/19.
9/1014 Brooke, Burton, Pte. Killed in Action, France, 5/6/16.
16/1469 Brown, Henry, Pte. Died of Wounds, France, 19/6/17.

9/908 Cameron, John Donald, 2nd Lieut. Killed in Action, France, 7/8/17.
16/572 Carroll, Tuahae, Cpl. Killed in Action, Gallipoli, 10/12/15.
16/567 Christie, Hapi, Pte. Died, United Kingdom ex Gallipoli, 10/12/15.
19423 Clark, Clark, Pte. Killed in Action, France, 19/11/17.
20787 Conrad, Paki, Pte. Died, United Kingdom ex France, 6/12/18.
16/1299 Cook, George Gray, Pte. Died, France, 12/10/18.
9/1412 Cooper, George Begg, Pte. Died, France, 8/12/18.
19564 Cootes, Taipua Skipworth, Pte. Died, United Kingdom, 29/10/19
16/260 Coupar, Simon James Stuart, Lieut. Killed in Action, France, 29/6/16.
9/1274 Crawshaw, Samuel, Pte. Died, France, 6/1/19.
19459 Curtis, Joseph, Pte. Died of Wounds, France, 8/10/17.

The Maori Roll of Honour. 163

23150	Dale, Charles Martin, Pte.	Killed in Action, France, 5/5/17.
16/575a	Danger, James, Cpl.	Died of Wounds, France, 3/9/17.
19703	Davy, Para, Pte.	Died of Disease, France, 8/11/18.
16/93	Delamere, Heremeta, Sgt.	Accidentally Killed, France, 13/6/16.
19699	Dickson, Harry, Pte.	Died, New Zealand, 13/11/18.
16/508	Downes, Albert, Pte.	Died, Malta ex Egypt, 9/9/15.
16/373	Duff, Matene Rangiamohia, Sgt.	Died of Wounds, France, 1/9/16.
38513	Edmonds, Bennie, Pte.	Killed in Action, France, 31/12/17.
16/579a	Ellison, Thomas, L.-Cpl.	Killed in Action, France, 14/9/16.
16/439	Emery, Peter, Pte.	Died, Egypt, 28/8/15.
16/1509	Epiha, Daniel, Pte.	Died of Wounds, France, 7/10/17.
16/580a	Eruera, Whiti, Pte.	Killed in Action, France, 7/6/17.
7/1461	Evans, James, Pte.	Killed in Action, France, 15/9/16.
16/982	Fairlie, Godfrey Alexander, T/Sgt.	Killed in Action, France, 5/4/18.
16/519	Ferris, Donald, Pte.	Killed in Action, Gallipoli, 8/8/15.
9/1007	Field, Alfred Thornley, Sgt.	Killed in Action, France, 18/9/16.
16/1046	Filitoua, ——, Pte.	Died, United Kingdom, 19/6/16.
8/3579	Fisher, Charles, Cpl.	Killed in Action, France, 18/6/17.
16/1480	French, Samuel James, Cpl.	Died at Sea, 17/8/16.
16/36a	Geary, John, L.-Cpl.	Killed in Action, Gallipoli, 8/8/15.
16/65	Grace, Abraham Turei, Pte.	Died, Egypt, 21/10/15.
19745	Grace, Samuel, Pte.	Killed in Action, France, 19/2/18.
20711	Graham, George, Pte.	Died at Sea en route to New Zealand, 25/3/19.
20811	Haenga, Heremia Tawhero, Pte.	Killed in Action, France, 31/12/17.
16/1558	Hakaraia, John, Pte.	Died, France, 14/11/17.
16/5	Hale, Richard, Sgt.	Killed in Action, France, 14/8/17.
16/6	Hamana, Kingi, Pte.	Died, United Kingdom ex France, 3/10/16.
16/536	Hape, Hona, Pte., M.I.D.	Died, United Kingdom, 11/4/19.
16/949	Hape, Tere, Pte.	Died of Wounds, France, 24/6/17.
16/750	Happy, Dick, Pte.	Died, France, 17/12/16.
19351	Hapuku, Manukea, Pte.	Killed in Action, France, 7/12/17.
16/267	Harding, Joseph, Pte.	Died of Wounds, Egypt ex Gallipoli, 14/8/15.
20769	Harding, Whetu, Pte.	Killed in Action, France, 6/8/17.
16/370	Hare, Heremaia, Pte.	Killed in Action, Gallipoli, 7/8/15.
19680	Harmon, James, Pte.	Died of Wounds, France, 18/3/18.
7/2018	Harris, Edward, Capt., M.I.D.	Died of Wounds, France, 18/9/16.
16/950	Haruiti, Henry, Pte.	Killed in Action, France, 23/12/17.
16/391	Hekiera, Remihana, Pte.	Killed in Action, France, 4/5/17.
16/1320	Hemi, Skipper Pori, Pte.	Killed in Action, France, 10/9/16.
16/176	Herewini, Hohepa, Pte.	Died of Wounds, Gallipoli, 21/9/15.
16/325	Heteraka, Haroe, Pte.	Died, Mudros ex Gallipoli, 16/8/15.
20069	Hetekia, Ngahana, Pte.	Died, France, 3/11/18.
20875	Hill, Hemi, Pte.	Died of Wounds, France, 7/6/17.
16/4537a	Hill, Percy, W.O.2., M.I.D.	Killed in Action, Gallipoli, 9/8/15.
16/597	Hillman, Charlie, Pte.	Accidentally Killed (run over by vehicle), France, 20/8/16.
16/1257	Hina, Pera, Pte.	Killed in Action, France, 21/7/17.
16/379	Hiroti, Rangihiwinui, Pte.	Died, France, 5/6/16.
9/1439	Hitchon, Frank Horton, Pte.	Died of Wounds, France, 12/9/16.

19786	Hohepa, Puehu, Pte.	Died, New Zealand, 30/12/17.
23/2204	Holmes, Arthur, Pte.	Died, United Kingdom, 20/12/17.
16/606	Houia, Wiremu Peha, L.-Cpl.	Died of Wounds, France, 27/9/16.
16/556	Hovell, George Woodward, Pte.	Died of Wounds, United Kingdom ex Gallipoli, 20/10/15.
16/1442	Huki, Raymond, Pte.	Died at Sea en route to New Zealand, 8/4/17.
7/2044	Humphries, Thomas James, Pte.	Died of Wounds, France, 8/6/16.
20856	Hunia, Te Ruawai, Pte.	Died of Wounds, France, 31/12/17.
19355	Hunter, Jack, L.-Cpl.	Died of Wounds, France, 6/10/17.
16/1339	Hura, Raukawa, Pte.	Died, United Kingdom ex France, 10/4/17.
16/1238	Huriwaka, George, Pte.	Died, France, 6/6/16.
20026	Huta, Meihana, Pte.	Died, United Kingdom, 24/3/18.

16/240	Johnson, William, Cpl.	Died of Wounds, France, 5/8/16.
16/1453	Jones, Charles, Pte.	Killed in Action, France, 23/2/17.

16/620	Kaa, Pekama, Capt.	Killed in Action, France, 14/8/17.
60875	Kahaki, Whare, Pte.	Died, United Kingdom, 19/2/19.
16/1062	Kaimanu, Pte.	Died, Egypt, 15/3/16.
16/10	Kaipara, Autiri Pitara, 2nd Lieut.	Killed in Action, France, 4/8/17.
19634	Kaiwai, Harold, Pte.	Died, France, 1/5/18.
16/629	Kaiwai, Reweti, Pte.	Killed in Action, France, 14/9/16.
16/634	Kanapu, Horomona, Pte.	Killed in Action, France, 30/11/17.
16/937	Kara, Taha, Pte.	Killed in Action, France, 5/4/18.
16/1491	Karapaina, Hakota, Pte.	Killed in Action, France, 14/9/16.
19948	Karapaina, Paratene, Pte.	Died, United Kingdom, 31/1/19.
19860	Karauria, Meihana, Pte.	Died, France, 24/7/18.
16/394	Karena, Wero Mohi, Cpl.	Killed in Action, France, 30/11/17.
16/271	Karetai, Stewart, Pte.	Killed in Action, Gallipoli, 21/8/15.
16/95	Kawhia, Eruera, Pte.	Died of Wounds, France, 8/6/16.
20678	Kemp, Kawenata, Pte.	Died, New Zealand ex France, 28/1/18.
20771	Kereama, Hori, Pte.	Killed in Action, France, 30/11/17.
20844	Kihi, Pua, Pte.	Killed in Action, France, 11/8/17.
16/802	King, Kohi, Pte.	Killed in Action, France, 14/9/16.
16/621	Kingi, Tauiti, Pte.	Died of Wounds, France, 2/1/18.
16/1018	Kohere, Henare Mokena, 2nd Lieut.	Died of Wounds, France, 16/9/16.
20/598	Kokiri, Tango, 2nd Lieut.	Died at Sea en route to United Kingdom, 21/4/17.
16/552	Konuke, Pat, Pte.	Died, France, 14/4/18.
16/643	Kopua, Whetuki, Pte.	Killed in Action, France, 4/8/17.
16/1477	Korako, H., Pte.	Killed in Action, France, 19/6/17.
16/399	Kumeroa, te Aohau, Pte.	Killed in Action, France, 25/9/16.

16/1418	Lazarus, Jack, Pte.	Died of Wounds, France, 24/9/16.
20715	Leefe, George, Pte.	Died New Zealand, 30/12/18.
16/807	Luke, Peter, Pte.	Killed in Action, France, 31/7/17.

9/165	McIntyre, William Nichol, Cpl.	Killed in Action, France, 15/9/16.
23255	McKay, Robert Patrick, Pte.	Killed in Action, France, 7/6/17.
19728	McLean, Thomas, Pte.	Died of Wounds, France, 17/12/17.
16/809	McNicol, Duncan Bannetyne, 2nd Lieut.	Died of Wounds, France, 4/8/17.
19562	Maaka, Henri, Pte.	Died, United Kingdom, 31/8/19.

INTERIOR OF THE MAORI WAR MEMORIAL CHURCH AT KAHUKURA, WAIAPU VALLEY, EAST CAPE.

This beautiful church, which has a memorial window symbolising the Maori effort in the Great War, was erected by the Ngati-Porou tribe in honour of their soldiers. The Governor-General of the Dominion, General Sir Charles Fergusson, took part in the opening ceremonies, February 16th, 1926.

The Maori Roll of Honour.

16/400	Mangaroa, Ngore William, Pte. Died of Disease following Wounds, Malta ex Gallipoli, 30/12/15.
25556	Mangaroa, Thompson, Pte. Died, New Zealand ex France, 9/6/19
16/189	Manihera, Waitere, Pte. Killed in Action, Gallipoli, 6/8/15.
16/656	Manuel, Josiah, Sgt. Died of Wounds, New Zealand ex France, 21/6/17.
16/340	Manuel, Richard, L.-Cpl. Killed in Action, Gallipoli, 8/8/15.
16/657	Manuel, Tiweka, Pte. Died, United Kingdom, 25/3/18.
10/117	Maraki, Tautuhi, Pte. Killed in Action, Gallipoli, 9/8/15.
16/139	Marino, Hohepa, Pte. Died of Wounds, Gallipoli, 2/9/15.
19621	Maranui, Pona, Pte. Killed in Action, France, 23/12/17.
19361	Mason, Harry, Pte. Died, New Zealand ex France, 12/1/19.
4/1128	Masters, George, 2nd Lieut., M.I.D. Killed in Action, France, 3/4/17.
16/663	Matana, Karauria, Pte. Died of Wounds, France, 19/9/16.
16/1189	Matau, ——, Pte. Died, France, 29/8/16.
16/810	Matenga, Tuheke, Pte. Drowned, United Kingdom, 14/5/18.
16/1557	Matheu, Wetini, Pte. Died, France, 28/12/18.
16/1285	Matai, Tuherini, Pte. Died, New Zealand ex France, 1/9/17.
16/385	Mete, Kingi Henare, Pte. Killed in Action, France, 14/9/16.
16/383	Mete, Kingi Teira Hoani, Cpl. Killed in Action, Gallipoli, 8/8/15.
16/207	Mihaere Taiamai, L.-Cpl. Died of Wounds, France, 9/12/17.
16/278	Mira, William, Pte. Died, Egypt ex Gallipoli, 9/2/16.
16/1378	Mitchell, Ernest, Pte. Killed in Action, France, 24/9/16.
16/1089	Mitikele, ——, Pte. Died, Egypt, 16/5/16.
16/1088	Moki, Pte. Died, United Kingdom, 30/6/16.
16/222	Mokomoko, Nopera Hape, Pte. Died, Egypt, 2/9/15.
16/555	Moore, Sunny, Cpl. Died, France, 24/4/18.
16/680	Morehu, Hakopa, Pte. Killed in Action, France, 2/6/17.
16/344	Morgan, Joseph Iraia, Pte. Killed in Action, France, 29/7/17.
19399	Morris, Benjamin, Pte. Killed in Action, France, 22/8/18.
20846	Murray, Raika Whakarongotai, L.-Cpl. Killed in Action, France, 31/12/17.
16/686	Newton, James, Pte. Killed in Action, France, 5/8/17.
16/185	Ngamu, Hoani, Pte. Killed in Action, Gallipoli, 6/8/15.
16/958	Ngatoro, Renata, Pte. Died, Egypt, 14/1/16.
19371	Nicholls, Frederick, Pte. Died of Wounds, France, 6/10/18.
16/164	Nicholls, Thompson William, Cpl., M.M. Died, New Zealand, 6/11/18.
20885	Nikorima, Fred, Pte. Killed in Action, France, 21/6/17.
16/689	O'Neill, John Irvine, 2nd Lieut. Killed in Action, France, 3/10/16.
10251	Ovens, John, Pte. Killed in Action, France, 29/9/16.
20625	Padlie, David, Pte. Killed in Action, France, 6/8/17.
16/1536	Paki, Rimi, Pte. Died, United Kingdom ex France, 10/3/18.
16/28	Paku, Akuhata, Pte. Killed in Action, Gallipoli, 21/8/15.
16/201	Paora, Paetaha, Pte. Died, Malta ex Gallipoli, 4/2/16.
16/493	Papuni, Kurei, Pte. Killed in Action, Gallipoli, 6/8/15.
16/346	Para, Paki Whetu, Pte. Died of Wounds, New Zealand ex Gallipoli, 9/5/16.
16/566	Parata, Paul, Pte. Died, United Kingdom, 17/5/17.
9/1086	Park, Douglas Murgall, Sgt. Killed in Action, France, 15/9/16.
16/931	Patara, Hiroki Rere, Pte. Died, Egypt, 2/11/15.

19740	Patara, Nele, Pte. Killed in Action, France, 31/12/17.	
16/30	Peka, Hohepa, Pte. Died, New Zealand ex France, 10/3/20.	
19732	Pene, Enoka William, Pte. Died, New Zealand, 22/10/19.	
16/284	Peneamene, Tumaru, Pte. Died, United Kingdom ex Gallipoli, 18/9/15.	
16/1115	Peni, Meta, Pte. Died at Sea en route to New Zealand, 23/6/16.	
16/703	Pera, Hue, Pte. Killed in Action, France, 19/2/18.	
16/33	Pera, Piana, Pte. Died of Injuries (Railway accident), France, 16/4/16.	
16/246	Pineata, Watarawi, Pte. Died of Wounds, France, 29/9/16.	
16/1126	Pineka, Pte. Died at Sea en route to New Zealand, 4/7/16.	
19427	Pirimi, Egbert, Pte. Killed in Action, France, 14/7/16.	
16/34	Pohatu, Renata, Pte. Died of Wounds, France, 13/7/16.	
60789	Pohipi, Waikura, Pte. Died, United Kingdom, 16/2/19.	
9/1091	Poole, Thomas Henry, Pte. Killed in Action, France, 15/9/15.	
16/410	Popoki, Te Ao, Pte. Died, Egypt, 15/8/15.	
16/287	Porete, August Paani, Pte. Died, Egypt ex Gallipoli, 11/9/15.	
19877	Potatau, Tipene, Pte. Died, New Zealand ex France, 10/6/19.	
16/388	Potonga, Tame, Pte. Died, New Zealand, 30/12/15.	
20743	Poutawera, James, Pte. Killed in Action, France, 18/12/17.	
16/198	Power, Hone Manahi, Pte. Killed in Action, France, 7/12/17.	
16/1107	Pulu, ——, Sgt. Died at Sea en route to New Zealand, 26/6/16.	

9/1725   Quin, Thomas George, Pte. Killed in Action, France, 15/9/16.

20402	Rakiraki, John, Pte. Died, France, 3/5/18.	
16/1574	Rameka, Percy, Pte. Died at Sea en route to N.Z. ex France, 26/5/18.	
16/37	Rangi, Hapi, Pte. Died, Egypt, 5/11/15.	
16/449	Rangi, Horima, Pte. Killed in Action, France, 4/8/17.	
60500	Rangitauwira, Wiremu, Pte. Died, United Kingdom, 31/3/18.	
16/580	Rapihana, Herewini, Pte. Killed in Action, Gallipoli, 6/8/15.	
16/525	Rapona, Kiri, Pte. Died of Wounds, United Kingdom ex France, 29/9/16.	
20736	Raroa, William, Pte. Died, United Kingdom ex France, 6/12/18.	
19411	Rata, Jerry, Pte. Died, United Kingdom ex France, 20/6/18.	
16714	Ratana, Wiremu, Pte. Died of Wounds, France, 30/7/16.	
16/91	Ratana, Nepia, Pte. Killed in Action, Gallipoli, 7/8/15.	
4/52a	Reid, Lestock Henry, 2nd Lieut. Killed in Action, France, 20/5/16.	
16/720	Reiroa, Martin Wesley, Pte. Died, France, 31/8/16.	
16/115	Rewa, George Rangitikei, Pte. Killed in Action, France, 31/8/16	
19755	Rewharewha, Henare, Pte. Died of Wounds, France, 31/12/17.	
20664	Rewi, Peremara, Pte. Killed in Action, France, 23/3/17.	
16/102	Richmond, Tom, Pte. Died of Wounds, Egypt ex Gallipoli, 9/9/15.	
16/723	Rickus, Thomas Samuel, Pte. Died of Wounds at Sea en route to New Zealand ex France, 5/8/17.	
60809	Rihari, Neri, Pte. Died, New Zealand, 19/2/20.	
16/199	Ropata, Pahia, Pte. Killed in Action, Gallipoli, 6/8/15.	
20630	Ruha, John, Pte. Killed in Action, France, 21/7/17.	
19303	Ruka, Willie, Pte. Died, Australia en route to United Kingdom, 28/1/17.	
16/61	Ruhinga, Waretini, Sgt. Killed in Action, Gallipoli, 1/9/15.	
16/1459	Ruru, Vivian, Pte. Killed in Action, France, 14/8/17.	
18707	Ryan, Edward John, Pte. Died of Wounds, France, 9/6/17.	

The Maori Roll of Honour. 167

16/888	Savage, Charles, Sgt. Killed in Action, France, 21/6/17.
19883	Savage, John Joseph, Pte. Died, United Kingdom ex France, 2/3/18.
13/2150	Saxby, Conrad Gordon, Lieut.-Col., D.S.O., M.I.D. Died, United Kingdom, 27/11/18.
9/1218	Scaife, Stanley Tancred, Cpl. Killed in Action, France, 15/9/16.
13114	Scully, Ernest Charles, Pte. Died of Wounds, France, 6/6/17.
9/1354	Short, James, Lt. Died of Wounds, France, 28/5/16.
16/591	Sidney, William, Pte. Killed in Action, Gallipoli, 21/8/15.
16/506	Simpson, George, Pte. Killed in Action, Gallipoli, 21/8/15.
16/869	Skelton, Harold George Nepia, Pte. Died of Wounds, France, 8/8/17.
19429	Slade, Joseph, Pte. Died of Wounds, France, 25/6/18.
16/735	Smith, Frank, Pte. Killed in Action, France, 15/9/16.
19417	Smith, Haka, Pte. Killed in Action, France, 19/11/17.
19394	Smith, Hoani, Pte. Died of Wounds, France, 11/4/18.
20015	Smith, Temete, Pte. Died, United Kingdom ex France, 27/12/18
16/1196	Solomona, L.-Cpl. Died, New Zealand, 3/4/17.

16/68	Taewa, Rawiri, Pte. Killed in Action, Gallipoli, 21/8/15.
16/358	Tahu, Ngakepa, Pte. Killed in Action, Gallipoli, 6/8/15.
16/113	Tairua, Joseph, Pte. Accidentally Killed (aeroplane accident) United Kingdom, 13/2/19.
16/933	Taiwhanga, Hirini, Pte. Killed in Action, France, 21/6/17.
16/474	Take, William, Pte. Killed in Action, Gallipoli, 6/8/15.
16/740	Takoko, Hori, L.-Cpl. Killed in Action, France, 24/12/17.
16/891	Takuao, Paul, Pte. Died of Wounds, France, 8/6/16.
16/1132	Taleva, Pte. Died, United Kingdom, 12/6/16.
16/418	Tamarapa, Waikohari, Pte. Died, Mudros ex Gallipoli, 12/10/15.
20656	Tamati, Poururu, Pte. Died, United Kingdom, 15/10/17.
16/963	Tamauahi, Papara, Cpl. Killed in Action, France, 5/4/18.
16/1504	Tangaere, Hori, Pte. Died, New Zealand ex France, 16/3/18.
16/840	Tapsell, Robert, Pte. Killed in Action, France, 16/9/16.
16/1199	Taringa, Pte. Died, France, 15/8/16.
16/1155	Tauetuli, Pte. Died, France, 9/6/16
19753	Tuakamo, Waata, Pte. Killed in Action, France, 31/12/17.
16/1165	Taumataua, Pte. Died, New Zealand, 19/12/16.
16/78	Taumaunu, Hare, Pte. Died, Mudros ex Gallipoli, 11/10/15.
16/955	Taupaki, Rameka, L.-Cpl. Killed in Action, France, 31/12/17.
16/1202	Taura, ——, Pte. Died, United Kingdom ex France, 7/1/17.
19524	Taurere, Tepana, Pte. Killed in Action, France, 4/8/17.
16/1479	Tawhai, Hohepa Taupaki, Pte. Died, France, 7/12/16.
19744	Te Ara, Nati, Pte. Died at Sea ex France, 5/4/19.
16/512	Te Awarau, Hori Karaka, Pte. Died, Egypt, 13/9/15.
16/964	Te Hau, Pera, Pte. Killed in Action, France, 5/4/18.
19528	Te Hui, Haora, Pte. Died, United Kingdom ex France, 25/4/18.
19398	Te Kauru, John, Pte. Killed in Action, France, 4/8/17.
16/753	Te Kuru, Piki-Kotuku, Pte. Died of Wounds, France, 4/8/17.
19770	Te Maro, Herewini, Pte. Died, New Zealand ex France, 19/3/20.
60895	Te Mete, Wiremu, Pte. Died, United Kingdom, 11/2/19.
16/477	Te Moananui, Mikaera, Cpl. Died at Sea en route to Egypt, 6/3/15.
16/181	Te Moni, Matehaere, Pte. Killed in Action, Gallipoli, 6/8/15.
20048	Te Moni, Ratapu, Pte. Died, New Zealand, 14/8/19.
16/42	Te Ngaio, Wharekete, Pte. Died, Egypt, 24/3/16.
16/183	Te Otimi, Pitonga, Pte. Killed in Action, Gallipoli, 8/8/15.

29104	Teparo, Hohepa, Pte.	Accidentally Killed (thrown from horse), France, 26/8/17.
16/922	Tepene, James, Pte.	Died, New Zealand, 10/11/16.
16/1222	Tepuretu, Apu, Pte.	Killed in Action, France, 30/9/16.
16/1389	Te Raina, Te Weka, Pte.	Died, New Zealand ex France, 15/6/18.
16/760	Te Rore, Te Hu, Pte.	Killed in Action, France, 3/6/17.
16/1390	Te Tuhi, Nikora, Pte.	Died of Wounds, France, 4/8/17.
16/846	Te Ua, Te Miere, Pte.	Killed in Action, France, 21/7/17.
16/421	Te Whare, Taiawhiao, Pte.	Died of Wounds, Malta ex Gallipoli, 31/7/15.
20621	Te Whata, Peter, Pte.	Died of Wounds, France, 23/3/17.
16/360a	Thompson, Richard, Pte.	Died of Wounds, at Sea ex Gallipoli, 9/8/15.
16/363	Tiatoa, Pita, Pte.	Killed in Action, France, 15/9/16.
16/364	Tiini, Hopa, Pte.	Died, Egypt, 16/1/16.
16/1134	Timoko, Pte.	Died, New Zealand, 21/9/16.
16/303	Timuiha, John, Pte.	Killed in Action, France, 7/6/17.
16/1133	Tionesini, Cpl.	Died, France, 31/5/16.
19572	Tipere, Wi Parata, Pte.	Died of Wounds, France, 11/4/18.
16/1164	Tiueatana, ——, Pte.	Died at Sea en route to New Zealand, 27/6/16.
20735	Toheriri, Moetu, Pte.	Died, New Zealand, 13/3/18.
16/98	Toheriri, Reupena, Pte.	Killed in Action, France, 14/12/17.
60599	Toi Tukapa, Pte.	Died, France, 30/12/18.
16/103	Toka, Taare, L.-Cpl.	Killed in Action, France, 9/7/16.
16/480	Tua, James, Pte.	Died of Wounds, at Sea ex Gallipoli, 14/8/15.
16/123	Tuati, Pareiha, Pte.	Died of Wounds, Mudros ex Gallipoli, 16/8/15.
16/46	Tuahiwi, Wiremu, Pte.	Died of Wounds, France, 19/6/17.
16/769	Tuhora, Potene, Pte.	Died, United Kingdom ex France, 13/1/17.
20616	Tuki Manu, Pte.	Died of Wounds, France, 7/6/17.
16/125	Tunoa, Hamiora, Pte.	Killed in Action, Gallipoli, 21/8/15.
16/1179	Vaihola, Pte.	Died at Sea en route to New Zealand, 28/6/16.
16/1177	Vasau, Pte.	Died, United Kingdom ex France, 11/6/16.
16/1203	Vavia, Pte.	Died of Wounds, France, 1/10/16.
20823	Waaka, Hapi, Pte.	Died, France, 27/12/18.
20816	Waaka, Hohepa, Pte.	Died of Wounds, France, 12/4/18.
16/1297	Waetford, Eugene, Pte.	Died, France, 5/5/16.
16/482	Wahia, Moa, Pte.	Died at Sea ex Gallipoli, 9/9/15.
16/426	Wahia, Thomas, Pte.	Killed in Action, Gallipoli, 6/8/15.
16/53	Wairau, Ra, Pte.	Died of Wounds, Malta ex Gallipoli, 11/9/15.
16/779	Wairau, Raniera, Pte.	Died, United Kingdom ex France, 30/10/16.
16/549	Waiti, Haureki, Pte.	Killed in Action, Gallipoli, 21/8/15.
9/227	Walker, James Alexander, Cpl.	Died of Wounds, France, 28/5/17.
16/564	Warakihi, Poihipi, Pte.	Killed in Action, Gallipoli, 21/8/15.
9/1620	Ward, Arthur, Pte.	Killed in Action, France, 9/9/16.
19661	Warena, John Tana, Pte.	Died, United Kingdom ex France, 1/11/17.
16/1354	Warena, Kitohi, Pte.	Died, New Zealand ex France, 20/10/17.
16/368	Waru, Henare, Pte.	Killed in Action, France, 8/6/16.
16/369	Waru, Kopa, Pte.	Killed in Action, France, 8/6/17.
9/96	Watson, Norman Forrester, 2nd Lieut.	Killed in Action, France, 12/10/17.

The Maori Roll of Honour.

47562	Watson, Rihari, Pte.	Died, France, 24/11/18.
11/2504	Webb, Roland, Pte.	Died of Wounds, France, 15/9/16.
19604	Webster, Jack, Pte.	Died of Wounds, France, 29/11/17.
16/382	Whakarua, Herewini, W.O.2.	Died of Wounds, France, 13/1/18.
20779	Wharepapa, Turi, Cpl.	Killed in Action, France, 23/12/17.
16/145	Whareraupo, Tuakana-Kore, L.-Cpl.	Died of Wounds, Gallipoli, 6/8/15.
19669	Whareihiti, Nikora, Pte.	Died, New Zealand ex France, 24/1/19
19726	Wharewhiti Rikihana, Pte.	Died, United Kingdom ex France, 28/10/18.
16/789	Whitau, Arapata Koti P., Pte.	Killed in Action, France, 8/6/16.
16/188	Whitau, Puaka, Pte.	Died, United Kingdom ex Gallipoli, 10/10/15.
20845	Whyte, Walter, Pte.	Died, Unted Kingdom ex France, 15/9/18.
19474	Wi, Henry Wi Waka, Pte.	Died, United Kingdom ex France, 8/2/18.
16/858	Wickham, Mema, 2nd Lieut.	Died of Injuries (shot by soldier), France, 31/12/18.
20665	Wiki, Frank, Pte.	Killed in Action, France, 3/6/17.
16/1291	Wiki, Whiro, Pte.	Died, United Kingdom ex France, 16/10/18.
16/371	Wikitera, Robert, Pte.	Died of Wounds, France, 19/11/17.
19779	Williams, James, Pte.	Died, United Kingdom ex France, 30/9/18.
16/112	William, Joe, Pte.	Died at Sea ex Gallipoli, 13/8/15.
20624	Williams, Willie, Cpl.	Died of Wounds, France, 4/9/18.
16/462	Winiana, Ponga, Pte.	Killed in Action, France, 14/8/17.
16/1398	Wipani, John, Pte.	Died, France, 31/12/18.
20778	Witana, Abraham, Pte.	Died, France, 1/11/17.
16/431	Wood, Charlie, Pte.	Killed in Action, France, 8/7/17.
16/308	Woods, George, Pte.	Died, New Zealand ex France, 10/12/19.
20704	Wynyard, John, Pte.	Died of Wounds, France, 8/6/17.

The following is a list of members of the Maori Contingents who have died since discharge from the N.Z.E.F. as a result of war service:—

16/310	Adams, James, Pte.		13358	Norton, Henry, Pte., 8/8/23.
16/1030	Alotau, Pte., 21/1/20.		16/1522	Paeroa, Nehe, Pte., 12/12/17.
19618	Awiti, Timi, Pte., 27/11/18.		16/694	Paneta, Wi, Pte., 12/7/20.
16/313	Brass, Rata, Pte., 2/2/19.		16/527	Paora, Reihana, Pte., 3/7/19.
16/564a	Brown, James, Pte., 6/8/20.		16/76	Paraone, Tapauri, Pte., 5/2/21.
16/570a	Clune, James, Pte., 5/12/18.		19664	Pene, Amo, Pte., 28/9/18.
37771	Cotton, Joe Bird, Pte., 6/11/21.		16/220	Pitama, te Kerikaihau, Pte., 5/8/20.
19940	Davie, Waru, Pte., 27/8/20.		16/288	Ransfield, Richard, Pte., 15/10/17.
20684	Ephia, Tame, L.-Cpl., 1/4/19.		16/184	Raponi, Hone T., Cpl., 4/5/16.
16/173	Franks, Samuel Osman, Pte., 11/11/21.		16/1273	Rawiri, August W., Pte., 23/8/18.
16/583a	Governor, Joe William, Pte., 26/11/17.		16/730	Rupene, Hoani, Pte., 8/4/17.
20786	Hadfield, Matthew P., Pte., 10/1/19.		19975	Savage, Daniel, Pte., 31/12/23.
19624	Hoko, Moa, Pte., 24/1/19.		16/1393	Tairua, Peter, Pte., 21/11/18.
16/1226	Holmes, Frederick, W.O.1., 1/3/18.		16/1460	Tangiora, Rewi, Pte., 20/12/19.
16/1478	Hopa, Murphy, Pte., 23/8/21.		19960	Tautau, John, Pte., 10/11/19.
16/511	Kaanga, te Kuru, Pte., 25/6/19.		16/571	Tawera, Barney, Pte., 11/5/21.
20893	Kanara, Ropata Wi, Pte., 16/5/19.		16/248	Te Muera, Wetini, Pte., 24/10/19.
60628	Kingi, Edward John, Pte., 14/1/20.		20807	Toheriri, Tangiwai, Pte., 11/7/20.
16/640	Kiri, Ben, Pte., 28/11/18.		16/54	Wainohu, Hemi, Pte., 9/4/20.
60543	Koti, Hone, Pte., 11/8/19.		16/1525	Walker, Taylor, Pte., 4/12/20.
16/276	Lucas, Joseph, Cpl., 8/12/18.		20758	Wawatai, Heta, Pte., 20/7/22.
57249	McKinlay, James, Pte., 10/6/23.		16/1328	Young, Charles L., Capt., 10/2/21.
16/1524	Mark, Ned., Pte., 21/10/19.			
16/546	Matiu, Hone, Pte., 18/10/19.			
16/669	Matthews, Joseph, Pte., 20/1/19.			
16/1096	Mitipauni, Pte., 24/3/17.			
16/23	Horete, Hone Henry, Pte., 24/5/19.			
16/279	Morgan, George, Pte., 28/11/18.			

The Following is a List of Members of the Maori Contingents who Died while Undergoing Training With Reinforcements in New Zealand.

84749	Chase, Tuti, Pte. 15/11/18.	19380	Poata, Akuira, L.-Cpl., 13/12/16.
16/1270	Denny, John, Pte., 27/4/16.	84733	Pukure, Te Riri, Pte., 4/11/18.
84481	Fati, Manuaho, Pte., 11/11/18.	84718	Tahi, Tame, Pte., 23/11/18.
—	Hihi, Rupena, — 16/11/18.	84744	Tapsell, Warena M., Pte., 4/11/18.
84703	Ihia, Te Hapa, Pte., 13/11/18.	84450	Tehiwi, Pitiroi, Pte., 7/11/18.
84494	Ilitomasi, Laligapata, Pte., 7/11/18.	84543	Teipo, Pai, Pte., 10/2/19.
19517	Keepa, Arama M., Pte., 15/1/17.	19324	Teiva, Yeaumarae, Pte., 14/9/16.
83270	Kerehama, Rangi, Pte., 13/11/18.	84489	Tonuia, Pte., 5/11/18.
90215	Kuka, Mangu, Pte., 22/1/19.	84714	Toto, Kiri, Pte., 12/11/18.
16/1213	Mataputa, Pte., 5/3/16.	84741	Turu, Te Kakama, Pte., 7/11/18.
24/233	Muriwai, John, Rflmn., 28/6/15.	20701	Uatuku, Te Iritima, Lieut,. 31/8/17.
84503	Ngaipu, Ingatu, Pte., 10/11/18.	16/1178	Vilipate, Pte., 25/12/15.
84750	Oneroa, Tiki, Pte., 2/11/18.	84501	Wycliffe, Peau, Pte., 27/3/19.
19296	Pirangi, Pte., 14/10/16.		

RAROTONGANS.

Nominal Roll of Members of the Rarotongan Contingent Who Died while Serving with the New Zealand Expeditionary Force during the Great War.

16/1184 Inga,——, Pte. Died of Disease, Palestine, 12/12/18.
16/1185 Kamate, ——, Pte. Died of Disease, Palestine, 4/10/18.
19250 Mataiti, Kai, Pte. Died of Disease, Palestine, 16/2/18.
60713 Matapo, Kaka, Pte. Died of Disease, New Zealand ex Palestine 14/8/19.
19281 Ngaia, Kapao, T/Cpl. Died of Disease, Egypt ex Palestine, 29/10/17.
60754 Rota, Rota, Pte. Died of Disease, At Sea en route to New Zealand ex Egypt, 6/1/19.
16/1335 Taliauli, Jione, Cpl. Died of Disease, Palestine, 12/10/18.
19239 Tapapa, Akava, Pte. Died of Disease, Egypt ex Palestine, 19/10/18.
19284 Tete, Nikau, Pte. Died of Disease, Palestine, 12/10/18.
16/1220 Tutavake, Pte. Died of Disease, Palestine, 15/10/18.
16/1385 Williams, Allan, Pte. Died of Disease, Palestine, 26/7/18.

DECORATIONS.

List of Honours and Awards Gained by Members of N.Z. Pioneer Battalion.

D.S.O.

16/593 Buck, Peter Henry, Major.
16/582 Ennis, Wm. Oliver, Lieut-Colonel.
13/2150 Saxby, Conrad Gordon, Major.

M.C.

11/445 Catchpole, James Henry, 2nd. Lieut.
9/688 Chapman, Albert Arthur, Capt.
16/1017 Dansey, Harry Delamere, Capt.
16/392 Hiroti, Tura, Lieut.
16/268 Jacob, Hohepa, 2nd Lieut.
9/393 Scott, Kenneth, 2nd. Lieut.
16/90 Stainton, Wm. Houkamau, 2nd. Lieut.
16/515 Tingey, Edward, Capt.
16/187 Walker, William Huatahi, Capt.

D.C.M.

16/1404 Barclay, Francis, Sgt.
9/529 Gustafson, William Alfred, R.S.M.
19289 Karika, Pa George, T/Sgt.
16/407 Paranihi, Tau, Pte.

M.M.

9/1522 Amos, Philip, L.-Cpl.
16/1252 Anderson, Andrew, Pte.
16/434 Angel, Richard, Sgt.
16/1321 Apa, John Twaine, Pte. (T/Cpl.)
9/104 Atkinson, Peter Hiram, Sgt.
13/24a Barclay, Walter, Sgt.
16/389 Bennett, Wm. Rakeipoho, Sgt.
16/1432 Brown, Tono, Pte.
23/2554 Conway, Alfred, Pte.
9/1379 Crawley, David James, Sgt.
16/212 Flutey, Robert Henry, Cpl.
9/935 Holmes, Arthur Leslie, Sgt.
20673 Hori, Kereapa, L/Sgt.
20752 Hughes, Edwin, L.-Cpl.
16/1474 Jones, Michael Rotohiko, Cpl.
20797 Leefe, Henry Tai, Pte.
16/18 McAndrew, Joseph, Cpl.
16/1306 McManus, Charles, Pte.
16/1396 Mano, Hii, Pte.
16/671 Maxwell, George, L.-Cpl.
16/1370 Morgan, Thomas Tutawake, Pte.
16/164 Nicholls, Thompson Wm., Cpl.
20776 Ngapo, Robert, L.-Cpl.
26156 Nunn, John, Cpl.
16/405 Otene, Rangi, Cpl.
16/821 Panoho, Jack, L.-Cpl.
16/832 Pomana, Hori, Sgt.
16/530 Rawhiti, Huki, Pte. Bar to M.M.
16/354 Rogers, Augustus, Sgt.
16/457 Rotoatara, Tupara, Sgt.
9/1611 Rowley, Francis Beyers, L.-Cpl.
16/590 Sidney, Thomas Phillip, Cpl.
16/739 Sparks, Alfred, Cpl.
16/742 Taiapa, Tamaki, L.-Cpl.
16/1275 Tangatake, Whiri, Pte.
16/360 Taua, Matiui, Sgt.
20860 Te Amo, Pa, Pte.
16/757 Te Patu, Tamati, Pte.

LIST OF HONOURS AND AWARDS. 173

M.S.M.

9/1009	Aitken, Arthur, Cpl.		4/714	Dawson, Alfred, Cpl.
9/677	Briscoe, Archibald, L.-Cpl.		16/396	Kerei, Hawea, Sgt.
11/280	Cameron, Duncan, Sgt.		16/681	Morris, Richard, L.-Cpl.
20891	Davies, Henry Marshall, Cpl.		16/108	Pahina, Whare, Pte.
			16/525a	Te Au, George David, Pte.

M.H.S.

16/544 Mabin, Frederick Burton, Capt. (T./Major).

FOREIGN DECORATIONS.

20680 Karini, Toi, Pte., Croix de Guerre (French).

11/680 King, George Augustus, Lt.-Col., Croix de Guerre. (French.)

9/1347 Richards, Charles Theodore, Pte, Croix de Guerre. (French).

20862 Tamehana, Puia, Rfm., Croix de Guerre. (French).

16/971 Geary, James Henry, Sgt., Belgian Croix de Guerre.

16/333 Kanara, Henare, Pte., Belgian Croix de Guerre.

16/1308 Karauti, Hori, Lieut., Belgian Croix de Guerre.

16/832 Pomana, Hori, Sgt., Belgian Croix de Guerre.

11/1492 Sloan, George Colin, C.S.M., Belgian Croix de Guerre.

9/310 Martin, Francis Roy, Cpl., Italian decoration (B.M.)

16/587 Gardiner, George, Pte., Serbian decoration (Cross of Karageorge, 2nd class)

16/544 Mabin, Frederick Burton, Capt. (T/Major.) Serbian decoration (Order of the White Eagle, 5th class, with swords).

16/545 Wainohu, Henare, Rev., Serbian decoration (White Eagle, 5th class).

MENTIONED IN DESPATCHES.

16/311 Auhana, Rewiti, Sgt. Sir D. Haig, 1/6/17; 31/12/17

9/670 Biggar, William Oliver, Arm/Sgt.

16/518 Broughton, Edward Renata Huhunga, Capt.

16/593 Buck, Peter Henry, Major. Sir D. Haig, 13/11/16; 9/4/17.

16/977 Bush, George Archer, Capt.

16/1017 Dansey, Harry Delamere, Lieut.

16/433 Emery, Thomas, Pte.

16/582 Ennis, Wm. Oliver, Major.

16/1486 Hale, Nathaniel, L.-Cpl.

16/590a Hall, John Henry, Capt.

9/466 Hancock, Fred Goffin, Sgt.

16/536 Hape, Hona, Pte.

7/2018 Harris, Edward, Capt.

16/1550 Hawira, Joe, Pte.

16/4537a Hill, Percy, Sgt.

16/510 Honeycombe, Charles, Sgt.

16/548 Hovell, Chas. Harry Pinika, Sgt.

11/680 King, George Augustus, Lt.-Col. (D.S.O.). 2/1/17, 1/6/17.

16/110 Kohere, Tawhai, Cpl.

4/112a Masters, George, 2nd Lieut.

16/343 Matiu, Reihana, Cpl.

9/469 Moffit, George Michael, 2nd Lieut.

9/629 Montgomery, Henry Steele, Lieut.

16/475 Muriwai, Tame, L.-Cpl.

16/29 Paputene, Tiara, Pte.

16/407 Paranihi, Tau, Cpl.

16/833 Paul, James, T/L. Sgt.

MENTIONED IN DESPATCHES—Continued.

9/1209	Pennycook, William Scott, Major.	10/1353	Thompson, Ralph James Lander, 2nd Lieut.
19438	Pitman, Warren, Cpl.	16/515	Tingey, Edward, Capt.
13/2150	Saxby, Conrad Gordon, Major.	16/161	Vercoe, Henry Ray, C.S.M.
		16/55	Waihape, Puke, Pte.
16/90	Stainton, Wm. Houkamau, 2nd Lieut. (Sir Ian Hamilton; Sir Chas. Munro).	16/187	Walker, William Huatahi, Lieut.
		16/427	Warahi, Rua, Pte.
16/1327	Sutherland, Frank Emanuel, Major.	9/1373	White, William Frank, Sgt. (Act. C.S.M.)

The Maori Contingent at Gallipoli.

MAORI PROTEST AGAINST SPLITTING UP OF THE FORCE.

After the Battle of Sari Bair, Gallipoli, in August, 1915, General Sir Arthur Godley, G.O.C., in a despatch to the New Zealand Defence Minister, wrote:—

"I have the honour to report that the Maori Contingent were in action for the first time between the 6th and the 10th instant. During this time they were heavily engaged and suffered casualties I regret to say of 17 killed, 89 wounded, and two missing. The Contingent took part in the attack on the Sari Bair position, and at various periods of the fight found themselves in line with units of the New Zealand Mounted Rifles Brigade, the 27th Infantry Brigade, the 13th Division of the New Armies, and the Ghurkas (29th Indian Brigade). All speak most highly of the individual bravery and courage of the men and their gallantry during the fight, but as the result of reports which I have received I have come to the conclusion that the Contingent did not have a fair chance in being utilised in this way as a small independent unit, and that it would have been of still more use and done even better, if possible, had it formed part of our New Zealand Brigades. ....Lieut.-Col. Herbert commanded the Contingent to my entire satisfaction, and did well, so much so that, by special request of the General Officer Commanding the 13th Division, I have lent his services temporarily to that Division to command a British battalion.....I have decided, after careful consideration, to temporarily attach half a company to each battalion of the New Zealand Infantry Brigade. Captain Ennis will be loaned to the N.Z. Mounted Rifles Brigade, and Captain Mabin's services have been lent to the Governor of Malta as Commandant of a convalescent depot, and the remaining officers of the Contingent, including Captain Buck (Te Rangihiroa) and the Reverend Wainohu, will continue to serve with it, and will be available to pursue the administration of the Maoris and to preserve a careful note of their records, etc., in case it should be found advisable to again reconstitute them as a separate unit. In the meantime I have explained to the Contingent, and I hope it will be clearly understood in New Zealand, that the incorporation of the Contingent with the N.Z. Infantry Brigade is done purely in the interests of the Contingent and of the Maori race, and that I will make it my business to see that their identity is thereby in no way imperilled or affected. Their fighting efficiency will be much greater, and they will be much more at home, and altogether have far better chances than they did during the late operations, when, as a small body they found themselves rather swamped amongst strangers.

"In conclusion, I wish to bring specially to your notice the very gallant bearing and conduct of the Contingent, who have thoroughly justified their right to fight alongside other units of the Army, and have more than worthily upheld the historic traditions of their race." -

This breaking up of the Contingent was greatly displeasing to the Maoris, and vigorous protests were made to the home country, where the matter was taken up by the Maori Recruiting Committee. On December 9th, 1915, the Committee (Hon. Sir James Carroll, Hon. Dr. Pomare, Mr. C. Parata, M.P., Mr. Tau Henare, M.P., and Mr. Ngata, M.P.) wrote to Sir James Allen, Minister of Defence:—

"In the two conferences with you on the 7th and 8th inst., relating to the Maori Contingent and Reinforcements we made the further request that the Maori Contingent be reconstituted with the reinforcements which were despatched last September, as a separate unit of two Companies. The information that the Contingent had ceased to exist as an independent unit, that it had been broken up, and platoons attached to companies of the N.Z. Infantry Brigade, was conveyed to you by General Godley in October, and has since caused the greatest dissatisfaction to us, to our people, and the members of the Contingent. During the period of training of the Contingent at Avondale last summer, the Maori chiefs by direct representations to yourself and the Prime Minister as well as by indirect representations through us, requested that the force be not split up into two companies, one for Samoa and one for Egypt. This was conceded by the Imperial Government, who accepted the Contingent of 500 for service in Egypt. It left the Dominion as a special force representing the Maori race. Though the individual members of the Contingent offered in New Zealand for active service abroad, the Imperial authorities accepted their services for garrison duty only, probably because they were an untried body of men, as to which no one in high command could say how they would comport themselves in the fighting line. The subsequent acceptance of their many repeated offers to serve at the Front was a compliment to the race, to their physical fitness and successful training as soldiers.

"The fortunes of this small force were, as you know, followed with the keenest attention by their people in New Zealand. The condition of their acceptance for active service, that reinforcements be found by the Maori race, was readily complied with. But you should understand that it was the existence of the force as a unit, however small, representing the Maori race alongside other races fighting for the one flag, centering the honour, good name, and reputation and the highest expression of the loyalty of the Maori people—it was this fact that the recruiting Maori tribes had always before them, it was this fact that appealed to them throughout the seven or eight months since the First Contingent left the Dominion. It is a matter to be seriously reckoned with by the Government and by the officers commanding at the Dardanelles. It is one that we, who have undertaken the responsibility for raising more men, have to face, and cannot get over.

"We do not object to the incorporation of the Contingent with the N.Z. Infantry Brigade. The proper place for the Maoris was with their fellow countrymen from the Dominion, and we do not understand why they were not so incorporated from the time they landed on the Peninsula. But we do not follow the General's view that the merging of platoons or half companies in various units of the N.Z. Infantry Brigade—leading inevitably to their being split up and being scattered over miles of trenches—does not imperil or effect the identity of the Contingent. We maintain that that identity has been lost. It is a fact that ever since the General's decision was given effect to we have heard nothing further of the doings of the

Contingent as a contingent. We have on the other hand received letters from the trenches with the wail—'Kua wehewehe matou'—'We are separated.'

"We cannot make our people understand, because we do not understand ourselves after reading General Godley's remarks, how the identity of the Contingent is being maintained and can be maintained after platoons which originally composed companies have been separated from one another and merged in companies of the New Zealand battalions.

"We must point out that the General in his despatch suggests that it may be found advisable to reconstitute them as a separate unit, and states that the administration is being pursued partly with that end in view. We urge that in view of reinforcements having been sent for the Contingent as a contingent, the opportunity is now offered for such a reconstitution. We think that it should be possible to form again two Maori companies to be attached together as such to any New Zealand battalion that General Godley may choose. The Maoris will then fight together and alongside their white fellow countrymen. We would regard the pursuance of the present policy of splitting them up as a breach of faith.

"General Godley should be informed that on this matter the Maori people are absolutely determined and unanimous. We could not ourselves go before our people to ask for further men to reinforce a Maori contingent that does not exist, except as reinforcements to the N.Z. Infantry Brigades. If Maoris are required to reinforce these brigades the Defence Department can recruit in the ordinary way. But we do not agree to raise a special force to reinforce a special contingent only to find these men scattered to serve the purpose of reinforcing the general New Zealand force."

This protest was successful, and to the great satisfaction of the Maoris the scattered detachments of the Maoris were reunited after Gallipoli, and the force was reorganised as a Pioneer unit.

"TE OPE TUATAHI!"

THE FIRST MAORI CONTINGENT.

(This was composed as a recruiting song, to raise men for the Maori Contingent and money for the Maori Soldiers' Fund. It proved an excellent stimulant for enlistment for active service, and it produced nearly £8,000 for the Fund, among the East Coast natives. Mr. A. T. Ngata, M.P., wrote the first and second verses of the Maori original.)—

E te ope tuatahi
No Aotearoa,
No Te Wai-pounamu,
No nga tai e wha.
Ko koutou ena
E nga rau e rima,
Ko te Hokowhitu toa
A Tu-mata-uenga:
I hinga ki Ihipa,
Ki Karipori ra ia;
E ngau nei te aroha,
Me te mamae.

E te ope tuarua,
No Mahaki rawa,
Na Hauiti koe,
Na Porourangi:
I haere ai Henare
Me to Wiwi,
I patu ki te pakanga,
Ki Paranihi ra ia.
Ko wai he morehu
Hei kawe korero
Ki te iwi nui e,
E taukuri nei?

E te ope tuaiwa
No Te Arawa,
No Te Tai-rawhiti,
No Kahungunu.
E haere ana 'hau
Ki runga o Wiwi
Ki reira 'hau nei,
E tangi ai.
Me mihi kau atu
I te nuku o te whenua,
Hei konei ra e,
E te tau pumau.

"TE OPE TUATAHI!"

[TRANSLATION.]

We greet our first war band
From Aotea-roa,
From the Island of Greenstone:
We sing of our warriors,
Our gallant Five Hundred,
The chosen heroes
Of Tu-mata-uenga,
The Angry-Eyed War God.
Some fell in Egypt,
Some on Gallipoli;
Now pangs of sharp sorrow
Our sad hearts are piercing.

From the Coast of the Sunrise,
Came our Second Contingent,
The men of Mahaki;
Men of Tolago Bay,
Warriors of Ngati-Porou.
Farewell, O Henare,*
Who led your company
And fell in war's thunder
Nobly fighting in France.
And who will survive there
To take the last message
To our own loved people
In dark sorrow bowed?

Our Ninth fighting Contingent
Comes from Te Arawa,
From the Coast of the Sunrise
From Kahungunu's land,
And now I am leaving
For France's red war fields.
There I'll remember;
My heart will send greetings
O'er far land and ocean
To my own constant love.

---

*2nd-Lieut. Henare Mokena Kohere, died of wounds in France, 1916.

"Tangata puhuruhuru" and "Poilu."

There is an interesting similarity of meaning between the Maori term "tangata puhuruhuru"—literally "hairy man"—in the famous haka song *"Ka maté, ka maté, ka ora, ka ora,"* and the popular French word for the soldier in the Great War, "poilu." The original diversion of "poilu," bearing the same significance as "puhuruhuru," to its war use was curious. In an article in the "National Review" (January, 1922), Mr. Edgar Preston said that the word was used by Balzac in his "Medicin de Campagne," when describing Napoleon's crossing of the Beresina: "General Eble, under whose orders were the pontonniers, could find only forty-two sufficiently intrepid (assez poilus) to undertake the work." The idea behind the word seemed to be an association of hairiness with manliness, and Mr. Preston quoted the French proverb, "Il n'a pas de poils sur le ventre," used as a term of reproach.

"Ka mate, ka mate," etc., is only a portion of a very ancient Maori chant. The original song begins, *"Kikiki, kakaka, kikiki, kakaka, Kei waniwania taku aro."*

The Ngati-Manawa Tribe.

Page 4.—The losses of the Ngati-Manawa tribe in the war out of twenty-one who served were three killed and two died of sickness; two were wounded. Besides those who enlisted in the Pioneer Battalion (twenty), Trooper J. H. Bird served in the Third Auckland Mounted Rifles, and was killed on Gallipoli, August 8th, 1915.

INDEX

Alderman, Major, 63, 67.
Allen, Sir James, Minister of Defence, 12, 19, 160, 175, 176.
Anafarta, Guns at, 27, 28.
Ancre Brook, 89.
Anzac, Gallipoli, Maoris arrive at, 26.
   „ fighting at, 27-66.
Antoine, General (France), 116-118.
Armentieres, 78-87, 101.
Armistice announced, 154.
Avondale, Maori Training Camp, 11, 12, 14, 17.
Ballots, under Military Service Act, 22.
Bapaume, 144, 145.
Basseville, La, 119-122.
Beauvois, 150.
Belgium, march through, after Armistice, 156, 157.
Bellevue, 125.
Bertrancourt, 136, 137.
Bezantin Ridge, 91, 93-100.
Beaudignies, 152.
Bevillers, 154, 155.
"Big Sap," Anzac, Gallipoli, 26, 30, 31.
Birdwood, General, 34, 52, 56.
Bournonville, 122, 125, 126.
Blackett, Lieut., 60.
Braithwaite, General, 119.
Broughton, Captain M., 71.
Bruce, Captain D., 114, 126, 132.
Buck, Major Peter H. (Te Rangihiroa) 10, at Gallipoli 29-67, in Egypt 68-73, appointed Second in Command Pioneer Battalion 71, service in France 76-133.
Bush, Captain G. A., 71, 106, 107.
Bush-fellers, Maori in France, 77, 78.
Cambrai, 136.
"Canada," transport (in Mediterranean), 74, 75, 76.

Carroll, Hon. Sir James, 10, 59, 84, 85, 160, 161.
Casualties, list of, 8, 162-171.
Chapman, Captain, 135, 145.
Chailak Dere, 36, 39, 45.
Charleroi, 155.
Chunuk Bair, battle of, 46-54.
Conscription, extended to Maori race, 21, 22.
Clifton, Major C. E., 71, 80.
Colingcamps, 136.
Cook Islands soldiers, 8, 72, 73, 99, 106, 107, 133.
Coupar, Lieut. S., 30, 80.
Dansey, Major Roger, 40, 41, 44, 81, 83, 84.
Dansey, Captain H., 68, 72, 90, 98.
Delamere, Sergt., 80.
Duff, Sergt., 89.
Duncan, Captain (N.Z.M.C.), 68.
Dunkirk, 157.
Edwin (Captain, transport "Warrimoo"), 16.
Egypt, Maori Contingent arrives in, 16.
"Emden," German cruiser, 16.
Ennis, Lieut.-Col. W. O., 32, 67, 71, 80, 89, 132, 134, 135, 140, 156, 159, 160.
Ehau, Captain Kepa, 71, 119, 120.
Estaires, 77.
Etaple, 88.
Ferris, Captain, 51, 126.
Ferris, Corporal, 46, 47.
Flers, 94, 95, 96, 98, 100, 145.
Forest of Nieppe, 77.
Forest of Mormal, 152, 153, 154.
French, Lieut., 125.
Frezenberg Post, Ypres, 135.
Fromm, Lieut., 79, 106.
Gairdner, Captain R. M., 71, 76, 77.

Gallipoli, Maoris' service on, 24-69.
Gannon, Lieut. A., 105, 134.
Gibbs, Captain, 98.
Gilmour, Lieut. J. H., 72.
Ghain Tuffhia Camp, Malta, 16.
Ghurkas, on Gallipoli, 48, 49.
Godley, General Sir A., 27, 38, 52, 54, 59, 67, 72, 102.
Gommecourt, 141.
Gustafson, R.S.M., W. A., 133, 172.
Hall, Captain J. H., 72, 156.
Hamilton, General Sir Ian, 34, 38, 39, 51, 56.
Haplincourt, 145, 146.
Harris, Captain E., 91, 94.
Hebuterne, 136, 137, 138, 139, 140, 141, 144.
Herbert, Lieut.-Col., 17, 25, 44, 60.
Hetet, Captain, 71, 119, 120.
Heuheu Tukino, Te, M.L.C., 19.
Hill, Sergt.-Maj., 49.
Hiroti, Captain T., 40, 51, 77, 159.
"Hokowhitu a Tu," 15, 16, 123.
Holmes, Major, N.Z.M.C., 43, 44.
Hughes, Lieut.-Col., J. G., 54.
Jacob, Sergt., 49.
Jennings, Captain, 95.
Johnston, Brig.-General F. E., 46, 48.
Jones, Captain A. E. M., 125.
Kaa, Lieut. Pekama, 68, 71, 84, 85, 90, 93, 121.
Kaipara, Lieut., 72, 119.
King, Colonel G. A., appointed to Command of Pioneer Battalion, 71; service in France, 91-122; killed 125.
Kohere, Lieut. H. Mokena, 68, 71, 73, 92, 93.
La Motte, 77, 78.
Leef, Lieut., 119, 120, 135.
Lemnos Island, 25, 67.
Large, Major J. T.
Le Quesnoy, 152, 153.
Larkhill Camp, England, 158, 159.
Longueval, 94.
Mabin, Lieut.-Col. F. B., 24.
MacLean, Lieut. J. C., 71, 78.

Mair, Captain Gilbert, 14.
Malta, 17, 24, 25.
Marseilles, arrival in, 76.
Masnieres, 149.
Massey, Right Hon. W. F., 9, 102, 140.
Messines, battle of, 106-115.
Mete Kingi, Lieut., 48, 134.
Metz, 146.
McGregor, Lieut., 123.
McKenzie, Major, 68.
McNicol, Lieut. D. B., 119, 120.
Moascar Camp, Egypt, 72, 73.
Montauban, 89.
Mudros Harbour, Lemnos, 25, 67, 68.
Narrow Neck Training Camp, 17, 22.
Niué Island soldiers, 8, 22, 73, 79.
Old Hindenburg Line, 147, 148.
O'Neill, Lieut. J., 96, 101.
Oosthove Farm Camp, Belgium, 104.
Paku, Lieut., 126, 129.
Parata, Taare, M.P., 10.
Peacock, Major, 14, 17, 21.
Pennycook, Major W. S., 71, 78, 103, 174.
Pitt, Captain, 51.
Pioneer Battalion formed, 70.
Ploegstreet Wood, 104, 118.
Polynesian volunteers, 22, 23.
Pomare, Hon. Sir Maui, 1, 9, 18, 19, 20, 21, 53, 59, 104.
Porter, Colonel T. W., 14.
Port Said, 74.
Pow, Colonel, 117.
Prince of Wales inspects Battalion, 73, 150.
Pussieux, 144.
Raiding parties, near Armentieres, 81-87.
Rarotonga soldiers, 99, 106, 107, 133.
Rawhiti, Pte. H., 49, 172.
Reid, Lieut. L. H., 78.
Rata Mahuta, 19.
Rau-angaanga, Te, 21.
Richardson, General, 140.

Ross, Malcolm, N.Z. War Correspondent, 27, 54.
Rossignol Wood, 140, 141.
Roto-a-Tara, Lieut., 104, 119, 120, 172.
Russell, General A. H., 27, 35, 39, 62, 74, 90, 95, 101.
Salmon, Captain C. W., 138.
Samoa, 9.
Samoan soldiers, 90.
Saxby, C. G., Lieut.-Col., 71, 94, 95, 98, 125, 126, 132, 133, 134, 141, 143, 154, 172, 174.
Sari Bair, Gallipoli, Battle of, 34-45.
Sarpi Camp, Lemnos Island, 67.
Scott, Lieut. K., 172.
Selle River, 149.
Shera, Captain, 40, 93.
Stainton, Lieut. W. H., 16, 33, 60, 71, 79, 159, 172, 174.
Stewart, Lieut.-Col. H., 74, 94, 98, 125.
Suez, 16, 72, 106.
Sutherland, Major F. E., 72, 174.
Suvla Bay, Gallipoli, 36, 37, 41, 44, 59.
Table Top, Gallipoli, 37, 38, 39, 42, 43, 44, 45, 47.
Tahiwi, Captain Pirimi, 16, 40, 41, 42, 47, 156.
Tahiwi, Cpl. H., 40, 42.
Tapsell family in the War, 4.
Tamati Taiapa, L.-Cpl., 138.
Thompson, Lieut. R., 138, 174.
Tikao, Lieut. J. C., 71, 80.
Tingey, Captain E., 62, 103, 119, 127.
"Toia mai te waka," 161.
Trench Warfare School, Armentieres, 78.

Tribes, Maori:—
  Arawa, 4, 7, 10, 12, 18, 103.
  Ngapuhi, 12, 25, 30, 103.
  Ngai-Tahu, 10, 103.
  Ngati-Apa, 9, 12.
  Ngati-Awa, 12.
  Ngati-Kahungunu, 12, 13, 25.
  Ngati-Manawa, 4.
  Ngati-Maniapoto, 13, 147.
  Ngati-Porou, 4, 7, 9, 12, 104.
  Ngati-Raukawa, 12, 147.
  Ngati-Toa, 12.
  Ngati-Tuwharetoa, 13.
  Whakatohea, 12.
  Whanau-a-Apanui, 12.
  Waikato, 18, 19, 20, 21, 22, 147.
  Urewera, 18.
  Whanganui, 9.
Tupu Taingakawa, 19.
Twisleton, Captain F. M., 54, 71, 74, 80.
Valetta (Malta), 16, 24.
Vercoe, Captain H. R., 71, 82, 83, 84, 85, 174.
Versailles, 77.
Viesley, 150.
Wainohu, Chaplain H., 32, 37, 48, 50, 62, 67, 68, 79, 128.
Waikato tribe, meetings with, 18-22.
Waite, Major F., 31, 45.
"Waitemata," troopship, 68, 104, 105.
Walker, Captain W. H., 71, 132, 172.
Walker's Ridge, Anzac, 30, 32, 33, 45, 60.
Ward, Right Hon. Sir Joseph, 102, 140.
Warnimont Wood Camp, 140.
"Warrimoo," troopship, 15, 16.
"Westmoreland," troopship, 160.
Wilkinson, Lieut., 149.
Wilson, Captain H., 71.
Young, Captain C. le P., 110, 112.
Ypres, third battle of, 124-131, 132, 133, 134, 135, 136.
Zeitoun Camp, Egypt, 16, 68.

www.ingramcontent.com/pod-product-compliance
Lightning Source LLC
Chambersburg PA
CBHW021837220426
43663CB00005B/285